Performance Perspectives

A Critical Introduction

Edited by

Jonathan Pitches and Sita Popat

Foreword by Mick Wallis

palgrave
macmillan

First published 2011 by
PALGRAVE MACMILLAN

Palgrave Macmillan in the UK is an imprint of Macmillan Publishers Limited,
registered in England, company number 785998, of Houndmills, Basingstoke,
Hampshire RG21 6XS.

Palgrave Macmillan in the US is a division of St Martin's Press LLC,
175 Fifth Avenue, New York, NY 10010.

Palgrave Macmillan is the global academic imprint of the above companies
and has companies and representatives throughout the world.

Palgrave® and Macmillan® are registered trademarks in the United States,
the United Kingdom, Europe and other countries

ISBN 978–0–230–24345–3 hardback
ISBN 978–0–230–24346–0 paperback

This book is printed on paper suitable for recycling and made from fully
managed and sustained forest sources. Logging, pulping and manufacturing
processes are expected to conform to the environmental regulations of the
country of origin.

A catalogue record for this book is available from the British Library.

A catalog record for this book is available from the Library of Congress.

PERFORMANCE PERSPECTIVES

What is 'performance'? What are the boundaries of performance studies? How do we talk about contemporary performance practices today in simple but probing terms? What kinds of practices represent the field and how can we interpret them?

Combining the voices of academics, artists, cultural practitioners, *Performance Perspectives* answers these questions and provides a critical introduction to performance studies. Presenting an accessible way into key terminology and context, it offers a new model for analysing contemporary performance based on six frames or perspectives:

- Body
- Space
- Time
- Technology
- Interactivity
- Organization

Drawing on examples from a wide range of practices across site-specific performance, virtual reality, dance, applied theatre and everyday performance, *Performance Perspectives* addresses the binary of theory and practice and highlights the many meeting points between studio and seminar room. Each chapter takes the innovative form of a three-way conversation, bringing together theoretical introductions with artist interviews and practitioner statements. The book is supported by activities for discussion and practical devising work, as well as clear guidance for further reading and an extensive reference list across media

Performance Perspectives is essential reading for anyone studying, interpreting or making performance.

Contents

List of Illustrations, Figures and Tables

Illustrations

Figures

Tables

Notes on Contributors

Matt Adams is one of the core artists and co-founders of the internationally renowned performance company Blast Theory. He is also Visiting Professor at the Central School of Speech and Drama, Honorary Fellow at the University of Exeter and works in close collaboration with academics in Computing at the University of Nottingham. He has taught widely on performance, new media and interdisciplinary practice at various institutions, and has contributed to research by Ofcom, the Technology Strategy Board and the Engineering and Physical Sciences Research Council.

Ralph Brown is Projects Officer at PALATINE, the Higher Education Academy Subject Centre for Dance, Drama and Music, based at Lancaster University. He manages and administers a programme of projects and events supporting the enhancement of learning and teaching activity in the performing arts higher education sector. Brown was awarded grants for and managed the HEFCE funded CAREER Project (2003–04) on employability, the DfES-funded PACE Project (2004–05) on entrepreneurship, the Higher Education Academy funded CoLab collaborative arts enterprise project (2006), the NCGE-funded project mapping enterprise and entrepreneurship in dance higher education (2007) and a Higher Education Academy-funded research synthesis on Employer Engagement in the Arts Sector (2008).

Steve Dixon is an internationally renowned researcher in the use of computer technologies in the performing arts and is the author (with Barry Smith) of *Digital Performance* (2007), the most comprehensive history and analysis of the field to date. As well as having worked in a range of professional roles across theatre, film and television industries, Dixon is the director of *The Chameleons Group* (established 1994), a performance research company exploring new approaches to the creation of multimedia performances using a diverse range of performance styles and electronic media. He is Professor of Digital Performance and Pro-Vice Chancellor (Strategy and Development) at Brunel University in London.

Anna Fenemore is a lecturer in Theatre and Performance at the School of Performance and Cultural Industries, University of Leeds, specializing in

Practice-as-Research, physical performance, site-specific theatre and contemporary devised performance. Fenemore's research interests include spectating embodiment, performer bodywork training, multi-sensory immersive performance, performance and phenomenology, theories of performance space/place and performance, and death studies. Fenemore is also artistic director of Manchester-based Pigeon Theatre, a solo perform-ance artist and performs for other contemporary performance companies.

Tony Gardner is a theatre academic at the University of Leeds with a particular interest in how compositional techniques might be applied to the creation of new performance works. Having created a number of dura-tional performances as well as theatre works, including a series of pieces involving communications technologies (*Phone-In, callerID, Massively Multiplayer*), he was drawn to Anne Bogart's Viewpoints and related Composition practice as a means of articulating approaches to time-based work in both theory and practice, and how this understanding might be extended to questions of training. He has previously published on the influence of Antonin Artaud's work on contemporary practice.

Ruth Gibson (see **igloo**)

Teo Greenstreet is Creative Director of sustainability/creativity venture Encounters, a CIDA innovation coach and a consultant/trainer. His fasci-nation is establishing the best environments for creativity to flourish. Greenstreet was CEO of The Media Centre, Huddersfield, and founder and CEO of The Circus Space, London. Projects include £4.5 million award-winning buildings, establishing conservatoire-level higher education in the circus arts, and training/creation producer for the Millennium Show in the Dome. His circus performing career was a clown double act touring for over five years, ranging from big top spectacles to school touring. Greenstreet is a Fellow of the Clore Leadership Programme and the Royal Society of Arts. Former roles include Vice President of the European Federation of Circus Schools, advisor to the London Development Agency and Arts Council England. Writing has included papers for *Mission, Money, Models* and NESTA.

Dorita Hannah is Professor of Spatial Design at Massey University's College of Creative Arts in New Zealand, where architecture and perform-ance form the principle threads that weave through her creative work, teaching and research. Her practice includes scenographic, interior, exhibi-tion and installation design with a specialized architectural consultancy in buildings for the performing arts. She has gained awards for her creative work, including a UNESCO Laureate and World Stage Design medals. Hannah publishes on practices that negotiate between art, architecture and performance. She is currently Vice-Chair for OISTAT's History/Theory Commission and is a board member of *Performance Studies International*.

Wendy Houstoun is a London-based artist who has been working with experimental movement/ theatre forms since 1980. She has maintained a practice that moves between devised company involvement, collaborative projects and solo practice. Her work with companies such as Ludus Dance Company, Lumiere & Son Theatre Company, DV8 Physical Theatre, Forced Entertainment, and Gary Stevens runs parallel with collaborations with performance artists, dancers, film-makers and writers (Rose English, Lucy Fawcett, Nigel Charnock, Tim Etchells, David Hinton, Jonathan Burrows, Matteo Fargion). Her solo works *Haunted, Daunted and Flaunted, Happy Hour, The 48 Almost Love Lyrics, Desert Island Dances* and *Keep Dancing* have all toured internationally, and all works weave a rich strand of text through a moving narrative and, in some cases, employ self-created video work. More recent choreographic work includes *In The Dark* (Sydney 2005), *DIY Theatre* (Verve – NSCD 2006), *NO Success like Failure* (Sydney 2007), *Dancing in Time* (Dansopolis 2009), *Imperfect Storm* (Candoco 2010), *Unruly Night* (VCA Melbourne 2010) and *Small Talk* (Antonio Grove 2010).

igloo comprises **Ruth Gibson** and **Bruno Martelli**. Their practice includes installation, intervention, virtualization, film and performance. igloo recreate environments and systems where coding joins hands with chore-ographies of the body. Their core concept is the intersection between tech-nology and the human spirit. Ruth Gibson studied performing arts with the Marcel Marceau Group and at the School for New Dance Development (Amsterdam). She was nominated for a Paul Hamlyn Award for Visual Art (2000). Bruno Martelli studied graphic art and set up a multimedia plat-form for interactive design. He is recipient of a Wingate Scholarship. igloo are UK-based.

Bruno Martelli (see **igloo**)

Alice O'Grady is a Lecturer in Applied Theatre and Intervention at the School of Performance and Cultural Industries at the University of Leeds. She is an active researcher in the field of interactive performance and play theory, particularly within the field of underground club culture and contemporary music festivals. She is Artistic Director of the performance company ... floorSpace ..., which makes interactive walkabout performances for festivals and club spaces. Much of her work is site-sensitive and examines the relationship between space, context and identity.

Scott Palmer is a performance academic and practitioner at the University of Leeds, UK. His research focuses on scenography, immersive performance, lighting design and the interaction between technology and performance. This research includes the AHRC-funded *Projecting Performance* project, in collaboration with KMA Creative Technology and Sita Popat, which has resulted in a range of performance outcomes including the interactive light installation *Dancing in the Streets*, an experimental production of *A Midsummer Night's Dream*, and a significant contribution to the digital scenography for DV8 Physical Theatre's *To Be Straight With You*. He is the author of *A Lighting Reader* in the Palgrave Macmillan *Theatre Practices* series.

Jonathan Pitches is Professor of Theatre and Performance in the School of Performance and Cultural Industries at Leeds University. His interests are in performer training, intercultural performance and performance documentation and (digital) archiving. He has taught in many different countries, leading masterclasses in Tokyo, Shanghai, Malta and within the UK – including the RSC's *Revolutions* season (in 2009). He is the author of two monographs, *Vsevolod Meyerhold* (2003) and *Science and the Stanislavsky Tradition of Acting* (2005/9), and is co-founder and co-editor of the Routledge journal *Theatre Dance and Performance Training*. His edited book on the influence of Russian actor training in the UK, *The Russians in Britain*, is due in 2011.

Sita Popat is Senior Lecturer in Dance and Head of the School of Performance and Cultural Industries at the University of Leeds. Her interests centre on performance in digital and new media contexts. She has choreographed for humans, robots and digital 'sprites', and she is fascinated by the inter-relationships between performers, operators and computers. Her research has been funded by the Arts and Humanities Research Council, the Engineering and Physical Sciences Research Council, and the Joint Information Systems Committee. She is author of *Invisible Connections: Dance, Choreography and Internet Communities* (Routledge, 2006), and Associate Editor of the *International Journal of Performance Arts & Digital Media*. She sits on the Board of Trustees for DV8 Physical Theatre.

Victor Manuel Ramírez Ladrón de Guevara is a Lecturer in Theatre and Performance at the University of Plymouth. His scholarly work is centred on the study of intercultural and physical theatre. He also has 16 years' experience as a performer and director working in México and England, and has trained in a range of diverse disciplines embracing aspects of Eastern as well as Western theatre praxis.

John Somers is Honorary University Fellow at the University of Exeter and Founder Editor of the journal *Research in Drama Education*. He is Artistic Director of Exstream Theatre Company and Tale Valley Community Theatre. He has written and directed a number of interactive theatre programmes, and has published widely on drama and theatre practices, and research methods. His interactive theatre programme 'On the Edge' toured nationally and was the winner of major awards. He works extensively internationally and is holder of the American Alliance of Theatre and Education Special Recognition Award.

Calvin Taylor holds the Chair in Cultural Industries at the University of Leeds. He has been teaching and writing about the cultural industries for 15 years, working with a range of organizations including UNESCO, WIPO, the British Council and the Arts Council, England. He is interested in innovation in the cultural industries with specific interests in organization and innovation. His most recent project was for an Arts and Humanities Research Council-funded Research Fellowship looking at the relationship between higher education and the cultural industries. He is currently developing new work on innovation, culture and society. His latest publication is 'The Creative Industries, Governance and Economic Development: A UK Perspective' in Kong and O'Connor (2009).

Gregg Whelan and Garry Winters have been collaborating under the name Lone Twin since 1997, and have developed an international reputation for creating performance pieces that are strongly grounded in particular settings and locations, often over extended time periods. They have worked freely between galleries, theatres, studios and public spaces across the world, and are frequently commissioned by festivals or arts organizations to realize community-based projects – including KunstenFESTIVALdesArts in Belgium, the Barbican Centre in London, Steirischer Herbst in Austria, and the Melbourne International Festival in Australia, among many others. In 2006, they established a new ensemble of collaborators under the name Lone Twin Theatre to tour theatre pieces, which were performed collectively as *The Catastrophe Trilogy*, most recently as part of the Barbican *bite10* season.

Louise Ann Wilson is a director and scenographer working nationally and internationally to create small and large-scale site-specific performance, and designs for theatre, dance and opera. She was Co-Artistic Director of wilson+wilson (1997–2008), makers of site-specific theatre, and is currently Artistic Director of Louise Ann Wilson Co., which creates site-specific performance exploring the relationship between landscape and human life events. The work is created in collaboration with artists and experts from many different disciplines. She has designed sets and costumes for Opera North, The Royal Exchange Theatre, The Unicorn Theatre, The Watermill, West Yorkshire Playhouse, and many other companies. She took up the post of Visiting Research Fellow at the University of Leeds in December 2010.

Jessica Wood is a freelance performance designer. She graduated from University of Leeds in 2008 with a first class degree in performance design. Since graduating, she has worked in various roles in theatre production and TV. She is currently working at Chichester Festival Theatre within the wardrobe department. Wood is planning to further her studies in performance design, working as design assistant and studying for a Masters degree.

Foreword

Mick Wallis

Models, maps and narratives

This book maps out six aspects of performance – body, space, time, technology, interactivity and organization – and brings three or more voices to bear on each. So, within a clear framework, we find a multitude of ideas, threads of thought, rhymes, differences, opinions, facts and questions. And that's where your contribution comes in. While each of the six chapter editors writes a summary of what has been raised with respect to that topic, the invitation is for the reader to do something similar for themselves.

You might find it useful to think in terms of maps and narratives. How might you map out the key definitions, ideas and questions raised by Steve Dixon, Gregg Whelan and Tony Gardner about time, for instance? And what narrative might we write to lead our own reader through that map? ('Let's start with the idea of stage time ...'.) A similar sort of map is the 'spider diagram'. Faced with an assignment topic or question, we begin with a blank sheet of paper and map down the essential starting categories – say, scenography as: (1) machine for acting; (2) sign-making vehicle; (3) sensory experience. And then we develop the diagram by plotting down associated ideas and questions – and then connecting these, corralling them into groups, *actively modelling* a field of material.

So, both maps and narratives are ways of actively modelling not only what we receive (through reading and other experience, like listening to a debate), but also what we want to write or otherwise do (like make an installation). And, if we think about it, any narrative makes a map – it sets things in relation to another. They are both models, in the sense that they arrange things so we can make active use of them in our thinking, writing and making.

The delicious invitation from this book is, first, to make maps of what is going on – both within each of the chapters and across them; and then to generate further maps and narratives as models or engines for future projects.

Practice

The voices in each of the chapters are various. Perhaps one way we could map them is by using a model of academics and artists, or 'practitioners'. Whether or not that last word is familiar to you in the sense in which is meant here will depend on particular things. For school or college students studying for the UK Advanced-level examination in Theatre Studies over the last few decades, it will signal 'Stanislavski, Brecht and Artaud' (and maybe Berkoff ...). And that focus on the practitioner was one of the ways in which theatre (and, more recently, performance) studies carved out a space of learning, teaching and research that was distinct from, especially, literary studies. In literature, one studies and interprets plays. In theatre studies, one studies 'practice'.

The French sociologist Pierre Bourdieu developed the useful model of 'fields of practice'. Secondary and tertiary education is one such field. It comprises many institutions, operates by various rules and is funded differently in different parts; but it also depends on particular norms of behaviour by the people involved in it (teachers, students, administrators, caretakers ...). We might usefully map school and university education in New Zealand as a field of practice, for instance. But even though that would be different from our map of education as a field of practice in, say, Canada or the USA, we would be safe in saying two things. First, there is a degree of coherence within the one field: it operates in a regular way, much like a machine. And second, the field of practice in one country will be similar in many respects to that in another – which is what makes the differences so interesting.

Bourdieu invites us both to define fields of practice for ourselves (as a form of modelling) and to recognize that different sorts of fields overlap one another. So, this book is situated at the intersection between the fields of education and of performance – as, presumably, are you. Performance 'out there' amongst the 'practitioners' is both an object of study for us 'in here' and a place many of us are aiming to arrive in. So, let's reflect a little on theatre and performance studies in higher education as a field of practice in itself. And let's note that, in this model, academics are practitioners, too.

Journeys

Broadly speaking, undergraduate theatre studies in the USA and UK were founded on different aims. In the early years of the discipline, an undergraduate in the USA might spend a great deal of time learning the practices of theatre-making – acting, directing, writing, stage management and so on. In the UK, the emphasis was on understanding theatre as a cultural practice; if the graduate were to become a practitioner, it was expected that this would be as a director, critic or, perhaps, playwright. We might say that the emphasis in the UK was more 'academic'. While some might argue that 'academic' means detached from the real world of practice, we might respond that academic practice is part of the real world. While both systems have taken their respective journeys since, we have here a generalizable model of theatre or performance practices and academic practices that are braided together in different ways and to different degrees in theatre and performance studies – not only in different countries, but also across different programmes and institutions in any one country.

Your own school education in theatre/performance will equally have had its own particular blend and articulation of academic and artistic practice. And many for whom this book is designed will not have studied theatre/performance at all. Likewise, beyond your university or college higher education, you will be preparing for any number of destinations – different roles within the field of practice of performance; or perhaps in another field altogether, where the 'cultural capital' (Bourdieu's phrase) gained in performance will still bear credit.

What this book offers all of us at our various stages in such a journey is a close-up conversation not only between, but also *with* practitioners at different positions in relation to the field of performance – that's to say, both inside and outside education; and, indeed, both inside and outside performance understood narrowly as only an artistic practice (see Chapter 7). And, of course, many of those inside education – as is increasingly the case in the UK – are also performance practitioners (choreographers, scenographers, performance artists ...) in their own right.

This is a book that both marks and enables your journey to a position in which you can bring theoretical (and historical) understanding to bear on performance. That's cultural capital that will endure for you, whether you become an artist, manager, educator, entrepreneur, theorist, activist or a combination of such roles when you graduate.

Lastly, let's reflect that universities and like institutions are not only places of education, but also research. Those who teach you are paid, of course, to be scholars; they must be up to date in their field. But many are also paid to be researchers: to ask new questions, and work out how to answer them. In the best higher education, you learn about the research your educators are doing. But not only that: part of the journey this book inaugurates is your own journey from learning by being taught to learning by researching. And it's active modelling that you'll need for both.

Have fun with it!

Acknowledgements

It has been a pleasure to work with such a dedicated team of scholars and practitioners, each drawing upon extensive knowledge and experience in the field of performance. We, as editors, are grateful to all of the contributors to this book for sharing this knowledge and for responding so positively to our suggestions. We would particularly like to thank the chapter editors, whose enthusiasm, patience and commitment have made this project possible.

Our thanks must also go to the students and staff of the School of Performance and Cultural Industries at the University of Leeds, for their invaluable feedback on draft material. From its inception, this project has been rooted in the realities of research-led teaching in performance, and many of the activities included are a product of this dynamic.

We are deeply indebted to Palgrave Macmillan and, most significantly, to Kate Haines, for her encouragement and expert management of the project from proposal to proofs. The support and advice of Felicity Noble and Jenna Steventon has also been essential to the successful completion of this project.

We would like to thank all of the people who have given permission for their images to be reproduced in the book. Their names have been included in the credit lines for each image. Every effort has been made to trace copyright-holders, but if any have been inadvertently overlooked the publishers would be pleased to make the necessary arrangements at the first opportunity.

Finally, we are eternally grateful to our respective families for their unfailing patience and support.

JONATHAN PITCHES
SITA POPAT

1   Introduction

Jonathan Pitches

Performance perspectives

'Performance' and 'perspective': two benign words, commonly used in everyday conversations and seemingly untainted by any specialized or terminological context. Yet, when they are considered individually (and even more so as a combination), these terms conceal a rich complexity. This book is designed to uncover that complexity and, in doing so, it offers a new means for interpreting the phenomenon of performance, based on six interconnected perspectives: *body*, *space*, *time*, *technology*, *interactivity* and *organization*.

In this introductory section, some fundamental terms will have their meanings debated. You will be given guidance in how to approach the book and there is one detailed illustration of how these chosen perspectives might be applied. It will conclude, in common with all the main chapters, with some further work for the reader, for this is a book that requires your input. You might say that that is true of all books – that one of the defining virtues of written prose is the demand it makes of its readers; the pages won't turn themselves. But, in this case, your activity can be characterized in a number of additional ways beyond a simple commitment to 'read on'. Here, we are asking you to make sense of the ideas and discoveries you make in reading this book in *practice* – either as a group or on your own, in a studio or in a seminar space. In this, we are echoing the tautology proposed by Huxley and Witts that 'performance is central to the study of performance' (2002: 3).

Consider the term 'perspective' as a starting point: there can be few words in the English language which are as inherently contradictory. On the one hand, perspective is an explicitly partial *point of view*, as in: 'I see it from a different perspective than you'. On the other hand, achieving perspective on a subject involves the pursuit of a more generalized and elevated overview – a new and objective vantage point. These contrasting understandings are evident in the first two meanings listed in the *Collins Dictionary*:

perspective, n. 1. A way of regarding situations, facts etc. and judging their relative importance. 2. the proper or accurate view or the ability to see it: objectivity: *try to get some perspective on your troubles*.

The first definition recognizes the *relativity* of perspective and acknowledges that it involves a level of comparison; the second defines perspective as a kind of universalizing eye, something which offers a unified, indeed, 'proper' view. The problem is all to do with how we view things (ironically, a problem of perspective!). In definition 2, the shift of viewpoint allows for a distanced reappraisal of the problem, one that only recognizes the singular new viewpoint. But, in definition 1, the observer has an already built-in contingency: he or she achieves perspective by recognizing other possibilities from the outset. It is this understanding – perspective as plurality – which drives the strategy and the structure of this book.

A different but related kind of tension is evident in the painter Leonardo's appraisal of perspective in painting: 'perspective is the bridle and rudder of painting' (Richter 2008: 110). Recognized for extending and innovating the use of perspective in Renaissance art, following the early development of the 'science of optics' by Brunelleschi (1377–1446) and Alberti (1404–72), Leonardo (1452–1519) captures the dual function of perspective, as both a controller of the artists' inspiration (the bridle) and a guide and facilitator (the rudder). These two metaphors resonate tellingly with the *Collins Dictionary* definitions: the bridle references perspectival *law*, the scientific rules of perspective which demand the identification of at least one vanishing point, and the steadfast adherence to rules created by Euclidian geometry and classical notions of beauty and logic. The rudder, by contrast, is not governed by any external control mechanism; it remains in the hands of the helmsman, responding solely to the specific desires of the sailor charged with steering the ship. It is this tension, between an external, notionally objective set of concerns and the personal, self-driven imperative which makes the term 'perspective' so interesting and which speaks, as we shall see, more generally to the practice of making and theorizing performance. Given this in-built conflict of ideas, it is perhaps not surprising that, at the very root of the word 'perspective', there are further tensions. Perspective (or *perspicere*) comes from two Latin words *per*, meaning 'intensive' and *specere*, 'to behold'. Taken together, the term thus denotes a rather delicious action of 'intensive beholding', a fusion of concentrated observation and naïve experiencing. It is this kind of attitude we would encourage the reader to adopt when encountering this book for the first time.

If 'perspective' is a difficult word, 'performance' is doubly so, even though its history as a term is much shorter. Philip Auslander, one of many critics hailing from the associated discipline of performance studies, cites seven meanings of performance:

1 A presentation of an artistic work to an audience, for example a play or piece of music.
2 The manner in which something or somebody functions, operates or behaves.
3 The effectiveness of the way somebody does his or her job ...
4 A public display of behaviour that others find distasteful, for example an angry outburst that causes embarrassment.
5 Something that is carried out or accomplished.
6 The performing of something, for example a task or action.
7 The language that a speaker or writer actually produces as distinct from his or her understanding of the language.

(Auslander 2003: 1)

The complications here are a little more extended. First, performance is understood both in strictly artistic terms – a play or a piece of music – and as a simple action in everyday life, something 'carried out'. Second, the manner in which somebody performs and the effectiveness of that performance are both included in this range of definitions. Thus, perform-ance can be the thing on offer and a measure of how good or bad that thing is. Third, performance can be used as a pejorative term, a use more in keeping perhaps with the term 'theatrical' in the mouths of frustrated parents! Putting on a performance connotes an illusion or a show, one which raises suspicion (not admiration) in its audience. This kind of charge might equally be levelled at politicians, as well as tired children for, in both cases, the accusation is that performance dissembles or gets in the way of the truth. It is an idea which recalls the ancient Greek philosopher, Plato (427–347 BC) and his critique in *The Republic* of what he considered to be the emotionally manipulative mimetic arts (1987: 435).

The sense of performance spanning both everyday and specialized cultural domains has been a dominant theme in performance studies over the last 20 years, and it remains important for this book. It marks a signif-icant ratchetting up of the responsibilities of the cultural critic and of the student of performance. For, if the definition of performance embraces the everyday, then it must also include the vast span of material *between* the highly specialized forms of dance, opera, theatre, music for instance, and the quotidian actions of daily human behaviour. This 'space between' has been likened by critics, such as Richard Schechner, to a continuum, a line stretching from identifiable cultural objects and events (performing arts, for instance) to variously organized human actions or 'special social situations', to performing in everyday life, with inexpressibly small gradations in between (Schechner 2006: 170–2). At the opposite pole of everyday life, Schechner includes shamanism and trance, which indicates that, for him, levels of immersion and transformation are the organizing principle underlying the continuum.

Whilst the diversity and richness of such an expanded territory is truly stimulating, there are clear and real problems with this widening of the field. At its worst, it can be seen as a kind of colonization of all behaviour, across cultures and geographies, and an indiscriminate collecting of these behaviours under the banner of 'performance'. In pragmatic terms, the danger for new students of performance attempting to gain access to the field is not knowing where to start and, more importantly, where to stop. One of the most difficult and thought provoking questions today is: Where does the field of performance begin and end?

This book will not address that question head on, but it will not duck it entirely either. The organization of the chapters into separate perspectives with, crucially, different points of view *within* the chapters, is a device to help establish strict parameters for discussion, crossing different kinds of learning spaces. Our perspectives are chosen to have as much currency in a studio space as in a lecture room or tutorial. Perhaps, ideally, they would operate in a space configured to support a *moving engagement* with the ideas, punctuated by reflection and further discussion. The common activity to unite these modes of investigation is, of course, reading but, as a reader, be prepared to encounter very different registers of writing in this book. Each chapter is co-written by three contributors, each one inevitably coming from a different perspective in relation to the guiding idea of the chapter. Consciously, we have mixed artists, academics, artistic academics and academic artists within the triads of chapter contributors to develop a multiplicity of ideas around a single series of lenses: our performance perspectives. Thus, the overarching model proposed here is in contrast to the linear continuum outlined. In this collection of essays, the idea is to establish what might be called three-point perspective in each chapter; that is, three subsections to each chapter with the focus on one organizing perspective. It must be remembered, though, that each contributor brings several preconceptions to the page, even before their ideas are juxtaposed with their co-writers. What is on view here, then, are performance perspectives at individual, at chapter, and at book level – more a concentric than a linear organization of ideas. Finally, these perspectives will be explored through the activities set as part of the chapters' conclusions and, thus, the perspectives are multiplied again, by you, in a further rippling of associations. In defence of the accusation that this approach is simply another method of diffusion, each chapter is organized and edited by one of the triad to keep a controlling bridle on the material.

This approach should satisfy what Robert Leach calls the framing function of performance analysis in his chapter on performance in *Theatre Studies*:

> Any piece of behaviour/doing/action which is in some way marked off, or framed, is a performance. The framing enables us to comprehend it as an entity and we can think about it in clear terms. (Leach 2008: 2)

For Leach, these frames are close to what the Russian director and actor Konstantin Stanislavski called 'Given Circumstances' (Stanislavski 2008: 36–59): '*where* it happens', *who* is present, *how* the performance unfolds (Leach 2008: 2). For this book, the frames are organized at increasing levels of distance from the performance material itself. Beginning with the *body* signals its core contribution to the phenomenon of performance, *space* and *time* add two further dimensions to the dramaturgical ingredients of a performance, and *technology* mediates the relationship between these three. *Interactivity* and, finally, *organization*, however, are at a further level of remove. Our intention is that, having finished the book, you are more sensitized to performance's inherent complexity and also to its relationship to wider cultural, geographical, political and industrial concerns. These frames or perspectives, taken together, constitute a holistic bracketing off of key performance aspects, so that the multiple dimensions of any one performance can be appreciated. Using one example and subjecting it to the perspectival scrutiny suggested by the book, all at once, can best illustrate this idea. I have chosen an example of everyday activity as performance – a 'special social situation', as Schechner calls it. In doing so, the efficacy of the perspectives is tested most explicitly.

Borth Bench

Context

For nearly 15 years, I have been documenting the growth of my family – not unlike many millions of parents, grandparents and guardians. But,

5

beyond the usual imperative to capture special moments and keep them (often digitally) for posterity, my task has been focused on a very strict, if simple, set of rules: a photograph, taken each year, on the same bench in the seaside town of Borth, in mid-Wales. At its inception in 1997, there was never any intention to produce an art object or, indeed, even to take another photograph the next year, but, once the second photograph *was* taken – by chance the following summer – a project has gradually emerged which, over time, has adopted an aesthetic quality. After 14 recurrent photos, one from each year (up to 2010), the quotidian act of a holiday snap has in some way been transformed into what might now be described as a domestic durational *performance*.

But what is it that underlies this transformation – from everyday activity to performance? What defines this delicate distinction? Is it performance simply because I have declared it as such, or are there more secure grounds to consider this collection of photos as a performative object? Applying the frames of our six performance perspectives should help answer these questions.

Body

Looking at the montage in Illustration 1.1 through the lens of the body brings out some specific qualities. The piece is, at one level, all about the body – or bodies, plural: ageing bodies, in essence; bodies which are visibly developing and therefore changing the dynamic of the larger body, that is the family. Three generations of bodies are represented here, but this is only evident after the first photograph, once the visibly extended body of the mother has produced the first addition to the group. This expansion is repeated in the years from 1999–2000 and, thus, the simple but universal process of childbirth is expressed; the one body that is blessed in producing this repetition stands for a far wider constituency of mothers – both actual and potential. The birthing body is juxtaposed here with the ageing body – perhaps most acutely through our view of the grandparents – and, although the figures themselves appear to be in perfect health, a bodily focus almost inevitably stresses a subtext of mortality as the photos progress.

The body also brings to the fore questions of *kinesics* – 'codes governing movement' (Aston and Savona 1991: 111) which are carried by the body. Of course, the movement here is frozen, but the *implication* of movement is as clear as anything. In these arrested movements, the bodies act as signifiers of much wider concerns – the weather, most clearly, but also the phenomenon of family itself. These bodies are subtly intimate with each other, connected not just by the strictly limited space of the bench, but also by their implied relationships – expressed, for instance, in the *movement* from (mother's or grandfather's) lap to a level of independence on the bench. Implied, too, in these connecting bodies is an indication of character – or perhaps, more accurately, archetype – for there is insufficient information to develop a sense of an individual: images of grandfather, mother, son are there to be filled in and individualized by the witness or reader of the work.

Space

It should already be clear that to focus on one perspective is to imply the existence of others: a brief consideration of body in this montage indicates both space and time immediately. The spaces indicated here are multiple and operate in different ways. Practically, the composition of the piece is determined by a fixed space – the bench – which, in contrast to the ever-developing bodies, is constant and ageless. The bench is one of the basic rules of the durational performance: it contains the family, but it also acts like a magnetic locus for the project itself, drawing them back each year to the very same location. There are modest resonances here of the great migratory stories of nature – the arctic tern flying thousands of miles and returning to its nesting point once a year – but this implied magnetism is in sharp contrast with the realities of the space itself. The Borth promenade, like many seaside resorts in the UK, is a pale shadow of what it was in the 1950s, a feeling evoked by the 'cost-cutter' supermarket in view behind the bench. Charm and neglect cohabit in this piece, then, and this, in turn, implies a narrative of sorts for the bodies on the bench: what is it that keeps bringing them back? There must be something beyond instinct that motivates their annual return...

Interestingly, the focus on space sharpens the viewer's awareness of the subtle *differences* in location, as well as the constants, for the bench is in fact not entirely the same one in each image. In truth, the photos are almost equally split across two locations along the same promenade, which changes the backdrop of houses and which echoes the subtly different arrangements on the bench itself. With everything ostensibly so controlled, these small errors or deviations away from the simple rules of the game create visual interest, and perhaps even suggest an understated dramatic potential. What happened in 2008 to so radically effect the ordering of the family? And why is that the father and grandmother never have a child on their laps?

1997

1998

2001

2002

2005

2006

2009

Illustration 1.1   *Borth Bench*
[Copyright: Jonathan Pitches]

1999

2000

2003

2004

2007

2008

2010

Time

Durational performance pieces are, by definition, preoccupied with the perspective of time – when the awareness of time passing is intrinsic to the experience itself, rather than supernumerary or unconscious. Of all the perspectives dealt with in this book, time is the most dominant here: not just because the component photos are explicitly marked with the years; not just because it constitutes a collection of visible temporal signs, as the young boys grow up in front of our eyes; but because the montage is as much about time lost as it is about time found or time secured. *Borth Bench* could be viewed as a hugely extended time-lapse film, but without the smooth computer-generated transitions used in television programmes such as *Honey, We're Killing the Kids* (BBC).[1] In fact, arguably, the most interesting temporal aspect of the piece is that it jars rather than smoothes the movement from one year to the next, drawing attention to the huge majority of missing time implied in these photos. In doing so, it speaks more generally about the impossibility of capturing our life experiences and begs the pointless but necessary question: What's in between?

Equally, as the piece grows year on year, it is as much about future time as it is about past time. For inscribed in this piece is a narrative of domestic hope and continuity, an implicit promise that the rules of the game will continue to be adhered to by its players *in perpetuity*: how long will it be before the bench is populated with a fourth generation? Will passing time dilute or concentrate the enthusiasm of the contributors to return to Borth? How will this simple arrow-of-time narrative be affected by much bigger concerns? Will there, for instance, even be a *Borth Bench* (at least, above water) once the world has warmed up by as much as three degrees in 2050?

Technology

Technological considerations reveal the context of the performance act itself: the back-stage activity necessary to capture the image each year. The photos are taken with a simple self-timer on a digital camera, but this technology has only been readily available over the last eight years. Looking carefully, it is possible to see a shift in framing from 2002 to 2003 caused when the camera was changed from a fixed 35-mm single lens reflex to an extended digital zoom. Despite the gear-shift 'up' to digital technology, and without a remote shutter release, it is always necessary for the photographer to rush from the camera, over the breakwater wall and to slide into position on the left of the photo as we look at it, within an eight-second window of time. It is another hidden movement in the margins of the piece, which dispels one of the mysteries of the performance and explains why the father never has a child on his lap!

Beyond the camera itself, it might be assumed that the technology is limited in this piece – no tripod even, which explains the blurred wall encroaching from the bottom plane in several of the photos. But technology has, in fact, augmented *Borth Bench* in several ways. In the footsteps of Eadweard Muybridge, who first juxtaposed stills' photographs to reveal hidden movement in the 1870s, these images have been placed along a *timeline* – in this case using a movie-editing package – to animate them with cross-fades and to add a soundtrack. Further layers have therefore been added to the performance (text, music and the animation of transitions); in doing so, the potential for more complicated or directed readings has been exploited: the inclusion, for example, of the soundtrack *Summertime*, interpreted by Larry Adler on harmonica, focuses attention on the seasonal and the atmospheric. One step further would be to distribute the now-moving collection of photographs using online technology, streaming it on the web or compressing it for viewing on a mobile phone.

Thus, it becomes clear how central technology is to our reading of performance. It is the prime mediator of this piece, the main vehicle for constructing a relationship between the work and its audience.

Interactivity

Technology is often thought to work hand in hand with ideas of interactivity and, in the case of the animated and streamed version of this montage, this is clearly true. The action itself is motivated by an interaction between technology (a self-timed digital camera) and six willing victims. This is a one-sided interaction for sure but one that, through the pressurizing impetus of the timer, animates the family and produces various individualized responses – from posing to pouting. Here, the singular focus on a staged interaction with a static camera isolates the family from the wider context and produces a set of performed behaviours which might not otherwise be evident if the camera were simply documenting play on the beach, for instance. At a more human level, the montage documents family interactions and their development over years. This is most evident in the promotions of the children from lap to bench – a narrative in microcosm of growing independence and maturation. But it is also suggested by the different levels of physical interaction between the characters which (accurately or not) suggests a hands-on role for grandfather and mother and a more distanced one for the two 'end players'.

11

Outside of the content of the montage itself, interactivity is a function of the way this work is disseminated and, thus, how it impacts on various audiences. At the time of writing, this set of photographs has been used in the context of an inaugural lecture, a visiting professorship, an introductory session with first year university students and in an article on the problems of actor training lineages (Pitches 2009). Each context elicits different kinds of interactions, but what is consistently true is that some kind of interaction *happens*. This is nothing to do with the relative success or failure of the piece and everything to do with the nature of performance itself – that it demands a present engagement from its audience. Importantly in this piece, the notion of present or live interaction is broken into two phases: the interaction of the family with the camera, and the interaction of these different audiences with the mediated artwork. There is no direct relationship between these phases; instead, they remain as separate interactions. But each event is no less a performance for that.

Organization

Thinking of *Borth Bench* through the perspective of organization, perhaps the most abstract of lenses in this book, focuses attention immediately on two areas: the local and immediate organizational choices, and those which occur as post-event decisions – what we might call curatorial choices.

In the case of the former, this piece has a backstory of organizational challenges which promise to grow in complexity as the age of the participants increases: these are largely issues of a pragmatic nature but, unless they are managed efficiently, threaten to undermine the success of the project as a whole. They might be summed up as: How does this extended family get to Borth, together, each year, at roughly the same time, armed with the right goods to document the event? Good organization thus includes decisions relating to body, space, time and technology from the start.

But this focus on *practical* organization – on the stage-management or project-management of the event – does not explain why this piece as a whole might be called 'performance'. It is the higher level, curatorial aspect of organization which fulfils that purpose. For, evident in this piece are the controlling organizational decisions of a director – at the moment of the picture being taken and at the post-event arrangement of the results. Organization informs both the choreography of the players on the bench and on the page, and the journey between the two is evidence of how the artwork has been constructed. Such construction is best thought of as 'creative organization'.

Finally, there is a wider circle of organization at work here connected to the audience's experience of the performance: organization as entity not as process. Each audience is situated in a different institutional or organizational context and this, in turn, impacts on the act of witnessing itself. Airing this montage-movie in a lecture hall or a cinema will have radically different effects on its reception; placing it on the web has an equally important impact. Such effects are a product of the latent influence imposed by an organization's cultural associations and structures, and a consciousness of this framing for critics is imperative.

Summary

This extended analysis of *Borth Bench* reveals much about our purpose in this book. First is the evident interconnectedness of the perspectives, as a discussion of one way into the work already suggests two or three other analytical frames. Second is the idea, already discussed, of a concentric shape to the perspectives, like ripples out from a stone tossed into the water. Applying all six perspectives to one example takes us from the fine local detail (the placement of bodies on a bench, for example) to a broad cultural dimension (its reception in different organizational contexts). Third is the way in which the perspectives provide clarity and direction to the complexity of performance: focusing on sharply defined territory helps facilitate deep and concentrated analysis, even if it also raises questions about what doesn't fit into any particular chosen frame. Fourth is the critical distance these perspectives provide, even for work that is closely related to its creator: I may have taken each of these photos, rushing to make the bench in time each year but, viewing it, here, through the agency of six *perspectives*, transforms my attitude and places me in that balanced state of 'intense beholding' (p. 2). Finally, the perspectival analysis goes some way towards answering the complex question already posed: What constitutes a transformation from everyday action to performance? For clearly, the application of these frames helps identify some key themes of contemporary performance: questions of composition and choreography; of character, narrative, setting and relationships; of stage management; of audience interaction and of mediation; of the big and little picture perceived; of creative materials and the means by which they may be (opportunistically) manipulated, controlled and organized. It is not so much that *Borth Bench* is a performance *in and of itself*, but that distinct elements of the entire work, abstracted and given value by the application of these performance perspectives, should be viewed in the performance domain.

13

Chapter summaries

What follows are full and detailed explications of each of the performance perspectives introduced here. Each chapter is a conversation-in-print between commentators who collectively bridge a very wide range of performance experience, from studio-based professional practice, to theorized performance discourse. Such binary distinctions, however, are not often personified in the contributors themselves, who relish in blurring all such boundaries, as will be evident from their triangular chapters. You must feel free to sample each chapter independently and in any order, although the chapters themselves are conceived to tell an incremental story of the perspective and should ideally be experienced as one. Inevitably, there is a logic to our organization of the chapters and a sense that, as one moves through, ideas accrue and can be recapitulated and/or revised, but there are other logics to be constructed by any independent user of this book and we would be delighted to hear about those, as the book begins to be used in different contexts. Further reading is identified at the end of each chapter, but the full reference list is collated in the Bibliography at the end of the book.

Chapter 2 considers the multiple bodies at work in any performance context. At a surface level, there are the bodies of the performers and the spectators. In this chapter, Ramírez Ladrón de Guevara, Houstoun and Fenemore peel back that surface to reveal the complexities beneath it. They introduce us to the many types of body that might be experienced by performers and audiences – and often both, including the fleshly body, the absent body, the 'at risk' body and the transformed body. In section 2.1, Victor Ramírez Ladrón de Guevara focuses on the performer's body, examining how it is experienced as a 'lived' entity and simultaneously 'read' as a text. Contemporary dance and performance-maker Wendy Houstoun pursues these points further in section 2.2, taking a personal and provocative look at her own body – a *some* body – in performance. Finally, in section 2.3 Anna Fenemore broadens the field to encompass the spectating body in its many guises. The activities at the end of the chapter encourage you to explore some of the bodies mentioned by the three writers, along with the vast array of other potential bodies *in* and *of* performance.

Chapter 3 examines how space is designed, organized and constructed in and for performance. It focuses on scenography as a holistic approach to performance design, acknowledging the intricacies of space as a concept and appreciating its interrelationships with objects, materials, light, sound, architecture. Space is understood as an element of performance with which performing bodies interact, rather than being simply a background or set.

Hannah, Wilson and Palmer discuss different aspects and functions of space, exploring how it can be manipulated to create meanings for audiences. In section 3.1, Dorita Hannah critiques the effect of theatre architecture upon the experience of performance, explaining that all spaces 'perform', whether they are empty studios or Victorian piles. In section 3.2, Louise Ann Wilson takes this theme outside of the theatre building, describing how she is inspired by the human histories of everyday locations to make site-specific performances. Palmer, in section 3.3, uses his personal experiences of Wilson's and other works to consider how space functions as a dynamic participant in the performance event, and how the activation of space affects the role of the spectator. The activities for this chapter invite you to consider the impact of spatial design on the ways in which performances may be 'read' or understood.

Chapter 4 addresses the unique nature of performance time. Time is neither linear nor continuous; rather, it is fragmented and flexible, individual and manipulable. Dixon, Whelan and Gardner explore the inconsistencies of time in a range of performance contexts. In section 4.1, Steve Dixon traces a brief history of human relationships with time, citing technology as a critical influence on changing perceptions and attitudes. He uses Uninvited Guests' *Film* (2000) to examine how contemporary media performance can reflect a sense of the *extratemporal* or 'time out of time'. In section 4.2, Gregg Whelan discusses the processes of durational performance with particular reference to the 12-hour-long *Ghost Dance*, created and performed with Gary Winters. He proposes that narrative structures and communal experience are key components in the shared space of an extended timeframe. Tony Gardner, in section 4.3, queries the nature of duration, ephemerality and transience in performance, referencing the multiple times of Antony Gormley's *One & Other* (2009). He concludes by exploring the transformative potential inherent in performance time, and offering some models for its analysis. At the end of the chapter, the activities are designed to develop your vocabularies for understanding and manipulating time in performance.

Chapter 5 considers the influences of technology on and in performance. This chapter refers specifically to digital and new media technologies, rather than the technologies of the stage environment (for example, lighting, sound, costume, set). Wood, Gibson, Martelli and Popat acknowledge the prevalence of such technologies in the twenty-first-century Western world, and they concern themselves particularly with gaming and communications technologies in performance contexts. In section 5.1, Jessica Wood examines dramatic narrative and identity at the intersection between computer games and performance to consider representation and action in virtual worlds. Ruth Gibson and Bruno Martelli discuss these concepts in relation to *SwanQuake: House* (2008) in section 5.2. This installation integrates gaming and performance techniques, bleeding together 'virtual' and 'real' to highlight the complex nature of mediated environments. In section 5.3, Sita Popat challenges claims that technology leads us inevitably down the path to disembodiment. She proposes that digital performance practices offer methods by which we might understand better how to negotiate and inhabit a mixed reality world. The activities for this chapter guide you through a series of investigations as to how digital technologies affect communication and representation in performance.

Chapter 6 presents interactivity in performance as both an aesthetic principle and a political ideology. Interactivity is often associated with technology, but the connection is not exclusive. The social interactions of day-to-day living are fundamental to how we make sense of the world and our identities within it. Somers, Adams and O'Grady address interactive performance both with and without technologies, prioritizing the quality and significance of the interaction over the method. In section 6.1, John Somers describes a type of interactive theatre developed out of the work of Brazilian theatre practitioner Augusto Boal. It engages audience members as active players within the drama, emphasizing social responsibility and choice. Matt Adams shares Somers' interest in interactivity as a process of collective meaning-making, but Adams' work focuses on technologically-mediated interactions. In section 6.2, he draws on Blast Theory's performance practice to discuss the philosophies and creative processes behind the design of interactive experiences. Section 6.3, by Alice O'Grady, concludes the chapter by highlighting different levels of participation and interaction, and examining what she terms the 'inbetweenness of things'. The activities at the end of the chapter invite you to examine the social, cultural and theatrical implications of interactivity in performance.

In Chapter 7, we see how organization is an underlying theme throughout the book. This chapter proposes three main categories of organization: process, structure and entity. Process is fundamental to the orchestration of resources for the performance event to take place. Structure covers the funding, marketing and management of that event. Entity refers to the artists, groups and companies involved in making it happen. The three categories are not mutually exclusive, and it is the relationships between them that concern Brown, Greenstreet and Taylor. In section 7.1, Ralph Brown explores the relationships between performance and the creative and cultural industries. He explains how the increasing international importance of this sector is raising the profile of performance 'creatives' as being uniquely equipped to operate effectively in contemporary social and economic environments. Teo Greenstreet, in section 7.2, expands on these points through a personal account of how his training and experience as a professional performer prepared him for work in the creative industries. In section 7.3, Calvin Taylor takes a historical look at this twenty-first-century correlation between organization and performance, and highlights the increased centrality of networking and collaboration skills in both fields. The activities for this chapter encourage you to notice and evaluate the implicit organizational processes and skills inherent in your day-to-day practices of performance.

In Chapter 8, the Epilogue, we revisit the idea of performance in the light of the six perspectives presented so far and address some of the problems with the concentric model of perspectives presented in the introduction. Instead, a 'flower' model of relationships is proposed, one which retains the singularity of each perspective as well as highlighting the many potential interactions possible. Finally, the Epilogue puts the ball firmly in the readers' court, asking you, personally, to define your future trajectory of performance practice and research.

Activities

Returning now to the main content of the chapter, here are a number of suggested ways you might test out, in action, the ideas of this chapter; these have been divided into individual work, group discussion and practical activity.

➤ *Solo activity*

Look closely at the montage of photos in Illustration 1.1.

- What resonances do they have with your own experiences?
- How does your reading of the groupings differ from the one described here?
- Are there photographs you can think of in your own collection which have performance potential?
- Why?

➤ *Discussion activity 1*

Recount a simple story to your partner – a folk tale or an oft-told experience of your own. Retell that story focusing on any one perspective introduced here.

- How does the story change when focusing on just one element?
- Are there new discoveries to be made about a well-known story from focusing down in this way?

➤ *Discussion activity 2*

In small groups, consider examples of how your own 'everyday behaviour' might be thought of as performance: contexts for this might include Freshers' week, an interview, a night out, Halloween, work experience.

- What distinguishes the activity from merely being 'performance-like' to being performance in a more grounded way?

➤ *Practical activity 1*

You will need a set of five photographs from your own collection that you are happy to share with the group.

- Arrange these photos to tell a particular narrative you are interested to develop: perhaps a growing-up story, or a disastrous or memorable holiday.
- Show your series to a partner.
- Now watch as they reorganize the photos to tell a different story of their own.
- Take this different story as a starting point for a one-minute devised piece of work.
- You must tell this new story with a predominant emphasis on either: body, space, or time.
- Present your piece and then re-devise another minute's work using the same story but a different perspective.

How have things changed?

➤ *Practical activity 2*

You will need a mobile phone with a camera or a digital stills camera, a laptop with simple digital photo editing software and a means to project images onto a screen.

- Decide on a simple theme to stimulate your thinking:
    spring
    decay
    heat
    tension
  Leave the studio and take exactly 50 pictures with a mobile phone or digital camera, responding to one of the themes or to an agreed theme of your own.
- Drop the photos into a slideshow software package – iPhoto or iMovie for Macintosh, Photostory 3 for PC.
- Experiment with *organizing* them on a *timeline* to enhance the theme further with simple embedded texts or soundtracks.

- How does this layering affect our reading of the montage?
- Project the images onto a screen or wall and add live *bodies* into the slide presentation, manipulate the space of the audience to exploit the theme further and to develop a clear mode of interaction, lengthen or shorten the *duration* of the slideshow.
- Discuss the piece, paying due attention to the different perspectives at work.

Notes

1   This BBC programme used a basic dietary assessment of a family's eating habits to project the effects over a generation. This often shocking projection, formulated as a 30-second film, was created using morphing technology so that the kids were seen to age, relative to their current diet, before the audience's eyes.

Further reading

Aston, Elaine and Savona, George (1991) *Theatre as Sign System: A Semiotics of Text and Performance*. London and New York: Routledge.

Auslander, Philip (ed.) (2003) *Performance: Critical Concepts in Literary and Cultural Studies*. London and New York: Routledge.

Huxley, Michael and Witts, Noel (2002) The Twentieth Century Performance Reader, 2nd edn. London: Routledge.

Leach, Robert (2008) *Theatre Studies: The Basics*. Abingdon: Routledge.

Pitches, Jonathan (2009) 'Spinal Snaps: Tracing a Backstory of European Actor Training', *Performance Research*, 14(2): 85–95.

Schechner, Richard (2006) *Performance Studies: An Introduction*. London: Routledge.

2   Body

Introduced and edited by Anna Fenemore

Introduction

This chapter will introduce the concept of the multiple bodies *in* and *of* performance:

> Human subjectivity is not constituted by one single discourse, but by the intersection of many, overlapping discourses ... the actor is constructed through not one body, but many. (Evans 2009: 170)

The three sections will offer insights into the multifarious ways in which bodies are used *in* performance (to frame, to represent, to act as subject for, to watch or experience), created *by* performance and become products of performance. It will do this through a series of contemplations on a number of different potential performance bodies. This chapter is written from a position of knowing that *the body* is of great concern today in media, in philosophical thought, in art and performance, and suggests that the body is being rethought and reconsidered by artistic work and philosophical thought for two primary reasons:

- technological and scientific advances/experiments have radically challenged notions of body 'authenticity' (live organ/tissue transplants, machine implants acting as human organs, Artificial Intelligence, cloning, genetics, IVF, cosmetic surgery, gender realignment, computer generated bodies (avatars) and virtual environments);
- these advances in technology and science, and also in philosophy, are breaking down binaries of *the body* in modern thought: mind and body, life and death, male and female, masculine and feminine, young and old, nature and culture. These distinctions are no longer as clear as they once were considered to be – or are, in fact, actively disputed, such that the boundaries are starting to bleed, and terms that conflate the historically opposed binaries are becoming naturalized ('bodymind', 'psychophysical'): instead of either/or, we are understanding these as both/and.

In section 2.1, 'Any body? The multiple bodies of the performer', Victor Ramírez Ladrón de Guevara begins to unpack some of the major concerns of 'the body' as an aesthetic and performative entity. The performer's body is introduced as both a site for representation (something that can be 'read'), and as a 'lived' entity. Ramírez Ladrón De Guevara addresses what might be termed the textual, the lived, the fleshly, the visceral, the unnatural and the imagined bodies.

In section 2.2, 'Some body and no body: the body of a performer', contemporary dance and performance-maker Wendy Houstoun offers a provocative section on her own body in performance. This section is deliberately designed to give a specific example of *some*body, and is therefore localized and personal, and acts as a point of specificity in this chapter. This section also enacts the political position that all bodies in performance are not just 'a' body, or 'the' body, but are always 'some' body. Picking up from Ramírez Ladrón de Guevara, Houstoun interrogates her position as *some* body at the level of both 'representation' (how it looks to somebody else) and 'livedness' (how it feels to herself). Houstoun addresses what might be termed *some* body, *no* body, the 'at risk' body and the ageing body.

In section 2.3, 'Every body: performance's other bodies', I draw together the themes of the two previous contributions and begin to consider the *other* bodies of the performance act – spectating bodies – through addressing what might be termed the social, the uncomfortable, the absent, the transformed and the irreplaceable bodies.

Finally, this chapter acknowledges the impossibility of the task it has set out to do, through introducing the vast number of *other* bodies that cannot, for both pragmatic and philosophical reasons, be included here. The chapter ends with a list of the many other bodies that might be attributable to performance, but asserts absolutely that this list is not complete, and that such a list would always remain inexhaustible and indefinable.

2.1   Any body? The multiple bodies of the performer

Victor Ramírez Ladrón de Guevara

Despite its apparent simplicity, the term 'body' is a contested concept. It is used in a great number of contexts and alluding to a wide range of different objects, organisms and concepts. In this way, it is possible to use the word 'body' to talk about *the body* of work of a director, *the body* of a wine, *the body* of a text (its argument), an organization's *body*, a *body* of water, and, of course, of human *bodies*.

Thus, it may be easy to understand why it is almost impossible to offer a single definition of what a body is. However, it is important to notice that the examples mentioned in the previous paragraph clearly show that, whenever someone refers to a body, he or she refers to something that is neither fixed nor homogeneous. Bodies are formed of a series of different elements that are combined, interrelated and, often, difficult to distinguish from each other. The body of work of a director, for example, will probably contain pieces produced in a wide range of styles and genres, unfinished works, latent projects, and, arguably, even those instances when that work has served as an influence for pieces produced by other people.

A body always is, to a certain extent, indefinable.

Therefore, rather than trying to define what a body is, it may be more productive to discuss the ways in which the body is thought of and the ways in which the body is acted *upon*, *on* and *through*. At first glance, the human body appears to be a singular, stable, homogeneous and harmonious entity that defies the multiplicity characterizing the connotations of the other bodies discussed earlier in this section. However, the human body is in a process of constant change (at least, at a biological and chemical level), and the human's perception of the body is limited. The body only makes itself present to one's awareness in a sporadic and fragmented way (in fact, this chapter argues, the body's *disappearance* is a key aspect of the way in which we experience our bodies; this will be further discussed later on).

This limited awareness of one's body provides a false sense of unity and continuity in those who perceive it (the continuous chemical and biological changes of the body, for example, tend not to affect the overall perception of the body). The body is therefore transformed into an *object* that comes into *being* only when it becomes present in one's own consciousness. In the West, during the last few centuries, the body has largely been considered an object that can be acted upon, a vessel that transports, a carrier, or a tool that can be used to achieve specific tasks. To think about the body in these terms renders it, to a certain extent, unproblematic (Welton 1999: 3). The body becomes unimportant in itself, and it is only relevant when associated with other objects, subjects, fields and concepts.

Meaningfully, the body has been largely absent from philosophical, sociological, political and theatrical discussions for the most part of the eighteenth, nineteenth and early twentieth centuries. It is only in recent decades that there has been an explosion in studies of the body. A great amount of contemporary literature discussing the body centres its analysis in cultural and ideological analyses *about* the body – largely influenced by psychologists such as Freud (1977) and Lacan (1980) and philosophers such as Derrida (1990), or Bourdieu (1990), or Foucault (1991). Feminist writers, such as Irigaray (1985), Grosz (1994) and Kristeva (1995) have positioned the body as a central theme in their theories. Advances in cognitive psychology have allowed writers such as Damasio (1999) and Lakoff and Johnson (1999) to reconsider the roles, functions and boundaries of the body in human experience. It is beyond the scope of the present chapter to offer a full account of the works and theories outlined here.[1] However, to a certain extent, all those theories and their different understandings of the body were coined as a response to a particular conception of the body first proposed by the French philosopher René Descartes in the seventeenth century. The body, for Descartes, is considered to be a separate entity from the mind (a separation otherwise known as Cartesian dualism).

The textual body

In the West, as outlined, the predominant approach to the understanding of the body has been largely based on a 'dualism'. In this approach, the body is largely subordinated to the mind and it is precisely our minds that are 'most essential to us as persons' (Welton 1999: 1). Descartes formulated his theory of the relationship between mind and body within a historical period known as the Enlightenment, which, amongst other things, privileged the acquisition of knowledge through the rigorous application of a scientific method. The world, reality itself, could only be apprehended by the rational capabilities of the mind. The mind looks at the world as a series of phenomena from which knowledge can be obtained. In this approach, the body itself is also transformed into an object of knowledge. Discussing Cartesian dualism, also known as the Cartesian split, Donn Welton signals the way in which Descartes:

> reduced the body to what is extended in time and space and, thereby, what is measurable. The body becomes an object whose true being is disclosed only by those natural sciences that attend to it. (Welton 1999: 2)

In other words, that which is 'true' in the body is only that which can be rationally and objectively observed, measured, tested and demonstrated. Thus, anatomy, chemistry, biology, and medicine became the disciplines that framed the understanding of the body (a trend that continues in our days with the development of fields such as sports science and ergonomics). The anatomical and the physiological body – the discovery and mapping of the body's muscles, bones, organs and their interconnections in *systems* (for example, the digestive and the nervous systems) – has been a direct result of this approach. Undoubtedly, studying the body through the natural sciences has offered human beings a great number of insights and benefits. Nowadays, we have the possibility of living healthier and longer lives in which new technological apparatus aids us to surpass our natural biological limitations.

This *scientific* approach is still largely dominant in the ways that we understand our minds and bodies. Knowledge, as taught in schools, is based on the acquisition and development of rational abilities. Even in those processes and techniques focused in the development of the body, it is commonly assumed that the body can be transformed and shaped by the sole employment of our rational abilities (after all, trespassing the body's limits is often claimed to be just an issue of 'mind over matter').

The body understood as an object of knowledge has also been a determinant factor in the way that human sciences (containing disciplines such as sociology and psychology), the humanities (philosophy, English and cultural studies, for example) and the arts (including theatre and dance) have dealt with the body. For most of the last three centuries, these disciplines have considered the body merely as reflecting (and being shaped by) practices, behaviours, and the ideas and theories that give them meaning. The body is thus treated as an object of representation. The body as a medium of representation does not mean anything in itself; it only stands for a text, a sign, a symbol or an ideological construct of something else (Csordas 1994: 9).

In this way, the body acquires a semantic value that is inscribed within a semiotic system.[2] The body is yet another text that needs to be interpreted and is open to be *read*. To date, a great number of theories and approaches that discuss and analyze bodies look at them from a primarily semiotic perspective.

Let's think for a second of the actor's body. In theatre, actors are commonly asked to express with clarity their character's meanings and intentions. Particularly when working in realist and naturalistic genres, actors use established conventions that the audience is then expected to decipher or decode. In fact, Erika Fischer-Lichte has argued that the history of acting in the last three centuries has been based on theatrical techniques that were modelled by treating the body as a text 'composed of artificial signs' (the declamatory acting style of the early nineteenth century), a text 'composed in the natural language of emotions' (the realist and naturalist acting styles of the late nineteenth and early twentieth century) or as a text with the 'raw material for sign processes' (the avant garde acting styles of the twentieth century) (Fischer-Lichte 1989: 22–9).

24

However, we just need to think of our own body and those concrete and specific bodies that surround us to realize that the body is *not* a text. Although it can transmit signs and meanings, the body resists signification and meaning. Certain aspects of the body can be selected and then interpreted in certain ways. But the human body (as the other bodies discussed at the beginning of this section) is formed of a series of elements that make it impossible to reduce that body to a single aspect, resisting a single definition and unitary, simple and definite significations.[3]

The lived body

Opposing the semiotic approach to the body, the philosopher Maurice Merleau-Ponty[4] (1964, 1968 and 2002) developed an approach called 'phenomenology', based on the body-as-a-lived-entity. Merleau-Ponty argued that our contact with external reality is always mediated by our senses and it is precisely our perception of the world that gives sense to it. In a Cartesian dualistic approach to the body, the 'subjectivity' (and therefore 'unreliability') of the senses is counteracted by the 'objective' abilities of a detached mind. In a phenomenological approach, the mind is not detached from the body's senses. The external reality, the body's senses and the individual's consciousness are perpetually and inexorably intertwined. For Descartes, thought was the essence of being (*cogito ergo sum* – I think therefore I am). For Merleau-Ponty, the body in its act of perceiving is what constitutes being, and this forms the basis of phenomenology. However, perceiving the world is not a passive act. As Alva Noë argues:

> Perception is not something that happens to us or in us. It is something that we do … the world makes itself available to the perceiver through physical movement and interaction. (Noë 2004: 1)

We *experience* and make sense of the world through the interplay of a wide range of senses, systems, internal and external stimuli. Merleau-Ponty refers to this dynamic grouping as one's being-in-the world. Our perception not only filters (and therefore articulates) reality but also, as Noë argues, it necessarily implies an active engagement with the world surrounding us.

Merleau-Ponty's ideas have had a profound effect on a wide range of performance studies scholars who have used a phenomenological approach to engage with diverse disciplines. Bert O'States (1987) was one of the first scholars who attempted to analyze theatrical phenomena in this manner. Garner (Jr) (1994) has looked into the work of a wide range of playwrights (such as Samuel Beckett and Caryl Churchill) and analyzed their work within a phenomenological framework. Machon (2009) has been inspired by Merleau-Ponty's ideas to create a (syn)aesthetic[5] approach. Through this approach, she has analyzed the practices of companies such as Punchdrunk,[6] and performers such as Akram Khan.[7] Theorists such as Zarrilli (2009) have used Merleau-Ponty's work to analyze acting processes; Fraleigh (2004) has employed his theories to understand and reconsider dance practices; and Sobchack (1992) has applied phenomenology to film analysis.[8]

However, the methods favoured by phenomenologists are still contested by many who are firmly inscribed within a legacy of the Cartesian approach. As mentioned at the beginning of this section, it is extremely difficult to understand the primacy of the body in a human being's existence when the body often tends to largely disappear from one's awareness (try, for example, to remember how much of your body was present to your awareness when you were reading the previous paragraph). In an attempt to rehabilitate 'the experiential core of Cartesian dualism, while at the same time identifying its fundamental error' (Csordas 1994: 8), Drew Leder in *The Absent Body* (1990) has suggested two distinct bodies articulated in co-dependent modes of experience: the ecstatic (or fleshly) body and the recessive (or visceral) body.

The ecstatic (or fleshly) body

Leder refers to the ecstatic (or fleshly) body as the sensorial and motor skills that mediate one's existence in relation to the world. The body engages with the world through its exteroception (the information/awareness elicited through hearing, seeing, smelling, touching, tasting and moving) and proprioception (that information/awareness obtained from the body's muscles and internal organs – for example, the heartbeat, spatial orientation and balance). It is the body's *fleshly* quality that helps to distinguish that which is felt as an internal sensation and that which is experienced as an external sensation. Yet, the ecstatic body does not only perceive, it also modulates the senses of the body by simultaneously foregrounding and filtering the stimuli surrounding it.

Think, for example, of driving a car. During this activity, the senses of the body are affected by a multitude of stimuli that *need* to be noticed (mainly stimulating one's aural and visual senses: the road, the other vehicles, passers-by, signs, traffic lights). However, the body's other senses will be mostly *inactive* while driving. The sense of taste remains mainly passive (that is, unless one eats whilst driving); one's taste and smell provide little feedback to one's consciousness; and, despite the great amount of movement necessary in order to steer the wheel, push the pedals and change gears, one's kinaesthetic sense (the sense that gives the body information regarding its movements and its spatial location/positioning) is largely disregarded. In other words, there are large sections of one's body that *disappear* from one's awareness.

There is, therefore, a double quality that sustains the ecstatic body. The first one is an 'active' quality. This body presupposes the employment of actions that define one's own engagement with the world. One's-being-in-the-world (one's subjective experience) is shaped by inhabiting a specific position within the perceiving/acting continuum (even when we enact largely passive actions, such as listening or thinking). Its second quality is a constant process of *disappearance*. Focused in the execution of the action, the ecstatic body continually denies itself as an object of experience and only offers a fragmented perception of both itself and the world that surrounds it.

The recessive (or visceral) body

If the world of the ecstatic body is one of action, the world of the recessive body is one of latent feeling. This body encloses the inner anatomical and physiological constituents of the body (such as organs, bones, tissues, cells, and blood), as well as the chemical and biological processes not dependent on one's will or present to one's awareness. To better understand the transition between the ecstatic and the recessive body, Leder gives the example of eating an apple (Leder, 1990: 38–9). The act of eating it will provoke a series of stimuli that will be perceived by the body's senses (its weight, texture, taste and smell). However, once that the apple has been swallowed, the apple's stimuli on the body's senses virtually vanish, whilst the apple itself remains 'within' the body and the body continues to act towards it (digestion and so on).

Yet, Leder argues that the recessive character of the body (its latency) can emerge at any time (for example, can be made present to one's awareness) by a process which he calls dys-*appearance*. By employing the prefix *dys* (generally used to signal something that does not work properly for example, a *dys*function), Leder indicates that the depth that characterizes this body only surfaces when the habitual conditions that surround it are disrupted and are 'apart ... from our ordinary mastery and health' (Leder 1990: 87). Pain (See Scarry 1985 and Morgan 2002) and discomfort are the main ways in which the recessive body becomes ecstatic. When a wound

27

occurs, blood makes itself present. When hungry, one can *feel* one's stomach. If a piece of the aforementioned apple gets stuck in one's throat, it would be possible to feel one's digestive tract. But, when the body is able to achieve a state of homeostasis (balance), the body then *recedes*, it makes itself *absent*. Our bodily experience is, in fact, largely recessive and even phenomena experienced by the ecstatic body have the potential to *sink* into the recessive. Leder argues that:

> I do not heal my scars, build my eyes, supervise the growth or loss of my hair. While it is within my province to move my hand, it was not I that first posited fingers, nor can I prevent their arthritic aging. Even my own hand movements elude control when motor reflexes come into play. Just as the visceral can surface to volition, as through biofeedback or yogic techniques, so surface motility can sink into the realm of the automatic. (Leder 1990: 56)

Therefore, large aspects of what was described as the ecstatic body tend to become elements of the recessive one. Arguably, the *dys-appearance* of the body is one of the main reasons that Cartesian dualism is so prevalent in contemporary Western culture. The fact that the body generally 'surfaces' through pain and discomfort has led to 'a bias elaborated in the Western tradition by construing the body as the source of epistemological error, moral error, and mortality' (Csordas 1994: 6). The effacement of the body (its gradual erasure) can clearly lead to the belief of an all-powerful inner sense of awareness or consciousness that rules and controls the body. However, one's awareness and consciousness are firmly rooted in the perception of specific inner and outer stimuli. One's awareness does not exist as an alien or separate entity of the body; it is necessarily mediated through the body's senses, and therefore *embodied* from a specific stand-point. More importantly, in order to act efficiently, the body needs to *erase* itself from its own perception (think what would happen in the act of driving if our awareness was centred on our own bodies). When stimulated, 'the body conceals itself precisely in the act of revealing what is Other' (Leder 1990: 22), making it possible to direct one's perception to the most tangible, urgent or desirable stimuli *outside* or *inside* its *fleshly* boundaries.

There is an already established tradition of performance artists who have experimented with the interplay between the ecstatic and the recessive bodies. Marina Abramovic,[9] Franko B,[10] and Dominic Johnson[11] (amongst many others) have made works in which they have cut themselves. In these performances, their recessive bodies (manifested through their blood) become visible and performative. But also, by doing so, the boundaries of their ecstatic bodies blur into visceral depths.

The unnatural body

Although there is a common tendency to think of our bodies as 'natural', the majority of what the body does is regulated by the culture where that body is situated. The way a body moves, the way it gestures, the way in which we eat, drink and even sleep are all acts that are culturally dependent. It is only necessary to look into the habits and traditions of different ethnic groups to realize that culture shapes most (if not all) elements of human activity. The sociologist and anthropologist Marcel Mauss (2004) argued that human beings are educated by 'techniques of the body' that are later assimilated by (or, to use Leder's terms, *recede* into) the body and then are considered 'natural' or 'normal'. A great number of aspects of the body that we consider 'organic' are, in fact, the result of the successful learning process of a specific 'technique of the body' (including, as Judith Butler (1999) argues, our gender).

For example, when my niece was three years old she was *learning* when to gasp. For a long time, she could not understand when it was appropriate to gasp or not and therefore she responded to a wide range of dissimilar questions with an equally surprising and convincing gasp (questions such as: Are you hungry? Which dress would you like to wear today? Would you like to go to the park?).

The opposition between what is considered 'natural' and what is deemed a 'learnt behaviour' is particularly important in relation to performing training techniques. A great number of performer training techniques emphasize the unnatural quality of the body (an aspect that will be developed by Fenemore in her discussion of the uncomfortable body in section 2.3), particularly in those training styles that are overtly *physical*. Yet, numerous performer training techniques strive to uncover the performer's 'natural' or 'neutral' body. The idea of a 'natural' body is, however, also a cultural construct. Evans has lucidly argued that:

> [s]ocial and cultural paradigms have influenced the development of the 'natural' body [which] in turn influenced the development of what is known as 'neutral' body training. The dominant paradigms continue to have a strong association with white, male/heterosexual, able-bodied culture ... The 'neutral' body, in its most abstract sense, is unattainable – it is quite literally and metaphorically a 'no-man's-land'. (Evans 2009: 117)

29

The training body of the performer is always unnatural, a constructed entity that responds to specific stylistic and aesthetic criteria. Aptly, Zarrilli has coined the term: 'aesthetic inner bodymind' to refer to the complex relation between performing training techniques and their process of embodiment by the performer (Zarrilli 2009: 55–7).

The imagined body

For the purposes of this chapter, I have decided to talk of the performer's body on stage as an 'imagined body'. The imagined body is the one that inhabits a performance act, usually associated with the creation of characters. The processes of creation of characters developed by Strasberg (1988), Chekhov (2002) and Stanislavski (2010) point towards the 'construction' of a body that is not the actor's but that belongs to a specific character. Character creation for these practitioners can be achieved through a combination of rational and cognitive abilities (such as the use of imagination in Chekhov's 'psychological gesture') or physical transformations (such as gaining/losing significant amounts of weight, as done in some method acting styles).

It is possible to relate the imagined body to Zarrilli's fourth mode of the performer's embodied experience: 'the aesthetic outer body' (2009: 58). For Zarrilli, this body does not centre on the construction of a character but, in a more general sense, it refers to the enactment of 'a specific performance score [shaped by] one's energy, attention, and awareness to the qualities and constraints of the aesthetic form and dramaturgy informing the score' (Zarrilli 2009: 58). Understanding the imagined body in this way allows us to include in this category dancers, musicians and most performance artists. Furthermore, Zarrilli's inscription of this body as 'aesthetic' allows us to understand that the forms that it attains are situated within a specific artistic style and genre. The body is (literally) moulded by the aesthetic form in which it is positioned (ballet bodies, for example, are significantly different from the bodies of dancers of other styles).

It is also important to remember that, as Joseph Roach has argued, aesthetics is always situated in and shaped by a specific ideological framework (Roach 1989: 156–7). For Roach, there are three 'ideological modalities' that affect the body. Roach uses these modalities to discuss key characteristics of the theatre in the eighteenth century. However, they are still relevant and appropriate to understanding contemporary relationships between ideology and our bodies. The first one is a process of idealization or appropriation by which cultures *create* an ideal concept/image of how a body should be. Men (see Dutton 1995) and women (see Brand and

Teunissen 2004) are equally subjected to this process, and even those of us who do not share these idealized characteristics are influenced and affected by them. Nowadays, the media (for example, film and television) plays an important role in the process of idealization of the body.

Roach's second ideological modality is a process of inscription and erasure:

> Inscription is the ideological production of bodily images and behaviours. As a process of constructing meanings from material forms, it provides idealization and appropriation with a technical means of expression. Inscription foregrounds and reiterates favoured representations; erasure occludes the undesirable ones. (Roach 1989: 159)

Roach's last ideological modality is a process of uniformity and specialization. Nowadays, bodies are trained in increasingly specific 'techniques of the body', a great number of which reject any sense of individualization. Bodies, particularly in commercial and mainstream performances, are treated as objects that need to be able to perform certain skills (have a specific singing/vocal range, know how to execute specific dancing steps, execute basic acrobatic exercises) irrespective of the body's age, gender or ethnicity.

There is, however, an undeniable tension between the ideological inscriptions of the body and the body as a lived entity. One of the aims of this section of the chapter has been to emphasize the latter and to question the former (the body as a text or as a site of representation). While it is impossible to negate the effects that our culture (its ideology) has on the way in which we experience our being-in-the-world, fixed distinctions between *textual* and *lived* bodies are becoming increasingly blurred. In this context, it is important to remember Herbert Blau's warning: '[t]here is nothing more coded than the body' (Blau quoted in Auslander 1997: 91). After all, ideologies are also always experienced as embodied modes of existence. Phelan (1997), Fraleigh (2004), Broadhurst and Machon (2009), Counsell and Mock (2009), Machon (2009) and Zarrilli (2009) are only a few of the many authors in performance studies who are making use of these interconnections and who are opening new fields of enquiry and practice through their explorations. No longer a mere object, the notion of the body as a fixed entity is fiercely contested by performance scholars and practitioners alike. The body is not a finished process; the body is always in a process of becoming. And, as a result of these processes, new ways of thinking, new ways of doing and new ways of experiencing are constantly emerging.

Introduction to 2.2

Through his application of notions of the textual, lived, fleshly, visceral, unnatural and imagined bodies, Ramírez Ladrón de Guevara's central concern with the 'presence' of performing bodies is made apparent. He argues that all bodies in the everyday and in performance fluctuate between moments of being present to themselves, being absent to themselves, being 'read' by others and being 'experienced' or 'embodied' by self and others. This fluctuation, or slippage between different ways of being in the world, can be picked up on in section 2.2 by performance-maker Wendy Houstoun.

Houstoun articulates in her writing a fluid slippage between Ramírez Ladrón De Guevara's different modes of being and, in so doing, reflects on the slippery nature of performing itself and the shifting nature of knowledge in the process of performing between knowing *that* you are doing something and knowing *how* you are doing it. With this in mind, it will be useful to note in the following section:

- moments where Houstoun's body is absent to her;
- moments where her body is very present to her;
- moments where Houstoun's body is 'read' as though text by others;
- moments where her body is described as 'lived' or 'embodied';
- moments where Houstoun knows-that she does something;
- moments where she knows-how she does something.

Simultaneously, be aware of how these moments are not occurring for Houstoun as absolute binaries (that is, either one *or* the other, absent or present, read or embodied). Instead, these moments begin to bleed into each other such that the overall experience is one of a shifting between, and simultaneity of, multiple ways of knowing and experiencing her body. These key ways of understanding bodily experience can be further noted in section 2.3, when they are applied to the 'other' bodies of performance: spectating bodies.

Houstoun also writes from the position of one particular performer with one particular set of experiences and understandings of her own performing body. Houstoun is, in a very real sense in this chapter, *some* body, but she is also at all times conscious that she is '*some* body observed'. As Melrose has argued:

Widespread uses of the term 'the body' are problematic in the context of performance-making ... The use of the term 'the body' is a nonsense

... because use of that term in such contexts tends to objectify, to generalise, essentialise, anonymise, and deprofessionalise the input of expert performers ... [and] what those who use the term 'the body' in the context of performing arts are actually dealing with is neither 'the body', nor 'a body', but rather 'some body observed'. (Melrose 2006: 1)

2.2 Some body and no nody: the body of a performer

Wendy Houstoun

Some body

I hit 50 last year and this episode has introduced the concept of history into my life. Or has introduced the concept that my life is history.

An eccentric training in the mid-1970s involved learning many dance techniques with a view to teaching them in a state school. I started working life in the 1980s – in Doc Martens with Ludus Dance Company – touring schools in content-based movement pieces. Movement pieces directed by theatre directors. Since then, I have maintained a practice that ebbs and flows between devised company involvement, collaborative projects and solo practice. Lumiere & Son Theatre Company, Rose English, Nigel Charnock and DV8 Physical Theatre were all meetings made in the 1980s and continued over the next decades with, perhaps, DV8's pieces *If Only ...* and *Strange Fish*, consolidating a reputation for emotional honesty and physical daring.

In the mid-1990s, my solo practice developed (*Haunted, Happy Hour, 48 Almost Love Lyrics, Desert Island Dances, Keep Dancing*), retaining a commitment to small and intimate spaces. As well, new collaborations with David Hinton (film-maker), Tim Etchells (writer/director) and Jonathan Burrows (maker/performer) extended my interests out into film, textual concerns and analysis of movement.

In the last decade, joining forces with Forced Entertainment on *Bloody Mess* (2004) and *The World in Pictures* (2006) and with Gary Stevens on his piece *Ape* (2008/2009) saw a move towards more performative territories. Their work on how movement copes with the rigour of logical thought and real time process has initiated a new thinking which has seeped into my solo projects and a new strand of practice creating/directing work with other people.

A lot of my moving and dancing life is beyond words. As soon as words start piping up, the body and its experience has a tendency to slip out of view and this is, for me, as it should be. My strongest impressions of moving coincide with memory and language disappearing. The briefest of moments seem to take a long time and all the other stuff that exists has led up to or away from those moments. The other stuff does, though, consist very much of language.

Whose body?

No body

I learnt very early on in dance training that how I feel is not necessarily how I look, and the journey through movement and performance practices has been a process of aligning my own internal perception with external commentaries. A journey of adjustments made in the attempt to eradicate discrepancy.

Over time, I have, among other things, been asked to: extend my leg, soften my back, extend my neck, drop my shoulders, release, contract, to open my feet out to the floor, to lower my eye line, make eye contact, be less emotional, to think more, think less, to smile, to use the space, to push into the floor, to have confidence, be less knowing, to listen to the music, listen to other people, to take more time, to be still.

And when I do move, it is possible to occupy different places simultaneously – the place where internal sensations and private ideas dominate. Ideas like: What if I move from everywhere and nowhere? What if I could get inside time and push it out? What if I imagined the air was a supportive structure? What if movement were a kind of marked dance of memory? What if I moved like a bad dancer? Ideas that have nothing to do with the actions I am carrying out and which are usually operating from some muscle memory beyond the brain. And, at the same time, occupying that other place where exterior commentaries cut in from the outside. Things like: 'relate more to the audience', 'don't hurry that bit', 'more stillness', 'don't try so hard', 'more shape', 'less self absorbed', 'give up the fight'.

In performance, these exterior adjustments are often articulated in response to yesterday's conditions. What follows is a lurch from one inept performance to another – until after maybe 25 renditions of inappropriate choices something settles into a place of stability.

A place where maybe what I feel finally meets how I appear?

Where internal and external commentaries find agreement.

One recurring thing I have noticed in moving and performing is that the more invisible and intangible I feel myself to be, the more resonant the response from outside is.

Is the ultimate aim emptiness? Not sure.

But I think this stuff has to do with inside and outside, and it's what the body is always up against. Even my own physique can contradict the intention of my actions. The first solo piece I made I thought was deeply meaningful and important but, when I performed it, people laughed. Going with the laughs has seemed like the best and only option.

A somebody or a nobody?

In dance/theatre pieces, I have taken the role of: Another worker in the *Karen Silkwood Story*, a girl in a forest, a girl in a rock band, a member of a bowling team, a punk, a mushroom on a hilltop, a butterfly, a turtle, a cheerleader, a Neanderthal, a barmaid, a crime victim, a clairvoyant, a dancer, a principal boy, a magician's assistant, the back half of a camel, the back half of a horse, a baby, a caterpillar, a soldier in a war, an interpreter of history, a rebellious member of a dance troupe, a person who ends up alone, a dancer who fights against injustice, a celebrity, a smoker, a drinker.

And now and then – a body.

I have been lifted, caught and dropped, I have dived into water, fallen from a ladder, pierced someone's shoulders with acupuncture feathers, been suspended from my feet upside down from a rope, rolled over stones, broken through a sheet of sugar glass, fallen backwards from a high tower, walked on wine glasses, been thrown out of a car driving at speed into my own performance, lurched around underpasses, tottered on high heels with my legs tied together carrying a large man, shouted through a megaphone under the spray of water, screamed into a microphone while losing my voice, run across a field for hours, danced in unison, collided with the group, moved alone and, now and then, just stood still.

I have (by critics and friends) variously been described as: louche, rebellious, idiosyncratic, eccentric, unlikely, a ghost, a fighter, honest, funny, irritating, boring, likeable, warm, energetic, daring, brave, vapid, silly, empty, stupid, experienced, clever, cerebral, humorous, quirky, casual, bossy, vulnerable, versatile, witty, courageous, engaging, too clever for my own good, a female Bob Dylan, a young Lynn Seymour, a brilliant renaissance woman, a small curly-haired woman whom one would hardly notice on an East Village street, a complete amateur, insincere and powerful.

These multiple actions, roles and observations are all joined not only in my memory. They are part of a continuity inside my body. All the same thing. Something to put my body into. And somewhere inside my body I am all and none of them. Inside the outer appearance is one continuous body – inside which I am – and they all occupy some similar process. They are me inside of time – or perhaps me escaping time. They are almost memorable because – at their best – they exist outside memory like the wordless place of a fall off a ladder, or a jump. The word jump is not a jump and – happily – never will be.

I am not my body.

The 'at risk' body

The acts I have described above have more similarity to stunts than they do to expressive movement. The meaning is tied up in the action and all that is required for the response is just to carry them out.

I say 'just', but that really is what is required. Just do the action and nothing else. Inherent in this 'just' is the speed the idea is operated on. If there is any kind of a gap between thought and action then the act becomes perilous.

I think this is what people mean by 'risk' but, to be honest, I have never quite been able to equate these actions with risk of any kind.

Activities that appear dangerous often carry with them less risk, as they are given their due attention. Appropriate levels of fear have been felt previous to the action itself. The fear is needed to focus the mind on the specifics of the action, so when I fall from a ladder I am definitely going to be concentrating.

A while ago, I strained a muscle due to looking out of the window while skipping. A careless and risky strategy for someone who, these days, is best off doing one thing at a time. On returning to some actions, it is hard to fathom how they were ever carried out and I find it hard to believe I was the person who did, in fact, balance on top of those wine glasses when I currently find it hard to drink out of one.

I recently saw the high heels I wore twenty years ago in DV8's *My Body, Your Body* and cannot even walk in them, let alone run while carrying someone. But, at the time, it seemed so important to carry out the act there was no risk at all.

When the emotion is connected to the action, there seems to be very little chance of physical damage. Injury seems to occur either when the ego kicks ahead of the body, when ambition moves the body ahead of its current capacity to the place where it 'wants to be', or when the mind can't find enough importance for doing it in the first place. A reminder that yesterday's risk is today's boredom.

The ageing body

This inside out stuff, the word 'stuff', the multiple and singular stuff is all beginning to collide with age.

With age – something very odd is starting to happen.

The commentaries are changing. Or, more to the point, they are disappearing. There seems to be an absence of language about witnessing the ageing body. Maybe a bit of fear? Maybe a bit of denial? I'm not sure what it is. Perhaps it is horrible to see a hip that won't bend, nerve wracking to notice the jumps don't work. (Or, like I say, maybe it's just lack of language).

Whatever it is, external commentaries are thin on the ground, and I have a suspicion the discrepancy is starting to increase the gap between how a move feels to do and what it looks like.

Maybe this accounts for the tendency of older dancers and movers to look as if they are lost in their own nostalgic dancing past. Looking like deluded idiots unwilling to surrender their prime – and unable to enter the present.

The body has imprints of moves running around it that reside in another era. They exist in a place of fast neurological connections and an unquestioned need to move. But they encounter a piece of machinery that is slowing, packed tight with commentaries and ideologies and producing ideas that have a tenuous relationship with the notion of excitement.

And so this thing I have spent a lifetime working at – balancing the inside with the outside – is becoming redundant and, in its place, there is an absence of sounding board, nowhere to bounce off of.

I have begun to be uncertain about how I am being perceived. It didn't even occur to me before. Didn't worry me.

But now, I find myself asking people if I look embarrassing when I move. If I look like I think I'm younger than I am. I did see a review saying I was doing the moves of someone half my age, but I couldn't tell if that meant I should stop doing them or carry on.

If there are commentaries, they seem to revolve around the notion of surviving, continuing, persisting. A kind of pat on the back for still being alive. Although the women get this more than the men, I think.

But at the same time, my body is showing signs of wanting to move just for its own sake in a way I am surprised by. It is showing signs of wanting to spin a lot. To follow its own track without shape and form. It wants to endure something difficult – it seems to have unlimited capacity to want to do – which is not the same as doing at all.

And at such an inappropriate moment in my life I don't know whether to follow it or tell it to shut up.

This makes me realize I am not my body.

Illustration 2.1   *Wendy's Body*
[Copyright: Hugo Glendinning]

I am somewhere else listening to it, not watching it but noticing it. Perhaps I am beginning to become the commentaries I have listened to all my life? Perhaps wisdom is the detachment from the body into some other place. Where I don't know. It still feels like the same as it ever did. Multiple and singular, and maybe heading for the delirious freedom of emptiness.

2.3   Every body: performance's other bodies

Anna Fenemore

As Ramírez Ladrón de Guevara has argued, it is possible to understand bodies as both preceding and exceeding representation, and Wendy

Houstoun, as *some body*, has addressed both 'representation' (that is, how her body looks to somebody else) and 'livedness' (that is, how her body is used and acts upon others, and how it feels to herself). And it is this 'livedness' that marks Houstoun's writing here, this 'livedness' that allows her to speak of the 'at risk' body and the ageing body, this 'livedness' that accounts for the very specific register used by Houstoun in this chapter, a register that recognizes the specificity of her experiences and that does not attempt to 'objectify, generalise, essentialise, anonymise' (Melrose, 2006: 1). Instead, Houstoun unpicks her position as *some body* in a personalized way, whilst simultaneously introducing herself as *'some body observed'* (Melrose 2006: 1). What the final section of this chapter will now do is begin to unpack these 'other' bodies of performance, the bodies that *observe* bodies performing. After all, '[t]heatre is an art of bodies witnessed by bodies' (Shepherd 2006: 73). Such bodies may be collectively titled 'audience', or individually titled 'spectator', or 'observer', or 'witness', or 'participant'. In this section, I will take some of the ideas from the previous sections on 'livedness', discomfort, transformation, the fleshly and the visceral, and apply these to the processes and experiences of the spectating body.

Some bodies observed

A small woman walks across a stage in high heels, her ankles tied together, she carries in her arms a large man.

There is a large man being carried in the arms of a woman in high heels, her ankles tied together.

There is somebody watching her, somebody watching this small woman walking across a stage in high heels, her ankles tied together, carrying in her arms a large man.

There is probably another large man watching the other large man being carried in the arms of the small woman in high heels whose ankles are tied together.

As somebody walks across a stage in some high heels, ankles tied together, carrying somebody else, somebody larger, somebody watches, somebody probably smaller and somebody probably larger watches.

The small woman understands and knows her body in one way, as restricted, as uncomfortable, as off-balance, as on the edge, as empty, as in pain, as 'at risk'. She understands the large body of the man she carries through weight, pressure, gravity, balance. She understands that somebody else watches her, and that that somebody does not know *how* her body is restricted, uncomfortable, off-balance, on the edge, empty, in pain

– but does know *that* her body is these things and most specifically *that* her body is 'at risk'. Somebody else watching knows *that* the man is large and therefore is probably heavy, and knows *that* it must be quite difficult for the small woman carrying him in high heels with her ankles tied together.

The spectating body

Trying to understand bodies in performance by just looking at performing bodies is like trying to understand a tennis match by just looking at one player. In the enactive approach to perception, as Ramírez Ladrón de Guevara mentioned earlier 'perceiving is a way of acting. Perception is not something that happens to us, or in us. It is something we do ...' (Noë 2004: 1). As spectators, then, we are active at all times, things are not happening to us or *in* us; we are *doing* something (much like the performer is *doing* something). Noë, then, is not separating perception from action. For Noë, the enactive approach to perception requires that we:

> reject the idea ... that perception is a process *in the brain* whereby the perceptual system constructs an *internal representation* of the world. No doubt perception depends on what takes place in the brain, and very likely there are internal representations in the brain ... What perception is, however, is not a process in the brain, but a kind of skilful activity on the part of the animal as a whole. (Noë 2004: 2)

Noë argues that perception is a 'skilful [bodily] activity', and is not just the reception and decoding/processing of information/data from the world out there. Instead, it requires that we move through, inhabit and act in the world – a kind of 'practical knowledge' or 'know-how' (Noë 2004: 11). So, it is not enough to *have* sensations, but to have sensations that we *understand*, and that this *understanding* comes from use, action, exploration and practical bodily knowledge or 'sensorimotor understanding', as well as from 'conceptual understanding' (Noë 2004: 33). So, when we are watching a small woman in high heels carrying a large man in her arms with her ankles tied, we are not just receiving a visual image of this, there is the skilful bodily activity of our eyes probing at the visual scene (constantly moving, our eyes only take in a small amount of the visual scene at a time, in the same way that we can only touch one bit of the object at a time), and there is our conceptual understanding of this (we need to know what a 'performer' is, we need to know what 'high heels' are, what 'being tied up' is, what 'carrying' is). But there is also understanding that comes from somewhere between these two – we know what a 'large' man is and we know, from our sensorimotor experience (that is, we have all tried to lift something large and heavy) that a 'large' man is going to be heavy. We perceive as spectators in performance through a combination of sensori-motor and conceptual understanding, a combination that has been – possibly not entirely usefully, because of the implication of time past – articulated as body *memory*. But these *memories* are, in the enactive theory of perception, our ability to know the body's potential for action in response to certain situations/limitations/restrictions. So, perhaps specta-tors don't only *know-that* Houstoun's body is at risk, they also have the *know-how* of that bodily risk. To perceive is to 'understand, implicitly, the effects of movement on sensory stimulation' (Noë 2004: 1), whether we actually move ourselves or not. The enactive theory therefore is not just relevant to the *active* performing body, but is also resonant and relevant for spectating bodies – we understand performance not just through concep-tual understanding, not just through a barrage of external information thrown at us, which we then process and decode. We understand perform-ance through our own bodies' potential for use and action, through a sensorimotor engagement (an *active* engagement that begins to put into question the notion that spectating could ever possibly be, as it is often considered, a *passive* act):

> Perceptual experience acquires content thanks to our possession of bodily skills. *What we perceive* is determined by *what we do* (or what we know how to do); it is determined by what we are *ready* to do … we *enact* our perceptual experience; we act it out. (Noë 2004: 1)

The social body

In looking at bodies in performance, we might conventionally understand the following:

- first-person subjective experience of performing: *I am performing for you*;
- third-person objective observation of physical behaviour/performance of performers: *You are performing for me*.

But this chapter also addresses:

- first-person subjective experience of spectating: *I am watching you*;
- third-person objective observation of physical symptoms of spectators by performers (both individual *and* social): *You are watching me*.

41

The small woman is both *singular* – some body (she is, in this instance, Wendy Houstoun) and *multiple* – she might be termed an uncomfortable body, an empty body, a political body, a gendered body, an entertaining body, a disconcerting body, an amusing body, a body for concern (how else might we react to a small woman in high heels with her ankles tied together and a large man in her arms, but be entertained, disconcerted, amused and just a little concerned?) There are also singular (small and large, and even some medium-sized) bodies watching her, bodies that are also living and breathing, and possibly uncomfortable, or empty, or absent. And certainly gendered and political. But, as well as there being some bodies that act, react and behave as singular bodies, these bodies might also simultaneously act as a *body* of bodies. *Body* as a group – a communal grouping that act and react, or *behave* as *one* some of the time (spontaneous applause, laughter). A football match energizes the bodies of the spectators; we all rise together with excitement as our team approaches the net.

Some types of performance, such as the immersive installation environments of Punchdrunk or Slung Low,[12] deliberately further this bodily awareness of the group. So, audience groups are taken on a tour of the performance work, are encouraged to move around, explore, make choices about where they want to go, what they want to see. In Punchdrunk's *It Felt like a Kiss* (Manchester International Festival, 2009), small groups of audience were terrified by a man wielding a chainsaw, and the group response was to run from the room screaming and holding onto each other (risk here is fictional, not real, and yet the pleasure from this fictional terror is overwhelming). We continued to take pleasure in the thrill of the fictional terror and in the thrill of the social contract between us and others in the space. In moments such as this one, the overriding perceptual means of engagement between the individuals in the group is one of *social* engagement. Each individual has a heightened awareness of the other individuals occupying the space and a heightened awareness of the activity of their own (whole) group, as well as a heightened awareness of their own physicality.

The uncomfortable body

At the centre of many teachings of the performer is the concept of discomfort. A greater physical discomfort in the performing body allows for a greater awareness of the body and an increased presence in the space. As Ramírez Ladrón de Guevara has already noted, in the everyday we know that our bodies are absent to us, we aren't aware at all times of every little part of our body, we rarely know how the backs of our knees are feeling, or our ankles, or the back of the neck just at the start of the hairline. Unless we are in pain, at which point the body part that is in pain is brought into sharp focus. Performers begin to use their bodies differently because of physical ageing processes or because of injury. Whilst pain alerts us to the material presence of our bodies, it is clearly neither a sensible nor useful strategy for most performers. Other tactics are, however – tactics that engage our awareness of our bodies through discomfort; a slight alteration of balance, a slight tension, an alteration in the habitual way of holding the body, or of walking, or standing, or sitting, so that our bodies remain present to us and, at the same time, present to the audience. Such tactics are explored extensively by Barba (Barba and Savarese 2006), who conducts extensive and comprehensive explorations of balance and tension across different cultural disciplines, which force actors to engage with bodily processes corporeally and presently, rather than absently. Zarrilli (2009: 60) also offers a detailed discussion of practices that can enable an actor to 'better inhabit the bodymind in space and through time so that it does not disappear but remains present to us'. Not only do Barba and Zarrilli offer a way forward for performing bodies, their discussions also offer a framework in which we might consider spectating bodies – as bodies that can (and often do – though to different extents in different types of performance) remain present in the moment. In the everyday, through familiarity, we experience a certain sensory fatigue (Noë 2004: 13) where we don't continuously feel the clothing against our skin, or the ring on our finger, or the glasses on our nose. In the same way, in performing and spectating, habit and familiarity of certain actions/gestures (especially sitting in a darkened auditorium for a spectator) means that these things recede into the background. I therefore don't notice myself sitting in the dark, until something irritates me (the person next to me sitting too close or brushing my knee, the big hair of the person sitting in front of me obscuring my view), or until certain strategies for discomfort are introduced (as in immersive performance work, where spectators are not allowed to disappear or relax into sensory self-fatigue). What this 'immersive' work attempts to do for spectators is require a certain kind of *energy-full* engagement with the work, and is what Zarrilli wants of his participants in training workshops:

> not to space out, zone out, or attempt to relax – rather, their task is, through specificity of focus, to enter a state of concentratedness in the moment which is not energy-less, but energy-full or energized. (Zarrilli 2009: 29)

The absent body

For Leder (1990), absence (with sensory fatigue being one symptom of this) is a fact of bodily existence. He argues that, when in action, an individual's sensorimotor means of surveying action recedes. So, even though in certain situations my attention shifts to my body here and now – for example, in moments of precarious balance – such experiences are not primary ways in which the majority of us live out our bodies. Using Heidegger's terminology these are 'deficient' modes of interaction with the world (cited in Leder 1990: 19). This deficiency implies not a hierarchy, but an extra-ordinary mode of embodiment such that absence is the norm and presence the 'deficiency' from that norm. For spectators of normative, traditional, 'visual' performance, spectating bodies are sometimes rendered unnecessary for the appreciation of the artwork before them, and are somehow forgotten, made absent, or recede from the direct physical experience of spectating. But, as we have now seen, there are always moments when our bodies come back into our consciousness when watching live performance. This might be through moments of discomfort (necks craning upwards to watch a circus trapeze act), or through moments of sensorimotor empathy (watching a small woman carry a large man in her arms, in high heels, ankles tied together), but also through the deliberate strategies of immersive performance work.

The transformed body

One (extreme) performing tactic is the use of what might be termed, 'the transformed body', where the body within the frame of performance is very specifically not fictional, and very really transformed. Such a non-fictional or transformed state might be achieved through bodies 'at risk' or in danger; or in extremely precarious physical states; or physically exhausted; or, like Wendy Houstoun's disconcerting and 'at risk' body, carrying a large, presumably heavy man when wearing high heels with ankles tied together (where both small woman and large man are 'at risk'); or through bodies that have been physically altered, as in the work of performance artists working through scarification, blood-letting, cosmetic surgery, and technological body alteration – for example, Ron Athey,[13] Franko B, Orlan,[14] Stelarc.[15] In these truly transformed bodies, the artists (and the spectators) cannot forget their bodies. But it must be understood that bodies do not surface only in dysfunctional moments, as some theorists would suggest (Scarry 1985, Leder 1990), but also in moments of pleasure or discomfort, and under varying – and not necessarily dysfunctional – conditions of precariousness and tension (as explored extensively by Barba, in Barba, and Savarese, 2006 and Zarrilli 2009). It is easy, however, to force such an engagement with performers who work muscularly; it is more problematic to force such an engagement with spectators due to ethical considerations of participation and safety/risk.

But imagine the different kinds of spectating bodies of carnival, clubbing, street theatre, or ritual, whose modes of embodied performer–spectator interaction are based on physical/visceral/fleshly/ambient pleasure and/or thrill. In these genres, demarcations between performer and spectator, subject and object tend to be less distinct than in theatre events. Such immersive performance spaces as those developed by Punchdrunk and Slung Low, and the spaces of carnival, circus, ritual, clubbing, and football spectating, use explicitly a *haptic* potential of sight and space. I use the term 'haptic potential' to denote the visual sense of touch (exploited by pornography) that is rigorously policed by ethical rules of physical engagement in the theatre space; but, in spite of this rigorous policing, this haptic potential persists in other live theatre and performance environments where spectators are perhaps simply sitting in an auditorium in the dark watching actors in front of them in the lighted patch. The *Concise Oxford English Dictionary* defines *haptic* as 'of or relating to the sense of touch', from the Greek, *haptikos* 'able to touch or grasp'. My usage of the term implicates, more directly, sight with the potential to touch, specifically following Deleuze and Guattari who distinguish:

> 'tactile' or rather 'haptic' space ... from optical space. 'Haptic' is a better word than 'tactile' since it does not establish an opposition between two sense organs ... [A] haptic space ... may be as much visual or auditory as tactile. (Deleuze and Guattari 1988: 492–3)

Different genres of live performance already explore and exploit this embedded and visceral potential of vision and touch. This can be seen at its most basic in the live performances of sex shows, strip shows, circus, and pantomime. But it can also be seen in the work of theatre companies such as La Fura dels Baus[16] and De La Guarda,[17] whose aesthetic relies on the tangible visual effects of circus (heart-stopping aerial routines) combined with the ambient systems of clubbing. It can also be found in the work of those 'immersive' performance companies whose approach is a more total sensory approach than that of more conventional theatre.

45

The irreplaceable body

Imagine the numerous different physiological or visceral 'symptoms' that you have had as a spectator at live performance events. You are likely to have experienced both physical pleasure and/or discomfort in a number of ways, perhaps similar to the following:

- boredom;
- irritation at other spectators;
- spine-tingling sensations from 'good' aesthetic quality (being 'impressed');
- physical responses (between revulsion and muscular empathy) to really transformed (or 'authentic' bodies);
- emotional (and physical) responses to fictional bodies – that is, fiction-ally transformed bodies (actors who inhabit another's body, the imper-sonation of somebody else, a character, *as though* they were somebody else);
- emotional (and physical) responses to fictional (and/or real – as in auto-biographical performance work) narrative;
- physical thrill on seeing the wielding of a chainsaw;
- physical thrill on seeing Houstoun's precarious 'at risk' body.

It is these symptoms that, despite numerous different kinds of disembod-ied (or virtual) bodies used today in performance environments (for exam-ple, cyborgs and avatars),[18] ensure that there remains a certain pull of live performance and the live human body (whether transformed or fictional). As Gómez-Peña argues:

> [D]espite innumerable predictions over the past thirty years, perform-ance art hasn't died, nor has it been replaced by video or outdated by new technologies and robotics. Stelarc's warning in the early 1990s that the body was becoming obsolete turned out to be untrue. It's simply impossible to 'replace' the ineffable magic of a pulsating, sweaty body immersed in a live ritual in front of our eyes ... Whatever the reasons, the fact is that no actor, robot, or virtual avatar can replace the singular spectacle of the performance artist's body-in-action. (Gómez-Peña, cited in Heathfield 2004: 79)

I will attempt to identify a potential reason here at the end of this chap-ter. A distinction can be made between different types of visuality (optical and haptic) and their relationship to tactility. Lying in bed next to a lover (in a perfect sensual encounter) and looking but not directly touching has a very different quality of tactility than does, for example, observing a stranger at a distance. It is the seven major structural components of this difference (and not the specifically sexually charged nature of this example) that might be used as the primary reasons for the persuasiveness of the live 'artist's body-in-action':

- the *potential* to touch through proximity, and the understanding and acceptance of certain rules;
- the *anticipation* of *being* touched, as defined by the context of the situation;
- the *thrill* of being witness to the other's transformed, transforming or at least transformable body;
- the *sensory immersion/sensual experiences* of other-than-visual communication (vibration, sound, smell, taste, excitement, arousal) which encourage individuals not to orient themselves purely visually to the other's body;
- the thrill of the *unknown* – what will happen next, and where and how (including the possibility of accidents or mistakes);
- the acute awareness and *presence* of our own bodies to us;
- the understanding that (like in a tennis match) there is a *social contract* between I and you, and that; as I watch you, you watch me, and vice versa.

It is these qualities of physical engagement: *potential, anticipation, thrill, sensual immersion, the unfamiliarity of the unknown, physical presence* and *social contract* that form the unique bodily relationship of performer and spectator.

Drawing together the three contributions in this chapter, we are able to see that every aspect of life is embodied. Thinking, speaking, listening, watching, sleeping, walking, working, playing, performing, spectating are all experienced through our bodies. Asserting semantic independence to 'the body', or even the multiple 'bodies' of performance, signifies a theoretical distinction; one that isn't apparent in the lived experience of our bodies (in the everyday, or as performers, or as spectators). The distinction we make in this chapter between these different bodies is both a relative one and a functional one – not an absolute or 'real' distinction. Theoretical distinctions like these may seem clear conceptually, at the level of theory or on paper, but in practice, in life, in performance, these distinctions are slippery, and it is precisely in their slipperiness that the real pleasure of grappling with them is discovered. 'Pleasure' is the important word here.

There has always been a bodily tradition in theatre, and a pleasurable one at that, and this pleasure is located precisely between the multiple bodies of the performance encounter.

Activities

The following activities are designed to get you to begin to think about the multiple different ways in which you inhabit, use, demonstrate, 'play at', read, your own bodies and those of others, in both the everyday and in performance. The activities encourage you to place yourself within the frame of this discussion around different kinds of bodies. They require you to become aware of everyday situations where you might begin to slip between different bodies, between everyday, dancing, mediated, exhausted and physiological bodies, for example. Through asking you to think about specific bodies, these activities lead you to consider how you might begin to slip between – or, indeed, inhabit simultaneously – the more widely applicable 'absent', 'present', 'read' and 'lived' bodies. How are these multiple bodies already present in the performance act and, more importantly, how might you actively make use of these different bodies in making performance?

➤ *Solo activity*

In preparation for understanding the many bodies that are available to you, this activity helps you to examine the nature of embodied experience. Leder (1990) suggests that Cartesian dualism is deeply entrenched in our lived experiences because our bodies tend to recede as part of our interaction with the world. Focusing your attention on your body will allow you to overcome that tendency at least partially, enabling you to analyze your embodied experience and consider how potential other bodies might be located in it.

- Stand with your weight equally spread across both of your feet, and allow your arms to hang in a relaxed manner by your sides. Become aware of the length of your spine. Think about your recessive body (Leder 1990). Can you feel yourself blinking, breathing? Can you feel your blood moving around your body? Can you feel your digestive system working?
- Experiment with tensing and relaxing groups of muscles in your back, arms, torso and legs. Observe what it feels like to tense and relax different muscles, and see how much you have to tense the muscles in order to cause your body shape to contort. Try to feel the ways that your muscles connect to your bones as your body moves. Be aware of your balance and how it is affected.
- Place the fingertips of your right hand against the back of your left hand. It may feel as if you are touching your left hand with your right hand, but actually both hands are touching and being touched simultaneously. Can you feel the 'being touched' sensation on both the back of the hand and the fingertips

at the same time? Can you feel your fingertips touching and being touched simultaneously?

- For the rest of the day, try to be aware of your body as much as possible, and to notice when it naturally recedes from your awareness. What effect does this have on the ways that you move and on how you experience the world around you?

Use the following list of bodies as provocations for the Discussion activity and Practical activity that follow. Remember that this list is not exhaustive, and that the terms are not fixed, stand-alone terms with established meanings. Rather, they are examples of different categories of bodies, which you may amend or add to as you see fit:

absent body	male body
ageing body	mediated body
apologetic body	physiological body
cybernetic body	political body
dancing body	sexual body
entertaining body	social body
erotic body	spectating body
everyday body	transformed body
exhausted body	uncanny body
explicit body	uncomfortable body
female body	unnatural body
fleshly/visceral body	unruly body
ideal body	virtual/disembodied body
imagined/fictional body	volatile body
irreplaceable body	

➤ *Discussion activity*

Choose a body that resonates somehow with you. (You can select from the list of bodies above, or use your own ideas.)

Consider the following questions and then share your answers with a partner:

- How does your chosen body manifest itself in the everyday, and how is this different to how it could potentially be used in performance?
- What examples of your chosen body can be found in performance practice?
- How have different practitioners used your chosen body, and to what specific ends?
- How have you used your chosen body previously for performance and with what effect?
- How might you physically (and non-fictionally) reveal your chosen body to others?

• What different discoveries have been made by the rest of the group, and are there any common findings?

➤ *Practical activity*

In groups of three or four, choose a body and unpack/reveal/demonstrate its significance for performance through a 10-minute lecture demonstration. (You can select from the list of bodies above, or use your own ideas.) The questions in the Discussion activity will help you to think about how to approach this task.

Notes

1   For an extended discussion on the contemporary 'body craze' present in academic studies, see, for example, Davis (1997: 1–23).
2   Semiotics is the study of signs, their meanings, their interrelationships with other signs and the processes by which they create meaning. Semiotics was first proposed by the linguist Ferdinand de Saussure (2006), who argued that all words were formed by a signifier (an arbitrary sign – the word 'cat', for example) and a signified (the thing in itself: the cat who actually sits in my lap). The relationship between signifier and signified (between the sign and its meaning) is what is called 'semantics'.
3   For an extended discussion of the body as a site of representation/the body as a lived entity, see Csordas (1994), whose text has served as the basis of the argument presented in this first section.
4   Maurice Merleau-Ponty was a French philosopher born in 1908, dying at the early age of 53 in 1961. His work was heavily influenced by phenomenological philosophers such as Husserl and Heidegger.
5   (Syn)aesthetics is based on the medical term 'synaesthesia', in which a stimulus directed to a particular sense provokes a reaction in a different one. For example, for people with this condition a colour may smell in a particular way. (Syn)aesthetics was devised by Machon as a holistic, all-encompassing approach in which the stimuli present in a performance have both a semantic and a somatic (bodily) effect on the audience.
6   Punchdrunk, established in 2000, is a UK theatre company making immersive theatre where active (rather than passive) audiences walk freely through the environments and narratives/worlds that are built for them.
7   Akram Khan is a British choreographer/dancer whose family is of Bangladeshi origin. Khan studied in Kathak dance from an early age and began presenting solo performances (classical Kathak and contemporary choreography) in the 1990s. In August 2000, he launched the Akram Khan Dance Company.
8   Please note that the works listed above are only indicative of the great number of people who have applied phenomenology to performance studies. An exhaustive and thorough review of the literature surrounding this area is beyond the scope of the present chapter.

9   Marina Abramovic is a New York-based performance artist born in Belgrade. Abramovic explores the relationship between audience and performer, and the limits of the human/performing body.

10   Franko B is an Italian live artist, living and working in London creating body art, performance, installation, paintings, photography and sculpture.

11   Dominic Johnson is a UK artist and writer who works through body-based performance art practices that include solo performance and durational performance.

12   Slung Low, established in 2000, is a UK theatre company specializing in making new work, and often working in non-theatre spaces, immersing their audiences in created environment.

13   Ron Athey is an American performance artist most commonly known for his work through extreme body art.

14   Orlan is a French performance artist living and working in Los Angeles. She uses photography, video, sculpture, installation, performance, biotechnology and cosmetic surgery in her work.

15   Stelarc is an Australian performance artist, born in Cyprus who makes perform-ance art that extends his own body through virtual space, cybersystems and technologies (low- and hi-tech).

16   La Fura dels Baus, established in 1979 and now based in Barcelona, have a number of different strands of their performance practice. One strand is their work in non-conventional theatre spaces making large-scale interactive performance environments, often using industrial sites/technologies.

17   De La Guarda are an Argentinian performance company co-founded by Diqui James and Pichon Baldinu, who first came to London with *Villa Villa* in 1997 (a spectacular acrobatic show performed mainly above the heads of the audi-ence). James and Baldinu developed a new show, *Fuerzabruta*, which came to London in 2006.

18   For further details, see Chapter 5, 'Technology'.

Further reading

Banes, S. and Lepecki, A. (2007) *The Senses in Performance*. Abingdon and New York: Routledge.

Barba, E. and Savarese, N. (2006) *A Dictionary of Theatre Anthropology: The Secret Art of the Performer*, 2nd edn. Abingdon and New York: Routledge.

Mauss, M. (2004) 'Techniques of the Body', in A. Blaikie (ed.), *The Body: Critical Concepts in Sociology, Volume 4: Living and Dying Bodies*. London and New York: Routledge: 50–69.

Shepherd, Simon (2006) *Theatre, Body, Pleasure*. London and New York: Routledge.

Zarrilli, P.B. (2009) *Psychophysical Acting: An Intercultural Approach after Stanislavski*. Abingdon and New York: Routledge.

3   Space

Introduced and edited by Scott Palmer

Introduction

Space is a fundamental concern of all performance practitioners but, as a performance concept that underlies practice, it is rarely foregrounded. In this chapter, we examine a range of approaches to understanding the organization of space in theatrical work, its importance as a signifier and the way it can be manipulated to make meaning for an audience. We shall explore the range of ways in which space functions, from the practical arrangement of the audience and the design of the performance area, to the ability of the space and the theatre architecture itself to perform.

A central focus in this chapter is the role of scenography and the function of the scenographer or theatre designer in the shaping and organization of stage space in performance. 'Scenography'[1] is an ancient Greek term originating from Aristotle, who informs us in *Poetics* (1932 [350 BC]) that Sophocles first introduced '*skenographia*' to the stage. The compound term derives from '*skene*' (stage-building) and the verb '*grapho*' (which means 'to make line drawings' or 'write'). So, the term 'scenography' might be considered not as drawing *for* the scene but drawing *in* or *with* the scene. In contemporary performance practice, the term is replacing that of 'theatre design' and has come to represent the complex interrelationships between space, object, material, light and sound that define the space and place of performance. Scenography therefore goes beyond the traditional art of 'scenic design', with its connotations of creating pictures and illustrating the stage with the use of painted backdrops, for example. Instead, the term advocates a more active intervention and a holistic approach to design for performance in which the design of space is central – a space created for performing bodies to interact with rather than against.

This chapter explores different interpretations of scenography, which range from the organization of stage space to wider notions which encompass architectural space. Scenographer and academic Pamela Howard in her book *What is Scenography?* asserts that this contested term lies at the heart of all creative performance processes:

Scenography is the seamless synthesis of space, text, research, art, actors, directors and spectators that contributes to an original creation. (Howard, 2002: 130)

This compositional contribution to the evolution of a theatrical event not only affects the performer directly (for example, how and where they move, what they wear), but also fundamentally the way a performance is understood. It therefore has a profound impact on the nature of the spectator's experience:

Scenography is not simply concerned with creating and presenting images to an audience; it is concerned with audience reception and engagement. It is a sensory as well as an intellectual experience, emotional as well as rational. (McKinney and Butterworth 2009: 4)

The scenographer is responsible for the construction and organization of the stage space as an elementary aspect of the creative process, not simply as a practical solution to the staging. In this chapter, we will consider a wide range of factors which impact on this contribution and explore how space makes meaning in performance:

[S]pace is the first and foremost challenge of the scenographer. Space is part of the scenographic vocabulary. We talk about translating space and adapting space; creating suggestive space and linking space with dramatic time. We think of space in action, how we can make it and break it, what we need to create the right space, and how it can be constructed with form and colour to enhance the human being and the text. Some play games with space, searching for its metaphor and meaning in the quest to define dramatic space. (Howard 2002: 1)

In working with stage space, the scenographer must consider the very nature and qualities of the site – the place of performance. Since ancient history, architects have wrestled with the fundamental problems inherent in organizing stage space and audience space, and in creating structures in which performance events can be housed. In section 3.1, Dorita Hannah examines the nature of the architecture of the space itself and how this organization of space forms a critical element of all theatrical events. Space is traditionally considered as a three-dimensional extent in which objects and events occur, but this volume is never static and its constantly changing nature suggests that we should acknowledge its fourth dimension – time. Hannah writes about this dynamic in developing the notion of *event-space* and how even what appear to be permanent spaces are changed or destroyed through time. She provokes us, through a series of examples, to consider how the space itself performs and how it needs to be considered as an integral aspect of the performance experience, reminding us that the space is never fixed but continually changing in an active state of becoming.

In section 3.2, Louise Ann Wilson concentrates on the role of scenography and, in particular, on the creation of performance space beyond the theatre building. This interview echoes many of the themes explored by Hannah, focusing on examples from Wilson's own work to explore the impact of the way theatrical space is designed in site-specific work. A given playing space not only changes as performers move within it, but the space itself also provides us with echoes of previous events – be they memories of previous performances or traces of histories. Both Hannah and Wilson see space as central to their creative practices, whether the space that they respond to is purpose built for performance or a found space for which a performance is specifically designed.

In section 3.3 of this chapter, I will provide an overview of some key aspects of working with space in performance, considering how approaches to organizing space (as a place of performance) and designing space (scenography) impact on the reception of a theatrical event. I will explore factors which influence our response to space and ways of understanding the use of space in performance through specific examples, highlighting key theories and practitioners for further study and investigation.

3.1 Event-space: performance space and spatial performativity

Dorita Hannah

Performing space

Space – whether a suspended pause, a blank area, an empty room or a limitless cosmos – *performs*. As a concept theorized over centuries by philosophers, scientists, artists and dramatists, space remains complex and elusive, although it is the fundamental immaterial-material utilized by designers creating sites for theatrical performance. Space is the stuff of architects (who construct it) and scenographers (who abstract it); experienced by inhabitants (immersed within it) and spectators (who regard it). However, the 'it' of space is multiple and fractured, as architect Daniel Libeskind points out:

But one can say that there is no space, but there are spaces, a plurality, a heterogeneity, a difference. That would also make us look at spacing differently. We would not be looking for one. (Libeskind 2000: 68)

Considering sites that accommodate staged events, this section outlines how space is a performative medium, and therefore an inherently active entity, which reciprocally acts on, and is activated by, its occupants, who need not be physically present within it. As a practising scenographer and theatre architect, one of my ongoing projects has been to develop the notion of *event-space* – a term that emerged toward the end of the twentieth century – in order to consider spatial performativity generally and performance space specifically. Approaching space by way of the transitory event – whether *historic* (epic incidents), *aesthetic* (theatrical displays) or *banal* (daily occurrences) – realigns the static object of built form with the dynamic flux of performance, thereby exposing an intricate system of active forces that undermine architecture's traditional role as a fixed, durable object designed to order space and those who inhabit it.

I will therefore argue how, through the *event*, space is an intricate and active player in our everyday lives. This notion of the 'evental' emerged from spatiotemporal revolutions in twentieth-century science, arts, and communication, whereby the static *spatialization of time* shifted to a more dynamic *temporalization of space*, which emphasized movement, relativity, and duration. Radical shifts in modernism exposed space as a temporal event, undermining the discrete object of architecture, and allowing us to perceive the built environment more in a state of active *becoming* than passive *being*. The well-constructed playhouse now seems as meaningless as the well-made play.

Event-space and spatial events

French philosopher Jacques Derrida suggested that:

The question of architecture is in fact that of the place, of the taking place in space ... an event. (Derrida, in Leach 1997: 302)

Event-space – bridging theatrical and spatial theory – becomes a useful paradigm for articulating how space performs and how performance is spatialized by the event, specifically in theatre architecture, long considered the 'proper' site of performance. The term is attributed to contemporary architect, Bernard Tschumi,[2] whose mantra has long been 'there is no space without event' (1996: 39). His alliances with thinkers such as

Derrida, as well as his belief in the active nature of the built environment, have served to influence and shape recent architectural theory as 'the discourse of events as much as the discourse of spaces', thereby challenging architecture to be more active (Tschumi 1996: 149). This link between event and space questions architecture's traditional association with continuity, coherence and autonomy by focusing on time, action and movement. If performance is, as theorist Elin Diamond (1996: 5) contends, both 'a doing and a thing done', then 'spacing' – like the words 'building' and 'construction' (a structure and the act of its making) – represents both noun and verb: thing and action. Because action in space has a reciprocal relationship with space in action, our banal everyday environments can be perceived and utilized as continually fluctuating performances. This is further confounded by how the so-called 'real world' is informed by the virtual worlds emerging from various media and our own imaginations.

Considering performance space as 'evental' repositions built and imagined space as both embodied experience and evolving time-based event, where the constructed environment itself (whether architecture or scenography) is no longer perceived as a static object but as a volatile spatial subject. A theory of the 'event' (with its fleeting elusive qualities) therefore undermines the proper place of both theatre and architecture, traditionally sited in the playhouse. Acknowledging that performance occurs all around us in the everyday or quotidian world results in its un-housing, and desire to leave the conventional stage and auditorium that discipline the spatial practices of spectators and performers; dictating how they act, re-act and inter-act. So, while the *dramatic* event negotiates between real time and fictive time, existing site and scenography – as well as between actors and actors, actors and audience, audience and audience – the *quotidian* event focuses on what Tschumi refers to as the 'spectacle of everyday life', (Tschumi 1996: 22) which is neither singular nor isolated, but fragmented, overlapping and mobile. As dynamic spatial action, event-space operates between the ordinary and the extraordinary, the subtle and the spectacular, the banal and the epic. Implicated in monumental, aesthetic and daily events, places are shaped by significant *historic* moments, such as natural and human-made disasters as well as socio-political and philosophical revolutions, which shift thought, by *dramatic* spectacles that demand and manipulate public attention, and by the overabundance of *quotidian* performances happening all around us.

The diverse nature of the event – as a turning-point, a dramatic presentation, and a singular moment capable of being perceptually isolated amid the plurality and chaos of reality – establishes the intricate system of forces at play in the constructed environment that, operating in the realms of reality and possibility, are both actual and virtual (see Grosz 2001: 12). This complex interplay is further complicated when leaving the confines of buildings built to house aesthetic performances, where the dramatic event intersects more overtly with the multiplicity of the *quotidian event-space* that often lacks the explicit architectural frame, collapsing the theatrical into the everyday.

This collapse opens up the ever-present abyss that haunts lived space, encapsulated in the darkly veiled stage houses and black box theatres which proliferated in the second half of the last century. Built as an instrumentalized theatrical void, both proscenium stage and black box negate the object of architecture itself by presenting a symbolic location cut off from concrete reality. As dark floating worlds – incorporeal, aspatial and atemporal – they are designed to admit the virtual, those ghosts and gods we have summoned on stage since ancient times. Constructed voids, they play host to the phantasmagoria and fleeting acts of theatre, undermining architecture's aim to be secure and eternal (see Phelan 1993).

The end of illusion

How did this void open up in theatrical space? The nineteenth century was brought to a close with the echoes of German philosopher Friedrich Nietzsche's proclamation that 'God is dead' (1974: 95). As a seminal modernist event, the death of God called into doubt the physical space of worship, and therefore architectural typology – 'What are these churches now if they are not the tombs and sepulchres of God?' (Nietzsche 1974: 95). More radically, it emphasized the disappearance of any absolute reference to a closed system of spatiotemporal coordinates previously defined by Cartesian perspectivalism.[3] This signalled the end of mimetic representation, which, since the sixteenth century, had bound art, architecture, and theatre through scenography, defining our ways of seeing and experiencing both architectural and theatrical space. The framed perspectival construction within the nineteenth-century proscenium arch simultaneously distances and centralizes the viewer in the event, integrating the monumental architecture of the house with the pictorial architectonics of scenery. The plane of the proscenium forms both window and mirror, beyond which a perspectival world is artificially constructed through spatial collapse and distortion. The spectator's gaze apprehends a spatial continuum via geometric projection that is dependent on a horizon line and vanishing point 'where infinity, aesthetics, mathematics, and theology meet on a unified plane whose grandeur and perfection symbolizes God himself' (Weiss 1995: 59).

However, Nietzsche's pronouncement declared the end of that classic age to be the end of illusion, wiping away the rational, stable and homogenous space defined by geometric projection. It coincided with a loss of desire to represent within the field of art, as a mimetic crisis in which the world had become unrepresentable. This, in turn, destabilized both architecture and the stage, neither of which could now play a role in representing a closed, complete universe as a finitely constructed totality. The edifice of classic representation was therefore in a state of slow and inexorable collapse, reconfiguring how space is constructed not only for events, but also as events. Since Nietzsche's proclamation, the monumental theatre with its picture frame stage has been continuously challenged and often abandoned.

The empty space

Theatre director Peter Brook famously stated that:

> I can take any empty space and call it a bare stage. A man walks across this empty space whilst someone else is watching him, and this is all that is needed for an act of theatre to be engaged. (Brook 1968: 11)

The idea that any given space is essentially an active site for theatrical encounter, where action (of performer) is watched (by spectator), was articulated by Brook as the archetypal 'empty space'. However, rather than vacant and vacuous, each apparently 'empty' space is actually redolent with character and action. Every location contains its own particularities that influence, shape, and are, in turn, shaped by multiple performances harnessed through the spatial programme and social codes of architectural inhabitation. These are made more complex during the theatrical performance by the production's *mise-en-scène*,[4] which, often acknowledging the virtual (out of body, out of space and out of time), is designed to admit other worlds – past, present and mythological.

Peter Brook's treatise, which coincided with political and social rebellion enacted on the global stage, was timely in its radical rethinking of the theatrical stage. In drastically reducing the event to a direct and more confrontational spatial encounter, Brook was insisting there was more at stake than comfortable middle-class entertainment staged for people who sit submissively in the auditorium waiting for the picture-framed performance to unfold before them. He was wiping away conventional notions of theatre architecture that endured well into the twentieth century and – despite radical demands from the historical and second-wave *avant-garde*

– continue to persevere in the early twenty-first century. However, Brook's demand was not for a modernist *tabula rasa* in which architecture and its history are obliterated in favour of a featureless spatial void, as evidenced in the continuing proliferation of black box studios since that time. Instead, his *Empty Space* challenged us to regard any space (with its intrinsic character) not only as a site for performance, but also as a performer in waiting. In reducing the staged event to a raw spatial encounter between participants, he was implicating the built and natural environment within the event and highlighting the role that existing space plays in both action and reception.

As a spatial event, architecture – traditionally perceived as rigid and enduring – admits the more dynamic, ephemeral and temporal aspects of performance. This idea of the built environment as a complex system of fleeting and fluctuating forces challenges the well-established notion eloquently expounded by Breton:

> Theatre transcends architecture. The architectural framework may foster or frustrate dramatic action but it is not the source of this emotion. Once the theatrical spell has been cast, the limits of physical space become irrelevant. Breton (1989: 4)

Like many scholars focusing on theatre architecture, Breton renders it a secondary scenic device that disappears when the lights are lowered. However, the construction of the live theatrical experience occurs through an intertwining of architecture, audience, performance and the fictive environment. It does not necessarily involve, as McAuley (1999: 76) contends, an 'inversion of interior and exterior' where attention is shifted from auditorium to stage when the curtain rises and the non-stage world 'loses its power temporarily in face of the superior power of the attraction of the performance'. Instead, a more intricate spatiality is always at work, which encourages or disturbs, and often complicates, the entire event dimension. This can be seen in staged site-specific events where the inherent nature of a found-space remains both relevant and powerful during the staged event – either co-opted as a major player, or silent and subtle in its performances.

Disciplinary manoeuvres

It is important to recognize that architecture mutely incorporates power systems into the built environment – defining, regulating, and limiting our daily practices. This has become acutely evident since the event of 9/11

(September 11, 2001) when New York and Washington experienced spectacular acts of terrorism, which were highly effective in a media-saturated global condition. Since these attacks in the USA, our freedom of movement and expression has been purposefully curtailed – locally and globally – in the very name of 'freedom'. It is interesting to note that architecture was deliberately attacked in that decisive terrorist event for what it represented. Surrealist writer Georges Bataille (1997: 21) maintained that architectural monuments were themselves violent phenomena that had to be eradicated because – as static, dominant, and regulated forms – they 'impose silence on the multitudes' and 'inspire socially acceptable behavior, and often a very real fear'. The philosopher Michel Foucault (1980: 149), who aligned the history of *powers* with the history of spaces, highlighted architecture as a disciplinary mechanism, as did his compatriot Henri Lefebvre (1991: 57), who believed the 'logic of space' conceals an authoritarian force that conditions the competence and performance of the subject who can experience it as a resistant element 'at times as implacably hard as a concrete wall'.

Since the multi-leveled and gilded baroque auditorium (an architectural model that dominated between the sixteenth and nineteenth centuries) was condemned for being monumental and over-decorated, theatre architecture representing the *status quo* – as state, municipal, commercial, or institutional performing arts venues – developed into a rigid and lifeless container that depends on the staged event to enliven it: within the seemingly passive vessel of its auditorium, a homogeneous plane of well-organized viewers' gazes transfixed at highly composed images enacted behind the technological frame of the proscenium stage. The archetypal twentieth-century public auditorium persists in its construction of the supposed homogeneity of what Lefebvre calls modernism's 'abstract space', effecting 'a brutal condensation of social relationships' by reducing spatial practice to conform to its apparent neutrality, transparency and functional logic (Lefebvre 1991: 57). This is enforced through building laws and strict regulations for places of public assembly: authoritative and authoritarian codes that fortify spatial control in the name of health and safety, often foreclosing on architectural experimentation and resistance. Even the contractual prerequisites of performers and the exigencies of surveillance systems can present insurmountable obstacles for architects (Khan and Hannah 2008).

The repeatable format of the internationally recognizable public auditorium reinforces behavioural expectations from venue to venue, and even from country to country. As an inveterate model, with established conventions for staging, managing and producing performances, this cookie-cutter theatre is the result of accepted interpretations of performance criteria – encapsulated by performance theorist Jon McKenzie (2001) as aesthetic *efficacy*, organizational *efficiency* and technical *effectiveness* – that tend to limit innovation and place demands on the architect, performers, audience and management. This shifts performance into the realm of behavioural expectations through social coding rather than aesthetic expression. Global replication of this familiar model also excludes cultural difference and the expression of varying spatial and theatrical practices specific to the locale. It is therefore my contention that the seemingly inert, neutral and 'democratic' form of the archetypal modern auditorium is, in fact, none of these things. Instead, it actively reduces the impact of audience and architectural presence, enacting a violent gesture against any potential contribution, which is feared as a disruption to the smooth running of the venue and event. Unfortunately, in October 2002 it took an incredibly violent disruption to reveal the inherent brutality of public gathering space when Moscow's Dubrovka Theatre was seized for three days by Chechen rebels, illustrating how such venues provide an ideal site for 'barricade hostage-taking' (Dolnik and Pilch 2003: 589).[5] Added to the tragedy of lives lost is the response of the authorities after such terrifying attacks, who react by strengthening the barricades rather than seeking more unbounded, communal and fragile architectures that are resistant to attack through their inherent openness and ephemerality.

Presencing architecture

In *Parables of the Virtual*, Brian Massumi (2002: 79) writes: 'What is pertinent about an event-space is not its boundedness, but what elements it lets pass, according to what criteria, at what rate, and to what effect.' Architectural theorist Ignaci de Solà-Morales (1997: 71) suggests we combat the brutal nature of disciplinary space with 'weak architecture' that utilizes the fleeting, vestigial and ephemeral, to construct a new type of monumentality 'bound up with the lingering resonance of poetry after it has been heard, with the recollection of architecture after it has been seen'. Solà-Morales refers to the tendency for architecture to foreclose on chance by attempting to create itineraries of control. In order for architecture to be transformed into a dynamic and co-creative event, the aleatory and temporal, found in the theatrical event, must be admitted: 'This is the strength of weakness; that strength which art and architecture are capable of producing precisely when they adopt a posture that is not aggressive and dominating, but tangential and weak' (Solà-Morales 1997: 71). Solà-Morales' notion of weak architecture can exert its powers as both performative and resistant in defying attack through transience, permeability and anti-monumentality. This could challenge architecture's conformist tendency in times of fear and crisis. And yet, ideally, theatre and the buildings that house it should provide a forum for open and radical dialogue that critiques the *status quo*. A free-flowing exchange of ideas can be made present by architecture that operates figuratively and concretely as an accessible platform.

Harnessing the virtual and housing the actual, an actively present architecture operates between the intangible acts of performance and the rigidity of tectonic form. As a combination of dynamic space and rigid form, the building refuses to disappear when the lights are dimmed, becoming an inscrutable force that must be considered within performance. Theatre artist Tadeusz Kantor (1993: 275) acknowledged this 'reality' of the built environment and sought to incorporate its particular essence and existence into his staged performance. The architecture was not to be neutralized by staging conventions, but encouraged to contribute with its own architectonic commentary.

Acknowledging architecture itself as a spatiotemporal event, with alternating and overlapping realities, brings the slow time of built form into play with the varying temporalities of performance and fictive space. On his *Impossible Theatre*, Herbert Blau (1964) wrote not only that 'we must take the risk of letting the architect's dreams infect our dreams so that something really new may indeed come to it', but that new spaces, like any new art form, must turn on those who utilize them: 'the question remains whether our theatre artists can break out at the challenge were it to materialize'. Challenging accepted models of theatre architecture allows us to combat not only the rigidity of built environments, but also the powers that shape them. This would allow us to reclaim public space as *The Empty Space* of theatrical expression, reminding ourselves that, no matter how empty it seems, space is full, multiple and highly active.

Introduction to 3.2

In Section 3.1, Hannah's focus lay at the intersection between space and performance with a specialization in the design of buildings for the visual and performing arts. She argued that we need to acknowledge the way that all spaces perform and that an awareness of the spatial context existing prior to the performance event is essential in creating work. In Section 3.2 artist and scenographer, Louise Ann Wilson discusses her particular approach to designing the relationship between rural landscapes and human life events. The audience experience is central to Wilson's work, which is characterized by collaborations with artists as well as experts from other disciplines not usually associated with performance, such as neuro-scientists, geologists, cavers and sheep farmers. Wilson's innovative response to place is fundamental to this experience, and lies at the heart of all of her creative activity.

In this conversation, Wilson begins by discussing her particular approach to designing for building-based theatrical performances, but the rest of this exchange is concerned with her work as a scenographer and maker of 'evocative' and 'resonant' multi-disciplinary, site-specific performance works. In focusing on the works *House* and *Mulgrave*, the interview explores how Wilson's innovative use of space enables audiences to engage with the nature and histories of specific places and how, through performance, they are encouraged to find new spaces and to rediscover familiar places in a new light.

3.2   Scenographic space and place

Louise Ann Wilson in conversation with Scott Palmer

How do you work with theatre space?
My interest in working in response to place and with space has informed my approach to designing productions in theatre spaces and non-theatre spaces alike. Whether it is The Royal Exchange in Manchester, England, or a derelict chemical salt factory in Essen, Germany, the space always provides some of the key starting points for my scenographic work. Sometimes I have added to extant architectural features. My design for Petrushevskaya's *Three Girls in Blue* (1996), for example, harnessed the evocative atmosphere and shape of the ramshackle White Bear Theatre in Kennington, London. The play is set in a leaky decrepit *dacha*, a room in Moscow and in various rural locations. I lime-washed over the black walls and apex roof of the main theatre space to give the impression of the *dacha*; I then covered the floor with soil in which vegetables and weeds grew and gradually invaded the space; I opened up surrounding rooms and corridors which were then crammed with Russian-inspired objects, and I added water pipes to those already suspended from the ceiling which gradually sprang leaks throughout the performance until eventually the space was engulfed in a dream-like rain storm and turned the earth to mud. With a lighting transition and a shift in the performance language, the audience were trans-ported from the cramped interior rooms of the play into a melancholic, poetic landscape that was Dostoevskian in atmosphere and scale.

On other occasions I have removed architectural elements of the space. At The Unicorn Theatre, London for a production of *Twelfth Night* (2009), my design responded to the unseen physical features of the building. I discovered when working in the model box that beneath the central floor of the theatre was a pit which I decided to open up. I filled one half with water to create a pool of sea and raised the other half up and planted it with a wild flower meadow. These two halves – split like twins – were then joined by stepping stones of flotsam and jetsam (objects I found in the theatre's prop store) to create an island – Shakespeare's 'Illyria'. By extending the usual seating into 'the round', I found that not only the shape but the whole atmosphere and dynamic of the theatre were changed.

How did you become interested in site-specific work?
I studied theatre design at Nottingham Trent University (1990–93), where my formal training was enhanced and informed by a culture of students creating work in found spaces. Site-specific work captured my imagination and I created a number of devised performances that took audiences into locations ranging in size from the claustrophobic interior of a small broom cupboard, to a dungeon in Nottingham Castle, and Park Tunnel – a vast subterranean coach tunnel in which I created a promenade production inspired by Persephone's journey into Hades.

Looking back, these early pieces laid down the key themes, preoccupations and methodologies that have continued to occupy me as a scenographer and site-specific performance-maker. For instance, all my work then, as now, originates from an in-depth investigation of a site and is made in response to the physical, material, dynamic, architectural and atmospheric features and qualities of the place for which it is being created. My work is frequently characterized by the re-telling or making of mythic stories (made for and born of a particular place), typically involving a journey through or into other worlds. I remain concerned with the nature of the audience's experience, and seek to create intimate, multi-sensory experiences where small audience groups move in and amongst the performance and travel physically with the action of the piece as it unfolds.

Although the performances I create are exploratory in their staging and use of space, my scenographic solutions can appear to be relatively 'simple' – a boat thrown up into a tree top, a painted blue sky glimpsed on a concrete wall at the end of a passageway, a police 'crime scene' set outside a solitary house. Frequently, I seek to find a juxtaposition of performer and space. In *Mapping the Edge* (2001), for example, these moments included a uniformed RAF officer and his WAAF girlfriend walking arm-in-arm down a Sheffield street whilst kids on bikes and spiky-haired punks passed by, and an exhausted Yemeni woman making her way to the 'workhouse', glimpsed leaning against a wall of colourful graffiti whilst her children (represented by puppets) peered out from underneath her shawls.

Through my work, I have found that each place, regardless of how ordinary it might appear initially, is full of riches. I don't use a space as a mere backdrop to the performance but, rather, environmentally; that is, as an integral part of the performance itself. Within this dynamic environment, the audience can re-imagine the everyday and see the familiar afresh. My concern is to create relationships between space, performer and audience, and to find ways of revealing, re-showing and re-enchanting a place by saying: 'Look anew at what is here; witness the surface of things, and then look again and you will see something more profound about *this* place and perhaps about the world, and how we experience it, and our place within it.' This type of site-specific work is born out of the place in which and for which it is made. Rather like an archaeological dig, making work like this involves an approach to performance-making in which I 'excavate' the performance 'out' of a specific landscape or place.

I first came across your work in House in 1998, when you and Wils Wilson had recently formed the creative partnership wilson+wilson. House made a substantial impact on the town and communities of Huddersfield. How did this piece come about?
House was wilson+wilson's first production, made in collaboration with the poet Simon Armitage and the sonic artist Robin Rimbaud aka Scanner.[6] The piece took just over a year to make and was created for and performed within two derelict nineteenth-century workers' cottages in Huddersfield. As London-based theatre practitioners, we wanted to return to our native Yorkshire in order to make a piece in and about a place of dwelling and belonging. Both Simon and Wils are from Huddersfield, so it was there we began our search for a house, but it took nine months and many detailed negotiations to secure a suitable one. The project became a reality when the Kirklees Council Leader persuaded the chief executive of a property developer to lend us two co-joined properties located in Goldthorp's Yard. The dwellings had been standing empty for years and were due to be renovated into an upmarket public house as part of the locally contentious Kingsgate Shopping Centre development, which was set to transform Huddersfield town centre.

With permission granted, and armed with a screwdriver, Simon, Wils and I found ourselves 'breaking into' the boarded up houses and beginning a process of excavation, in which the fabric of the building and the objects

65

that we discovered inspired the poetic and creative content of the piece. We incorporated this material within the performance and found objects were exhibited alongside their imagined histories. We undertook extensive research into the houses, discovering the names and occupations of all the inhabitants since they were built in the early 1800s. The realization that 3 Goldthorp's Yard had been the meetings room of the Huddersfield Naturalists' Society from 1866 to 1882 widened the thematic interest of *House* to include the evolution of the species and a journey through deep time. This source material was a jumping-off point for the artistic team, feeding our growing preoccupation with time, change, the evolution of buildings and private space, and raised questions relating to how we read the past. Many local individuals and organizations became involved in the making of the piece, including the neighbouring shop-keepers, workers and residents around Goldthorp's Yard and, in a wider sense, the people of Huddersfield.

Can you explain how the performance of House unfolded?
An audience of 15 journeyed from space to space, room to room in a piece which combined visual art, installation, poetry, live performance, live and recorded sound and music. It was performed over five weeks by a company of four actors. The piece began with a walk from the nearby Lawrence Batley Theatre to Goldthorp's Yard. Once inside the houses, the audience progressed through the rooms – sometimes split into groups of five, some-times brought together as one audience – whilst events and images unfolded around them. Fragments of human stories past, present and future were interwoven to create a rich narrative texture (see Illustrations 3.1 and 3.2)

Description
You enter the performance space by opening the front door. An old man sleeps in front of the fire, surrounded by the shored up fragments of his life. You can hear his breathing. On the mantelpiece, a clock is ticking loudly. Books, maps and paintings – Genesis and Darwin provide clues to how far we will travel. There is a model of *The Beagle*, fish in a tank and two finches in a cage. We hear a poem 'To the Occupier', written in response to the un-opened letters, dating back over many years which we found on the door mat when we first entered.

In the tiny kitchen a young woman stands at a sink of icy water peel-ing potatoes – her hands are red and chapped. She speaks as she dreams of escape and gazes out of the window but, rather than looking across the hills to Castle Top, as was once possible, she cannot see beyond the solid stone wall of the Lawrence Batley Theatre which, when built, was the largest Methodist Chapel in the world.

You descend stone steps into an even smaller cellar. Lace, thread, tapestry and needlepoint catch the dim light from the sewing machine. A doll's face found in this room peers out from the wall. A dodo egg nestles in the folds of a christening dress, and a spidery voice caught in the thick stone walls whispers a magical web of dreams and of escape.

Upstairs, the wall of the bathroom has been cut open and we peer through glass to see a man wearing pyjamas suddenly swing down from the ceiling and past our noses like a live specimen in a case. He evolves from ape to human through a few minutes of precisely choreographed and executed movement.

In the bedroom, an old woman sits at her dressing table in warm candlelight. The air is heavy with the evocative perfumes of face powder, rouge and cologne. A young man bursts in. He is dressed in black and, as the poem is spoken, you realize that he is dressed for her funeral.

We follow a sound that takes us up to the attic – someone has just left ... but not by the door. The old man's pipe and slippers hang in the air, the floor is covered with a young boy's toy aeroplanes (cut in half), the music is airy and meditative, you hear a poem about evolution spoken by the old man's voice – a poem of fingertips becoming feathers, of a desire to fly.

You crawl through a hole in the wall into a different space. It is a laboratory, full of found objects which have now become specimens: an archaeology of Goldthorp's Yard. Each one is meticulously labelled, numbered and classified. You realize that an experiment is in process here: an experiment into the nature of time. A young woman scientist sings a song like a nursery rhyme to herself as she works endlessly on her lonely obsession. She is dissecting objects, cutting them in half and placing scrapings of them under the microscope in search of their essence and the memories they hold. There is a [pre-Damien Hirst] sheep cut in half and a half hedgehog and, in the corner, Seth Moseley is studiously painting specimens of local flora.

In a small room, beyond a heavy curtain, you put on a headset. The poet's voice speaks in your ear telling of breaking down the door and entering the house for the first time. The incident turns into a polar expedition, a desert trek, an odyssey. Slides flash up on the walls: pictures of the derelict, rubbish-filled house, interspersed with Antarctic vistas, icebergs, hazy desert horizons and lonely lunar landscapes.

Dark, pulsating music draws you downwards and you descend two steep flights of stairs into the cellar. A man greets you from behind a

Illustration 3.1 *House* (1998) Created and Produced by wilson+wilson (Montage 1)

[Copyright: Fiver]

Top left: The Attic, 'then rock that chair forwards and upwards off its feet, and let fly' (extract from *Bird Brain's Big Night In* by Simon Armitage)

Top centre: Photograph from the first expedition into number 5 Goldthorp's Yard

Top right: Old Man and Woman (Leader Hawkins and Ruth Mitchell) in Eden eat apple pies whilst playing Snakes and Ladders

Middle left: Old Man (Leader Hawkins) in the Front Room nodding off over *The Origin of Species*

Middle right: Young Man (Nick Bagnall) evolving from Ape to Man swings from the bathroom ceiling to the floor

Bottom left: Scientist/investigator (Nicky Barnfield) examining, dissecting and labelling objects found in the house

Bottom right: Woman (Grace Mitchell) conjured up from memory by her son/lover (Nick Bagnall)

Illustration 3.2 *House* (1998) Created and Produced by wilson+wilson (Montage 2)

[Copyright: Fiver]

Top: Man (Nick Bagnall) preaching on the nature of time in the cellar whilst fish swim at his feet and rain falls from the ceiling pipes

Middle left: The 'Huddersfield Half Sheep' amongst found objects in the Specimens' Room

Middle right: Scientist/collector/investigator (Nicky Barnfield) in the Specimens' Room dissecting found objects

Bottom left: Seth Moseley (Leader Hawkins) painting a botanical study of a Primrose

Bottom right: Child's jacket and light bulbs found in the house during the first 'excavation' of the house broken window – a preacher? A mad scientist? He starts to speak – a sermon about time in which you are 'both witness and proof, audience and evidence, observer and specimen in the same breath'. Time unfurls before you and behind you as he speaks. You look down to find that you stand on the edge of a black abyss. It suddenly fills with light and you see that it is a swamp filled with brightly coloured fish, swimming at your feet.

You climb upstairs, into the light, where an ancient couple – the old man and woman that you have met before – are sitting drinking tea and playing snakes and ladders in the Garden of Eden. Real grass grows under their feet, there are primroses and you can hear birdsong. The young couple are there as well, putting the finishing touches to the walls of this, their new home. The walls are painted with the Huddersfield skyline in beautifully rich blues, greens and pinks – it is the once visible view. All four actors speak directly to the audience, a poem about their lives and all our lives: the past, the present and the future.

The space was a fifth, silent performer in this piece, and audiences responded to this key element of the work. What did your audience make of the performance? Audiences came from far afield and from just around the corner. We often found the people who came did so because they had a personal connection to the place, or were intrigued by what we were doing. Some were former residents, who brought with them memories of growing up there; one day, three sisters in their seventies and eighties came to re-visit the house in which they had lived in the 1920s. There were also a few accidental 'guests'; on one occasion an inquisitive, elderly lady who was out shopping was 'scooped up' with the audience and only towards the end of the piece did she call out 'Can I leave now, I have a bus to catch?'!

Following each performance, we asked the audience to write their comments in a visitor's book and their responses included: 'A new emotional experience – it opened parts of my mind and senses that other media has never touched before'; 'it was one of those occasions when you know theatre is the essence of life'; 'very moving: I know much more about what it is to be human'; 'it was so evocative, so compelling: the resonances live on for some considerable time afterwards'.

House demonstrated that site-specific performance of a particularly poetic and innovative kind has the ability to juxtapose many different references which can bring to the surface deep layers of personal and cultural memory. The overwhelmingly positive responses from audience members indicate that people's identities are inextricably linked to their sense of place, and that place itself holds the memory of the people who have dwelt there.

In complete contrast, in Mulgrave *(2005) you chose to locate your performance in a heavily wooded part of the North Yorkshire coastline!*
Initially inspired by Italo Calvino's *The Baron in the Trees*, where the world is seen from a treetop perspective, *Mulgrave* came about because we wanted to create a piece in rural North Yorkshire that took audiences up into the tops of some trees from where they could look across open sea whilst being close to the sky. We were interested in how naval explorers such as Captain Cook, native to this part of the world, traversed the oceans by astronaviga-tion; how boats such as *The Endeavour* were built from the wood of differ-ent types of tree, and how many maritime journeys were dedicated to bringing non-native plant specimens back to the UK. To add to these lines of enquiry, we discovered that Whitby was home to the crow's nest.

With all these ideas in hand, and after an exhaustive search, we discov-ered, by happenstance, the well-hidden Mulgrave Woods a few miles north of Whitby. Working closely with poet Amanda Dalton and composer Hugh Nankivell, our early visits to the woods soon revealed unexpected treasures that shifted and informed our ideas and creative thinking about the piece. As well as having inspired many local folk stories and myths, they contained an astonishing array of tree species from around the world and were the home to two castles, a hermit's cave, two valleys, two rivers and extensive pictorial landscaping designed by Humphrey Repton. We read accounts of visits by Joseph Banks, the plant collector; Omai, 'the noble savage' – brought back from his Tahitian island on one of Cook's ships; and the story of Maharajah Duleep Singh who, following military defeat in India, had been forced to give up the famous Koh-i-noor diamond, which was re-cut and incorporated into the crown jewels by Queen Victoria. Duleep Singh hired the Mulgrave estate, walked his elephants on the beach and took to dressing in the style of an English country gentleman.

Gradually, over many months, we wove this research into a production that was deeply rooted in and inspired by the woods, their atmosphere, their topography and their stories past and present, and so created a piece where, travelling mostly on foot and sometimes in six-seater buggies, audiences of 40 were taken on a four-mile journey whilst music, visual images, live action, song and installations unfolded around them. Their journey – from the sea, into the woods, and back down to the sea – was like a great wave, and was fundamental to the structure, narrative and visual imagery of the piece.

The woods themselves were stunning and dramatic, so the designed 'worlds' I created were placed in specific locations or experienced whilst on

Illustration 3.3 *Mulgrave* **(2005) Created and Produced by wilson+wilson**

[Copyright: Dominic Ibbotson]

Top left: 'The Boy Who Ran From The Sea' (Asif Khan)
Top centre: Carriage conveying Joseph Banks, Omai the Polynesian and Sea Captain Phipps into the woods
Top right: Mrs Clough (Sally Armstrong), amateur naturalist gives a talk on Shield Bugs
Middle left: Gull, the feral girl (Cerianne Roberts) on the castle ruins
Middle right: Sea Captain Phipps (Martin Pirongs) surveys the horizon.
Bottom left: Victorian Girl (Cerianne Roberts) on the lawn with 'stolen' items
Bottom right: Footman (Deka Walmsley) and Victorian Girl (Cerianne Roberts) in the tree house

the move. Many had a dream-like quality: a ghostly-suited drowned man walks in the river, searching for his life; a colourful rickshaw rattling past carries an Indian dowager as hunters with nets and guns congregate in the woodyard before speeding off in a Landrover; a fishing boat and buoys are seen marooned in the treetops and shoals of driftwood fish are suspended amongst the branches, as if the woods had been engulfed by a huge wave; a summer tea party is seen, and the Maharajah appears atop an elephant; a feral girl peers from the undergrowth where she hides out from conventional society; we see trails of stones and chairs set out for a woodland lecture; Banks leaps from a horse-drawn carriage laden with plant specimens; a girl perches on a platform in an oak tree, surrounded by hanging objects 'stolen' from the castle (see Illustration 3.3).

Recently you have established your own company and are exploring new creative possibilities. How does your current work with the Louise Ann Wilson Company differ in approach?

My work is still concerned with making performances through an extended period of immersion in, and investigation of, a chosen place. I have recently embarked on a series of new works which focus on the rural landscape as a place for performance in which the relationship between human beings and the environment can be re-imagined. These works seek to explore ways in which live performance can dramatize, articulate and reflect upon significant life events, creating multi-sensory experiences that make resonant the life experiences of the people of the locality. The form, shape and content of the pieces respond to the physical nature of the landscape of a place (which could cover many square miles), its geology, topography, geography, history and archaeology. The works incorporate the experiences and 'knowledge' of people who through living, working or spending leisure time there have intimate and specific understandings of the place and its landscape. And it is their activities, combined with different live art forms, that become the tools through which the piece is constructed and performed.

You describe yourself as a scenographer? What does this mean for you?

Even when working as a designer for theatre and opera, my work involves more than what is often 'traditionally' seen as the work of a designer; that is, the design of the costumes and set. In addition to creating the visual and spatial landscape of the production, I am equally interested in the performance language, the soundscape, the lighting and the relationships between the space, the performers and the audience – elements that fuse, juxtapose or interweave to create the physical world of a production. If I

73

am not directing, I work closely with the director, and always in close collaboration with the lighting designer, sound designer, composer and choreographer in order to create the whole 'world' of the piece.

I have only recently begun to use the term 'scenographer' when describing myself and, as the term finds currency, it becomes increasingly helpful to me. My work combines and synthesizes many different aspects and disciplines, and it feels inadequate to categorize it using the more conventional – and, at times, frustratingly undervalued – term of 'designer'. When I am making site-specific work, I describe myself as an artist and scenographer, and I credit myself as the creator and director of the work because I envision the whole production.

I think the current discourse around 'what scenography is' makes it a good time for practitioners such as me to evolve and define the scenographer as an artist with a unique set of creative, technical and collaborative skills with an inter-disciplinary approach to theatre and performance-making.

3.3   Audience space/scenographic space

Scott Palmer

Hannah's and Wilson's perspectives on performance space have raised some important questions about how we use space in contemporary performance. Hannah has outlined how architectural space performs on its own, whilst Wilson's work reveals how scenographic space is manipulated and conveys meaning in performance. Theatre spaces by their very nature seek to organize people and place them in specific relationships to the performers and to each other. In this section, I explore these relationships, and attempt to draw some parallels and highlight a number of associated factors which impact on our understanding and response to space in performance.

Performance space and the audience

The Marxist philosopher Henri Lefebvre (1991) suggests that place emerges as a particular form of lived space – and that such places are created and defined through the distinctive activities which take place there. Michel de Certeau (1984) also argues that place is a practised space, and that space becomes place when it develops significance by its inhabitants or users. The theatre, then, would seem to be more than an 'empty space'; rather, it is a practised space for bodies to perform and to be observed within.

The theatre (from Greek '*Theatron*' or 'seeing place') is both a noun and a verb. It is not only a place which is defined by the activities that it contains, but also by the way in which space is organized within it – both onstage through the scenography, which establishes the world of the performance, and also through the overall qualities of the space of the theatre itself. The relationship between the architecture of the space, the positioning of the audience space and the stage or playing area dictates the very nature of the experience that the audience will have in performance. These complex inter-relationships condition the reception and extent of audience engagement and are of fundamental importance – especially since, once the staging conditions are established, they are rarely able to be changed during a performance.

I recently attended a performance of *The History Boys* (2010) at The Quarry Theatre at the West Yorkshire Playhouse, and was seated high up towards the back of the amphitheatre-style auditorium. Whilst this meant that I had a good overview of the stage and could appreciate the way in which the entire space was used both during and in between scenes, I felt distanced and detached from the events on stage. During the interval, however, I was able to change position and moved to an empty seat in the front row. The second half of the performance was therefore experienced from a totally different perspective. With this new proximity to the stage, I was more fully engaged in the dramatic action whilst also able to notice the subtler nuances of the actors' performances, which had not been possible from the rear of the auditorium. The play felt like a totally different experience.

The relationship between performers' space and audience space is a primary concern of architect and theatre consultant Iain Mackintosh (1993), who argues that there is much we can learn from *ad quadratum* geometry, a classical system of proportions based on the square. It was employed by Renaissance theatre architects and is typical of the eighteenth-century Georgian playhouses, such as those at Richmond and Bury St Edmunds in the UK. In these spaces, the proscenium divide is equidistant from the rear of the stage and the back wall of the auditorium. This ensures that the actor, when standing on the forestage, is positioned at a critical intersection – in a powerful sacred space or *vesica piscis* at the centre of the whole space's volume (see Figure 3.1).

The relatively small scale of these playhouses ensures that the audience member is never far from the playing area, and this proximity helps to ensure their success as performance spaces for audience and performers alike. This shared sense of intimacy suggests that there is a clear link between the feeling of such spaces and their overall volume. The end-on arrangement, where the audience is arranged at one end of a space and the performance takes place at the other, originates from the indoor spaces converted for theatre since the

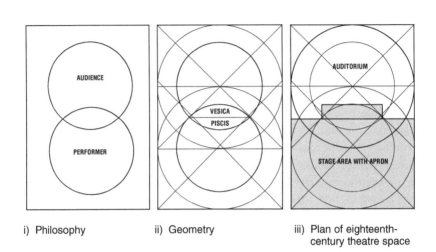

i) Philosophy   ii) Geometry   iii) Plan of eighteenth-
century theatre space

Figure 3.1   Sacred Space (after Mackintosh)
[Copyright: Scott Palmer]

Note: Ad quadratum geometry shows that eighteenth-century theatres are focused
on the *vesica piscis*. The thrust (or apron) stage extends beyond the proscenium to
create a powerful area where the space of audience and performer intersect.

Renaissance. These 'found' rectangular spaces, such as halls or tennis courts,
suggested a particular arrangement of audience and performers which has
since become the dominant format for Western theatre spaces.

The introduction of the proscenium formalized this relationship by
segregating the players from the spectators. The auditorium therefore
became a separate physical space to the stage area, which could then be
isolated further by the introduction of the curtain. Theatre buildings with
the characteristic picture frame stage dominated in the eighteenth and
nineteenth centuries. Whilst this form enabled the viewpoint of the spectator to be easily controlled, it created a legacy of a theatre-building which,
as Hannah suggests, can be little more than 'a rigid, lifeless container'.
Crucially, the proscenium divide prevents the spectator from directly experiencing the space that the performers inhabit:

A conventional theatre experience displaces the senses from the word
go. We sit in a dark auditorium, watching actors in costume and make-
up move about a set under artificial light, and willingly suspend our
disbelief ... Though conventional theatre-going is a real time, real space
experience and thus has the potential to be sensually immersive, it is
more often than not an audio-visual experience that offers little to the
other three senses. (Hill and Paris 2006: 48)

In contrast, alternative arrangements of playing area and audience area seek to offer a more dynamic relationship between player and spectator in which the sense of illusion and theatrical artifice is diminished. The thrust stage, where the stage area advances into the auditorium and the audience are positioned on three sides, was used in both Greek amphitheatres and Elizabethan playhouses – and regained currency in the twentieth and twenty-first centuries. A prominent example of this shift is provided by the Royal Shakespeare Theatre in Stratford-upon-Avon, which in 2011 has been radically transformed from a proscenium-bound, end-on space to one with a permanent thrust stage in which the audience find themselves much closer to the action. Alternative arrangements of performance space allow the audience to surround the action. The arena or island stage where performances are staged in-the-round is an ancient arrangement of performance space which, when championed by practitioners such as Stephen Joseph, has resulted in dynamic permanent theatre spaces such as Manchester's Royal Exchange Theatre.

Where performance space is not organized in such a formal way, dramatic action happens within and around the spectators in shared space. Richard Schechner coined the term *'environmental theater'* to describe such work, which developed from Allan Kaprow's Happenings of the late 1950s and early 1960s.[7] The re-evaluation of the performer–audience relationship is at the heart of such work, which, although considered by some as 'experimental', builds on a long legacy of 'non-frontal' performance styles employed in folk and non-Western theatre. Although not continuous, this environmental tradition extends back throughout the history of theatre (Aronson 1981: 15) where the divisions between audience and performance space have been blurred. There are clearly times when the need for less rigid and more spontaneous styles of performance-making seem not only to be relevant, but vitally necessary. In the UK, this has been evidenced in the work of companies such as Punchdrunk, Grid Iron and Shunt, by the growing interest in making performances outside of theatre buildings, and by the proliferation of city-wide celebratory public performance festivals.

De La Guarda's *Villa Villa* (Buenos Aires, 1996) was a promenade-style multi-sensory performance which has been adapted for a variety of spaces throughout the world. Its arrival in London in 1997 appealed to the zeitgeist by offering a carnivalesque celebration of life in an Artaudian rave-like experience that proved particularly popular with youthful audiences. Immersed within a theatrical environment, which was at first partly obscured by a gigantic paper ceiling, the audience were surrounded by performers who bombarded them from all directions, including from above on aerial ropes. In separate parts of the performance, little plastic toy objects rained down onto the audience, water was sprayed and audience members were assaulted by light, sound and wind. The audience became physically incorporated into the performance in a number of ways; encouraged to dance along with the performers to a heavy Latin drumbeat, or lifted above the floor by performers on ropes in an extreme sensory experience.

Performance place and scenographic space

Whilst promenade-style or immersive environments offer a radical alternative to the more traditional and static relationship of performer and audience, the use of a specific place for performance introduces further qualities to the experience, as we have seen from the work of Louise Ann Wilson. The feelings stimulated through site-specific work are evoked through an embodied response to the particular space. Often, it is precisely the richness of this phenomenological, multi-sensory experience of place that makes the event so memorable, as visual, aural, olfactory and tactile elements become an integral and often heightened part of the audience experience.

The poignancy of the final scene of *Mulgrave* (2005) was created through the combination of the visual framing of the action, live haunting music and the physical sense of place experienced through our bodies. The sea could be smelt, the wind felt on our faces and, standing on a grass bank, our legs ached from the distance travelled and the range of surfaces which had been traversed during the performance. We watched the drowned man, still dressed in a suit, stumbling despairingly in the river past us and out to sea, where he disappeared into the waves. (See Illustration 3.4)

The sense of taste had also been invoked earlier in the performance as a cup of tea had been served in the ruins of a thirteenth-century castle. This mid-performance 'interval' in the journey had a practical function but also worked on another level, as the taking (and tasting) of tea suggested direct connections to key themes of the performance and linked the exotic, non-native plants of the estate to English social customs and the histories of the sub-continent. Scenographic elements which acknowledge the sensory and stimulate embodied responses are able to evoke profound responses and create meaning through drawing subtly upon the themes of the piece.

Space is traditionally considered as a three-dimensional extent in which objects and events occur but this volume is never static, and its constantly changing nature suggests that we should acknowledge its fourth dimension:

Illustration 3.4   The Final Moments of *Mulgrave* (2005)
[Copyright: Dominic Ibbotson]

The surprise reappearance of the Maharajah Duleep Singh's elephant, which crosses the bridge at Sandsend whilst 'The Boy Who Ran' (Asif Khan) returns to the sea.

time. In section 3.1 of this chapter, Hannah addresses this dynamic in developing her notion of *event-space*, explaining how even what appear to be permanent spaces are changed or destroyed through time. She urges us to think again about the apparent permanence of architecture and, in particular, the playhouse in relation to the fleeting moments of theatrical activity which are staged within it.

A given playing space not only changes as performers move within it, but the space itself also provides us with echoes of prior events – be they memories of previous performances or traces of past histories. Louise Ann Wilson draws on these past events as rich material in her site-specific work, but theatre buildings also have their own unique echoes, whether they be Ariane Mnouchkine's adapted Parisian gunpowder factory La Cartoucherie, or Peter Brook's Bouffes du Nord in the same city, where the theatre's past has been consciously exposed and can be seen etched into the fabric of the auditorium walls. Each theatre space therefore has its own particular history that forms a part of each performance – one cannot, for example, escape from reflecting on actor-manager Henry Irving when attending a performance at London's Lyceum Theatre. His presence is also etched, both literally and metaphorically, into the very fabric of the space in which he practised in the late nineteenth century.

Yi-Fu Tuan writes about the sensual and emotional dimensions of space, and our unseen attachments to it. We assign particular feelings to places which may be evoked by fleeting moments which touch our consciousness:

> Intimate experiences lie buried in our innermost being so that not only do we lack the words to give them form but often we are not even aware of them. (Tuan 1977: 136)

These barely remembered feelings can create a poignancy which can be evoked through the experience of theatrical performance. The emotional attachment to place, known as *topophilia*, is evident in my own unseen attachment to a bland street in Huddersfield, for example. I cannot walk along it without remembering wilson+wilson's extraordinary *House*. Even though the space in which that performance occurred has long since been lost to commercial development, my experience on a winter's night in 1998 has created an intangible bond to the locale.

A physical response to space is central to our understanding of performance:

> We are spatial creatures; we respond instinctively to space ... it is the apprehension of space that may be the most profound and powerful experience of live theater although, admittedly, it is one that is most often felt subconsciously. (Aronson 2005: 1)

Punchdrunk draw directly on this practice through allowing their audience freedom to choose what they watch and where they go within the spatial environments that they create. The audience is therefore not viewed as passive but, instead, is encouraged to roam the performance space, experiencing and exploring the unknown:

> What we do differently is to focus as much attention on the audience and the space as we give to the performers and text. (Punchdrunk, http://www.punchdrunk.org.uk)

Scenographic space was the key component of Punchdrunk's *It Felt Like a Kiss* (2009), an ambitious collaborative production in which small groups of audience explored six floors of a semi-derelict central Manchester office building. A multitude of spaces were experienced, in sequence rather like an exhibition and, strangely, largely devoid of human performers. The spaces provided evidence of human activity with their many objects, film sequences, sounds and smells which were redolent of 1960s America, whilst the audience were left to piece together a series of narratives rather like a detective story. The journey through these ghostly spaces culminated in an experience akin to a visceral computer game in which senses were gradually heightened. In navigating labyrinthine corridors, the small groups of audience found themselves treated like rats in some large-scale laboratory experiment. In this uncomfortable world, where the American Dream had clearly turned to nightmare, the audience were chased by a man with a chainsaw, before finding themselves in a dark basement where they became systematically segregated in space. Passing through a series of turnstiles, the audience were no longer able to rely upon the security of the group as it became repeatedly subdivided until, in conventional horror movie style, each individual found themselves, in a narrow black corridor, alone and in the dark.

This way of working echoes Schechner's *environmental theater* practice in advocating a more active role for the audience:

> Spaces ought to open to each other so that spectators can see each other and move from one place to another. The overall feel of the theater ought to be a place where choices can be made. (Schechner 1994: 30)

The empty space and the performer

As Hannah mentions in section 3.1 of this chapter, Brook's famous proposition (see p. 58) prompts many questions for the scenographer. Where is this 'empty space'? How big is it? What are its volume, height, width and depth? What defines this space? How is it reached or approached? From where is the audience experiencing it? What is beyond the space or located around it? What else can be seen? What does the space sound like? How does it smell? What does it feel like? How is this space lit? What is its history? And, in terms of the 'man' walking across this space, there are perhaps an even greater multitude of questions that need resolving.

We have already explored the impact of the scenographer in shaping dramatic space, and how the way that spaces are designed and manipulated directly affects the experience of the performance by an audience. Scenographic space is, of course, also created for and through the actions of performers, and the scenographer needs to consider carefully the way in which designed space impacts directly on the performer:

Understanding the dynamic of the space means recognising through observing its geometry, where its power lies – in height, length, width, depth or the horizontal and vertical diagonals. Every space has a line of power, reaching from the acting area to the spectator, that the scenographer has to reveal and explore. This line of power is actively felt by performers on the stage, as they look into the auditorium and assess where they feel most strongly placed. (Howard 2002: 1–2)

Howard echoes the notion of Mackintosh's *vesica piscis* in establishing the importance of particular zones in a given performance stage. Space is felt kinaesthetically through multiple senses – it dictates how we feel and how we relate to others. In the theatre, the space also imposes conditions. The arrangement of seats, the number of people in the space and the sightlines all impact directly on the performer, who needs to react by altering how the voice is used to communicate, for example. Brook recognizes that the spatial relationship is the essential ingredient of performance practice:

To my mind, the theatre is based on a particular human characteristic, which is the need at times to be in a new and intimate relationship with one's fellow men. (Brook 1988: 147)

Space defines our very being: *'Je suis l'espace ou je suis'* [I am the space where I am], Noël Amaud asserts (Bachelard 1968: 137), but it also extends beyond the body and from the performer to all parts of the theatre space. Edward T. Hall pioneered the study of humankind's perception and use of space through his study of *proxemics*, which defined human activity into distinct types of space.

Oskar Schlemmer undertook experiments in the theatrical power of space at the Bauhaus in the 1920s, where the idea of haptic space – *Raumempfindung* or 'felt volume' – was explored from the perspective of the performer. Schlemmer sought to exploit the dynamic properties of space – its scale, texture and sound, as a material with theatrical potential. He developed a series of dances based upon sensations of space, to achieve a fusion between the performing figure and the architecture of the performance space. Radical costumes were developed as a physical articulation of the felt space, such as those for *Stick Dance* (Weimar 1919–27) and *The Triadic Ballet* (Weimar 1922).

In performance terms, it is useful to think of space not in abstract terms but in relation to and centred upon the human body, and an understanding

Table 3.1 Spacing Behaviour

Bodily distances*	Imperial measurement	Metric equivalent	
Public space	10 feet and beyond	Over 3 m	Domain of impersonal and relatively anonymous public interaction, such as in a shopping precinct or public park.
Social-consultative space	4–10 feet	120 cm–3 m	Typical of routine social interactions, and includes interactions with acquaintances and strangers and more formal social occasions.
Personal-casual space	18 inches–4 feet	45–120 cm	Area of interaction with good personal friends and people who you know well. This category tends to have the greatest variation between cultures.
Intimate space	0–18 inches	Less than 45 cm	The closest 'bubble' of space, beginning at the body. This is a space reserved for the closest of friends and family. Interactions may include hugging, whispers, close conversation, kissing and touch.

Note: *The measurements in this table are based on studies of Western, primarily North American social conventions over 50 years ago. Importantly, Hall acknowledges that other cultures set different norms for bodily interaction and social closeness, and that being too close or too far away can lead to significant intercultural misunderstandings.
Source: After Hall (1959, 1966).

of proxemics can assist us in creating performance work. An audience will decode the arrangements of figures on the stage and will read the relationship of characters to each other in terms of the changing spatial conditions, as well as what they might do or say in the theatrical environment which we observe them moving within.

I believe there is an actual, living relationship between the spaces of the body and the spaces the body moves through; that human living tissue does not abruptly stop at the skin ... human beings and space are both alive. (Schechner 1994:12)

In concentrating on the theatrical space with which performing bodies and audiences engage in an act of performance, this chapter has high-lighted a key concern of performance-makers, and has identified a range of approaches which have informed a new interest in experimenting with the use of space as the primary ingredient in performance-making. A sceno-graphic sensibility can assist in both designing new spaces for performance and creating events where the role of the audience itself is questioned – no longer seen as simply passive viewers but, rather, a dynamic entity and active participants in the performance.

Activities

➤ *Solo activity*

By way of reflecting on the material of the chapter, consider the following simple question: What is Scenography? It might help to break this down into sub-questions:

- How does scenography contribute to the performance event?
- Why is the arrangement of space/bodies and visual and aural signs within the stage space important?
- What implications are there for practitioners of performance?
- Are there moments from performances that you have experienced that you remember specifically for their scenographic impact?
- Can you identify precisely why a particular moment stands out? How did it make you feel?
- How can scenographic images in performance be explained and analyzed?

➤ *Discussion activity*

- Think through, in detail, the definition of event-space (p. 55).
- What major historical events have shaped your understanding and feeling for space?
- List places you have visited on holiday or on a day trip which are shaped by their history and the events that occurred there.
- Share them with the group, and discuss how this collapsing of time-into-space affects experience.
- Contrast this with examples of personal and everyday event-space.

➤ *Practical activity 1*

You will need six matching chairs for this task, which is a variation of an Augusto Boal activity for actors and non-actors. It introduces key scenographic principles, which are valuable for performers and designers alike, as it explores relationships between objects and stage space. It is useful to analyze the resulting arrangements critically, from the perspective of an audience. Referring to Table 3.1 will help.

- Take six identical chairs. Arrange the chairs so that one appears to be domi-nant in the group. Step back and look at the resulting image. Discuss whether the chair is in a dominant position, and why you read it in that way.
- Invite another group member to enter the space and try to improve on the arrangement, or to suggest an alternative. Review the new arrangement. Is it an improvement? What qualities are heightened or weakened? What does the new arrangement suggest? Do some arrangements in space work better than others? If so, can you identify why this is?
- Review and note the multitude of possibilities. (You might find it helpful to sketch the arrangements you find most successful.)
  - How is the arrangement of objects and space communicating to us?
  - What do these images suggest? Perhaps it is a particular space or place that you know or remember? (for example, a classroom, a bus, a doctor's waiting room).
  - Can these arrangements suggest anything else beyond a space/place? Do they evoke particular emotions in us or suggest a feeling?
  - Can you arrange the chairs to create a space that evokes feelings of: 'isola-tion', 'rejection', 'togetherness', 'opposition'?
  - How is space communicating in each of the solutions you have found? Is it to do with evocations of public, social or intimate space?

➤ *Practical activity 2 – Space as a dramatic score*

You will need a space large enough to experiment with different staging possi-bilities. Building on your developing knowledge of proxemics and the arrange-ment of objects in stage space, this exercise encourages small groups to combine these findings through exploring scenographic solutions to a specific dramatic moment.

- Select a well-known scene from a play text and use a short extract as a start-ing point (Macbeth's meeting with the three weird sisters, for example). You need not concentrate on the words but, instead, focus on action and move-ment. (Reducing the text to single key words or short lines may help to punc-tuate the scene and to root the movement.)
- Some members of the group should act as 'performers' and others as observers, commenting and feeding back. Then swap over.

- Experiment with variations in spatial arrangements between the characters. Observe the meanings created simply by changing the placing of bodies in space, and how they stand/move and relate to each other.
  - What do the variations suggest?
  - Are some arrangements stronger than others? In what way?
  - What principles are at work in creating these images?
  - From where should these arrangements be viewed? How does the viewing point make a difference?
- Try the same movement arrangements for a thrust stage with the audience on three sides. What difference does this make to the performer and the reception of the scene?
- Experiment with placing the audience in different positions – for example, surrounding the playing area (in the round), at either side (traverse staging) or with the audience in the middle and the action surrounding them.
  - Can you create an environment where the audience and performers experience the same space and there is little distinction between them?
  - What effect does this have on the performance?
  - Which arrangements seem to work best?
  - Can you identify the reasons why?

Notes

1   The term's likely origin is between 469–56 BC, when the plays of Sophocles and Aeschylus were first staged. For a detailed discussion of the origins and problems associated with the term, see Beer (2004: 26–7).

        Roman scholar Vitruvius c. 25BC refers to *scenographia* as perspective in relation to architecture (*De Architectura*, Book 1, Volume 2, 1970: 15), and describes how Aeschylus employed Agatharchus of Samos to paint a perspective background for the stage in around 458 BC (*De Architectura*, Book VII, preface: 11.) The Renaissance architect and theatre designer Sebastiano Serlio also refers to *scenografia* as a means of integrating the science and craft of architecture, scenery and painting into a combined space of both stage and auditorium (*Architectura*, Book II, 1545: 45).

2   Although Bernard Tschumi's specific mention of this term is not prevalent in his texts, K. Michael Hays has cited him as its progenitor in *Architecture Theory Since 1968*: 216. Hays states in an interview with Izabel Gass that 'the term "event-space" belongs to Tschumi' (*Manifold* 2007).

3   Cartesian perspectivalism is also referred to as the *ancien scopic* regime, whereby space, its subjects and objects, are constructed and perceived through Euclidean geometry.

4   *Mise-en-scène*, which literally means that which is 'placed on stage', folds scenography with directorially determined performance to create a mediated experience for spectators.

5   On 23 October 2002, the *Dubrovka Theater* in Moscow was seized by Chechen rebels who infiltrated during the musical performance of *Nord-Ost*, interrupting and transforming the show into a prolonged international spectacle of terror that ended after three days with Russia's Spetsnaz soldiers storming the building, having filled it with a narcotic gas that killed over 170 people.

6   All wilson+wilson performances were co-created by Louise Ann Wilson and Wils Wilson – websites: http://www.wilsonandwilson.org.uk/ and http://www.louiseannwilson.co.uk/

7   Happenings are theatrical events that involve aspects of spectator participation, and aim to break down the barrier between the audience and the artwork. The first Happenings are considered to be the forerunners of performance art. Kaprow's *18 Happenings in 6 Parts* (1959), for example, created an environment of separate spaces constructed within a New York gallery in which a series of activities, with which the audience was encouraged to interact, were presented simultaneously.

Further reading

Baugh, Christopher (2005) *Theatre, Performance and Technology: The Development of Scenography in the 20th Century*. Basingstoke: Palgrave Macmillan.

Collins, J. and Nisbet, A. (eds) (2010) *Theatre and Performance Design: A Reader in Scenography*. London: Routledge.

Howard, Pamela (2002) *What is Scenography?* London: Routledge.

McAuley, Gay (1999) *Space in Performance: Making Meaning in the Theatre*. Michigan, USA: University of Michigan Press.

McKinney, Joslin and Butterworth, Philip (2009) *The Cambridge Introduction to Scenography*. Cambridge: Cambridge University Press.

Schechner, Richard (1994) *Environmental Theater*, 2nd edn. New York and London: Applause.

4   Time

Introduced and edited by Tony Gardner

Introduction

This chapter will address the centrality of time to our understanding of performance as a live art form. It deals with the issues and questions that follow from the unique experience of performance time, as distinct from our everyday sense of time. As Peggy Phelan (1993) has pointed out, live performance exists perpetually in the present, and yet is always disappearing into the past at the very moment that it is made. Unlike the visual arts and recorded media, time in performance is not under the control of its audience: live performance can neither be rewound nor paused for later viewing, the experience of it cannot be slowed down or speeded up by its audience. Nevertheless, a dynamic tension may exist between what Hans-Thiess Lehmann has termed the 'fictional' or 'dramaturgical time' of the work and the real 'time of the representation' (2006: 153–62) experienced by the audience in a way that is unique to each example of performance.

Given how important these factors of time are in helping to define the specific nature of any one performance, it is surprising that relatively little critical attention has been given to it. Alan Ayckbourn notes that '[Time] is an area that's rarely talked about as much as it should be' (2002: 20). This chapter will therefore provide some critical tools that may be applied to both understanding and working with time in performance, as well as exploring some key terms in our contemporary vocabulary for describing different aspects of time. Steve Dixon begins by providing a historical and theoretical overview, and then reflects on the different dynamics that are engaged in new media theatre practice, where technology serves to create a unique type of 'time out of time', or *extratemporality*. This section introduces a set of key ideas related to how time is experienced, measured, conceptualized and manipulated in everyday life and performance contexts. The increasing interest of contemporary artists in creating performances that shape an audience's experience of time as *duration* is then explored through a discussion of the work of Lone Twin's Gregg Whelan and Gary Winters. In the final section, I consider how live performance creates a special quality of time passing, and how this may generate a sense of *occasion* or *event* that parallels the way that space may be transformed into *place* through performance.

4.1 Theatre, technology and time[1]

Steve Dixon

Understandings of time – its nature, structure and experience – have varied throughout history; time has never been a shared, continuous or linear notion. There is no universal temporality and, as Sylviane Agacinski points out in her wonderful study *Time Passing*: 'awareness of time is neither pure nor originary, and it cannot be separated from the empirical contents that structure it' (2003: 33). She explores different systems of temporality, how events respond to different tempos, and how nature-related tasks (harvesting, herding, hunting) and the cyclical rhythms of the sun and the seasons imposed particular notions of time on humans, who lived according to particular and necessary rhythms. In the West, since the nineteenth century, the social impacts of industrialization, technology and media have displaced older date-event traditions of dividing and calculating time in religion (births of prophets and dynasties) and politics (wars and conquests), to become the new force in its ordering, measurement and meaning. Time was once as religious and political as history, but is no more.

Understandings and meanings of time changed particularly radically, as one might expect, following the invention of the mechanical clock in 1354. But the standardization and unification of a global temporal order took centuries, and evolved through many stages, including a move from solar time to clock time announced in Geneva in 1780. The setting of World Standard Time (through Greenwich Mean Time) in 1884 inculcated a sense of 'State-time' in what Peter Osborne has discussed as an imperialist gesture of enforced temporal conformity. It was not until the twentieth century that consistent and thorough global synchronization came about; Holland, for example, only aligned itself with global time-keeping in 1940, and the Uniform Time Act was passed by the US Congress as late as 1966 (Osborne 1999: 42).

No sooner had this uniformity been agreed than postmodern theorists[2] began to postulate both the demise of history, and of time itself (at least, as it had been previously understood). By the end of the twentieth century, as the speed of technological progress accelerated, Francis Fukuyama declared *The End of History* (1992), and Fredric Jameson suggested that history could only be approached like the reflected shadow images of Plato's cave,[3] but now 'by way of our own pop images and simulacra' (1991: 25). As a digital clock on top of the Pompidou Centre in Paris counted down the seconds to the end of the millennium, Jean Baudrillard (1997) reflected on time not as progressive and accumulative, but as a system of reversal and subtraction.

Postmodern time

On the surface, it appears that certain examples of recent new media theatre practice examine and present ideas of time (and time's relationship to space and technology) in relation to 'classic' postmodern conceptions theorized since the 1970s. These conceptions might be summarized here as: a rejection of the linear 'grand narratives' of history – as named by Jean-François Lyotard in *The Postmodern Condition* (1984), doubts about whether the present can ever fully replace the past, and with it a suspicion about any claims of originality or innovation in the arts, which is often expressed in a blurring of 'old' and 'new' forms, or a self-conscious 'quotation' of the past in the present. Andreas Huyssen saw the acceleration of technology as effecting 'the draining of time in the world of information and data banks' (1995: 9), whilst Lorenzo Simpson (1995) suggested that new technologies sought time's very annihilation. Paul Virilio took up a similar theme, discussing the aesthetics of acceleration in *Vitesse et Politique* (1979) and later maintaining in *The Lost Dimension* (1991) that, rather than extinguishing time, computer culture emphasized the recurring and permanent present tense. 'Computer time', he insisted, 'helps construct a permanent present, an unbounded, timeless intensity' (1991: 15). Michel Foucault spoke of living 'in the epoch of simultaneity ... the epoch of juxtaposition, the epoch of near and far, of the side by side' (cited in Manovich, 2002: 72). Emmanuel Levinas (1991) conceived a present enveloping all tenses, and so saturated by different temporalities that it becomes a 'present perfect', where time does not move, but merely dilates.

However, postmodern notions of time provide only partial understandings of the expression and representation of temporality within new media theatre practice. Changes in conceptions of time within contemporary technological culture (and not simply in technological performance) emphasize a new sense of pre-medieval 'mythic atemporality' which may be theorized not only as a challenge to linear, chronometric time, but also as a type of return to earlier notions of time as static, mythic, cyclical or sacred. This is now reflected acutely within digital performance practice, where time is commonly seen to operate within a new and dynamic relationship between modern understandings of progressive, chronometric time and its contrasting ancient, theocratic, cyclical conception: between the secular and the sacred.

Postmodernism's denial of the possibility of anything new also denies the possibility of a future; time is theorized as a recurrent present which envelops and is saturated by the past, but never looks toward the future. But the best new media theatre is characterized by the very forward impulsions that postmodernism lacks. The 'present tense' of digital performance is marked by excitability and forward vision, in contrast to the static, backward-looking, 'groundhog-day' present of the postmodern experience. Digital performance often ignites a sense of the 'new' by creating representations and experiences which are extratemporal, a notion I will develop in more detail later in this section.

Zulu Time, the $1 million 'techno-cabaret' created by Quebec multimedia theatre luminary Robert Lepage and musician Peter Gabriel in 2001 (Montreal, Canada), provides a fascinating example of this dynamic, as the highly emotive critical response to it from Patrice Pavis makes abundantly clear. The production, which explores the unreality and disorientation of time as experienced in airports and during air travel, is so 'modern' and futuristic that Pavis pleads a passionate humanist case for the live body and for theatrical text in the face of such digital and robotic spectacle:

> Every technology, every computer is a foreign body at the heart of theatrical performance. The more complex, sturdy, omnipresent the technology, the more derisory it is to our eyes. (Pavis 2003: 188)

Lepage's stage machinery, robots, and digital effects swamp the human beings, he says, pulling them into the machine, whilst the audience searches desperately but in vain to connect with a speaking, living body.

Pavis' essay, however, is not a crude piece of conservative, Luddite criticism. It is a serious reflection on the future of performance itself, and the manner in which works such as *Zulu Time* signal how theatre, and the role and status of the performer within theatre, have changed fundamentally. Without acknowledging or using the word, Pavis places both contemporary performance and the performer into a *posthuman*[4] frame. Theatre's age-old humanism based on words, emotions, live bodies, and intimate, ritualized exchange has been superseded by posthuman theatre, and what is more, that succession is now irrevocable: 'triumphant ... technology has got the upper hand on the human for good' (Pavis 2003: 188).

Extratemporality

I would like here to theorize areas of digital art and performance from the distinct viewpoint of the *extratemporal*. In some ways, this viewpoint borrows ideas at play within postmodern theory, but postmodernism generally emphasizes the *atemporal* – a negatively configured 'non-time' of contemporary experience. The extratemporal relates to primitive and prehistoric (as well as some modernist) notions of time, in the way, for example, that Claude Lévi-Strauss conceptualized societies that 'refuse to accept history' as operating 'with reference to a mythic order that is itself *outside time*' [original emphasis] (Agacinski 2003: 8). This idea – that certain societies or practices operate according to an extratemporal order – lends itself well to an understanding of much digital arts practice, particularly where time constitutes the central theme or metaphor. The prevailing theoretical wind that currently perceives and celebrates artistic explorations of time in terms of ruptures and disjunctions provides one important perspective; but the idea that these explorations may operate within a system moving outside of time (at least, conceptually and metaphorically) opens a different and equally fertile analytical landscape.

Extratemporality has been a defining feature of Richard Foreman's unique brand of theatrical performance art for over 30 years. Foreman has held ideas of time and its suspension at the centre of his company Ontological-Hysteric Theatre. An early experimenter with video in his work in the late 1960s and early 1970s, Foreman nowadays uses little or no video or digital visual media, although complex audio soundscapes and live microphone voices provide key mediatized elements in his works. As in Robert Wilson's work, highly stylized and ritualized 'acting' performances, slow-motion movements and repetitions all contribute to a sense of time's manipulation and disruption. But Foreman's work is far more manic, Dadaist[5] and comic than Wilson's, exciting a quite different sense of extratemporal dreamscape and dreamtime. In *Maria del Bosco* (2000), a disorienting type of 'madness' is set up using Foreman's trademark elements: densely crammed and cramped design, oversize surrealistic costumes and props, processions of strange or sinister characters, and short scenes and *tableaux vivant* played with Gothic intensity. It ends with a *tour de force* sequence of controlled hysteria combining a hypnotic and insistent soundtrack, extreme stylized movement, and repetitive dramatic climaxes. Throughout the sequence, at the back of the stage a performer pulls out a ten-foot long wooden board from a gap in the set, and then quickly pushes it back out of view. This action is continually repeated in a fast, sawing motion about once every five seconds. Writ large on the board are the words: 'Resist the Present'.

Influenced by, and following the lead of Gertrude Stein, Foreman tries to induce, by artistic means, a highly attentive type of supra-real consciousness (which he calls 'semiconscious') which opens for the spectator a sense of a continuous present tense. In multimedia theatre and dance, the bombardment of different time-based projections working in conjunction with the live bodies of performers is frequently used to similar ends; that is, to disrupt cognition of time's linearity in order to achieve moments (particularly climactic ones) of extratemporal catharsis.

Freezing time

In the late nineteenth century, Henri Bergson's *Matter and Memory* (1896) provided an important and highly popular study of the flux of time as the fundamental element of metaphysics. His notion that 'what I call 'my present' has one foot in my past, and another in the future' (quoted in Rush 1999: 12) became an aphorism and an inspiration for many modernist artists' that is, those mainly working in Europe and America in the first half of the twentieth century who emphasized the creation of new works and techniques to replace the traditions of what was perceived to be a wholly decadent past, hence the frequent calls for a *revolution* in Western culture. This included those interested in employing the new technologies of the early twentieth century, although Bergson himself disdained technological intervention into the arts, believing instead in ideas of pure, unmediated perception and human intuition. Martin Heidegger similarly mistrusted the imprisoning effects of machines on consciousness, and his epic study *Being and Time* (1962 [1927]) elaborated upon Bergson's theme to hold time's impossibility of capture as a central tenet of philosophical thought.

However, halting time's wingèd chariot is not impossible in the practice of digital performance, where at least a *visual* capturing of time or freezing of the present has been used to great aesthetic and temporal effect. The digital frame capture or video freeze-frame is a simple computational task, and its employment in live performance contexts has created effects which are at times atemporal, but at others are distinctly extratemporal, as in Uninvited Guests' theatre performance *Film* (Bristol, 2000). *Film* manages to place Bergsonian feet in the past and the future, and repeats a freeze-frame effect with such compulsion and hypnotic repetition that even Heidegger's great truth of time's impossible capture seems suddenly (if only momentarily) a shaky proposition.

The performance locates film as a repository of memory and nostalgia, and the script incorporates material taken from interviews the company

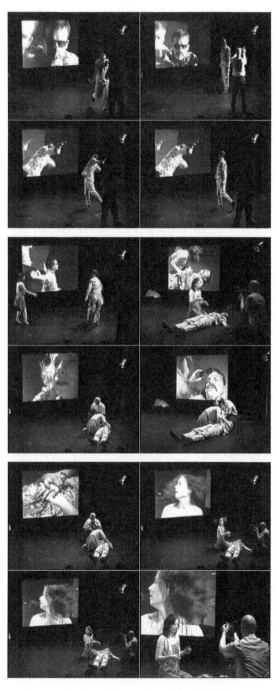

Illustration 4.1   Uninvited Guests' *Film* (2000)

[Copyright: Steve Dixon]

conducted at cinemas, where they asked film-goers to recollect memorable movie images and narratives. *Film*'s publicity material describes a 'theatre made for camera but not recorded; a bastard theatre obsessed with the movies'. Set in a private members club some time in the future when films have been banned, lost or destroyed, the performers recall, invent, and enact sequences from movies. A digital video camera and a hand-held miniature surveillance camera relay the live action onto a television monitor and a large screen, upstage centre. In the second section, one performer narrates the climax to a film; two performers act out its key dramatic moments; and a fourth films them, with the live video footage relayed onto the main projection screen. The sequence is the end of a formulaic gangster movie, where the male protagonist is pursued and shot, and his lover runs to the scene, and cradles him in her arms as he dies. The visual sequence onstage begins with her throwing off her coat in order to run faster. Thomas, the camera operator, says 'ready' and the performer swings her coat violently into the air. At the point it leaves her hand, Thomas presses the 'photographic still' button on the digital video camera and the image is frozen on the screen. The freeze-frame is perfectly composed (the timing between actors and cameraman has been meticulously rehearsed), and full of dynamic energy: her distorted, angled body at full stretch, the blurred coat caught as a violent swirl in mid-air. The image recalls the long-exposure 'motion captured in stasis' images of early twentieth-century Futurist[6] chronophotography.

The male protagonist, wearing an over-sized false moustache, sunglasses and a Hawaiian shirt, then prepares for his frozen image. Thomas returns the camera to running live footage, before calling 'ready'. The actor points his gun, takes a short step, and lunges aggressively towards the camera. With the actor in an intense, looming close-up, the 'still' button is pressed, once again at the point of greatest movement and dramatic impact. The sequence continues in this pattern, as the narrator describes the action.

At one level, the stage action is a nowadays relatively passé theatre pastiche of a film genre: an affectionate homage to the charm of pulp gangster movies, told through microphone-mediated narration and melodramatic, tongue-in-cheek performance reconstruction. But the use of the digital video camera's 'photographic still' facility renders it powerful and memorable on a number of levels. The relationship between the live performers' actions and the relayed video images on the screen is violently ruptured by the suddenly frozen screen moments. The continual and systematic puncturing and discontinuity of the time-flow adds strength and poignancy to both the stage and screen action.

On screen, the video-relayed stage action operates in real time; it is present as a synchronous mediatized mirror of the live, but then its place in linear time is suddenly lost, it becomes absent. In its place is a still photographic record of a moment, synchronous with the real-time stage action at the moment of the digital click, but now suspended in time within the screen space, as the stage time moves on and completes the action. The formalist repetition of this cycle – the camera constantly being switched back to live continuous time, only for its flow to be interrupted by yet another still – is key to its temporally disconcerting (yet also, for the audience, highly arresting) and pleasurable effect. The spectator becomes accustomed to the pattern and how the technique operates, and begins to anticipate the moment the photo-still button will be pressed.

Prior to the clicking of the photo-still button, both stage and screen action operate together in real time, in the present. But the freezing of the *present*, which in the image's stationary form immediately reverts it into the *past*, locates the live continuation of the performers' actions not only in the continuous present, but also in the *future* – of the trajectory of the still image – which becomes the central 'theatrical sign'. The theatrical action does not, first and foremost, serve liveness; rather, the performers act out the 'bringing to life' of stillness – time's stasis. Theatre is sutured through the digital video camera to switch the fluid, continual becoming of the theatrical present to the nostalgic, solid, classical image of the recorded past: the movie still.

Conclusion time

The commonly slowed-down or speeded-up projection images in multi-media theatre and performance 'play' with time, but their signification has long since ceased to mean simply 'time slowed down' or 'time speeded up'; rather, the images signify 'out of time'. As civilization's chronometric temporality appears to be accelerating ever faster, the dialectical twin pulls the other way, putting a brake on the tempo to pull it back to the centre, to reorient experience in relation to older ideas of cyclical and mythical time. The contrapuntal elements of intense live performance and temporally altered digital imagery spark a feeling and experience not of time standing still, or going backwards or forwards, but of stepping to one side or outside of it.

The depictions of time in digital performance (and the conceptions of creative artists about temporality) have developed beyond postmodern theories and explanations to take a much closer account of the future. Or perhaps, as Ursula Heise observes in *Chronoschisms*: 'the culture of time in the late twentieth century has evolved faster than the theoretical reasoning which has accompanied it' (Heise 1997: 31). Time is a vital, recurring theme of new media theatre, and its artists and companies continue to explore and exploit the unique particularities and peculiarities of extratemporal effects that are achievable only through the conjunction of the live and the digital. The results range from the sensorially disorientating to the pleasurably hypnotic, and equate both with understandings of an ancient, mythical time.

Introduction to 4.2

Steve Dixon makes clear that different historical periods have witnessed varied understandings of the nature, structure and experience of time. He argues that changing technologies have been a key influence, and reflects on how the use of video and other digital technologies to manipulate the passage of time in contemporary media performance can create a sense of the *extemporal*, or 'time out of time'. There are many other examples of performance-makers who share this expanded awareness of time, even if they do not make use of such technologies directly. The possibilities of working directly with the audience's experience of time passing are especially evident in *durational performances*, which have become increasingly popular in recent years. Works falling under this category generally defy expectations of how theatrical events should be structured and organized, and invite new kinds of relationships between performer and audience.

Durational performances may range in length from a few hours to weeks, months or even years,[7] and are usually set up to allow audiences to attend as little or as much as they want. The experience can therefore be very different for each audience member: they can stay the course and experience the same endurance test as the performers, or they can be sample it at different times across its whole running length. Even if not all of the performance is witnessed, there is still often a heightened consciousness that the performance is still continuing 'elsewhere', and this can stimulate an imaginative connection between the work and the audience as they go about their everyday lives. Durational works can, in this way, mark out and frame a special time in the ongoing flow of the everyday as a privileged space of performance. They may also invite a type of active involvement that creates a unique community of participants while the performance lasts.

This is particularly clear in the various durational performances created by Gregg Whelan and Gary Winters of Lone Twin, of which *Ghost Dance* is the best known example. This piece was created initially for gallery spaces rather than theatres, and was performed most recently by Lone Twin in 2008, but has also been performed by other of Lone Twin's collaborators. It lasts for 12 hours, and features the two performers in mock cowboy costumes, blindfolded and slowly moving through a repeated line dancing sequence, perfectly synchronized with each other. In common with other durational works, the performers focus on realizing a relatively simple set of tasks (that is, *task-based*) within an agreed framework of rules. What is quite remarkable about this piece is that audience members frequently elect to join in with the dancing and, in doing so, establish a special kind of bond with the performers. In section 4.2, Gregg Whelan discusses the importance of this piece within their larger body of durational works, and also how these works have influenced the short-form theatre pieces they have made in recent years with their collaborators under the name of Lone Twin Theatre.

4.2   Ghost Dance: time and duration in the work of Lone Twin

Gregg Whelan in conversation with Tony Gardner

What was the first impulse for you both to begin working with durational performance? Was it underpinned by a particular understanding of time and how it is experienced in live performance as opposed to other, everyday experiences of time?

Our first performance, *On Everest*, began before the audience arrived and finished three days or so after the performance proper had concluded – we asked the audience to think of each other three days later as their daily walking quota completed a descent of Mount Everest. Three days after the performance is when we'd all arrive back at sea-level, the performance itself ending on the mountain's summit. Using this extended time frame, or a time frame that exceeded the amount of time we were all in the room together, felt necessary – we were making a piece about ideas of 'great' travel and exploration, and there was something inherent there about time, about needing more than 90 minutes by which to have everything completed. It increased, albeit conceptually, the performance's scale and offered us the possibility of creating this liminal group of people, which would include ourselves, that would have the next three days of our every-day life framed as something quite heroic. It was perhaps the idea of how using an extended time frame created a social event, or a link between people, that in retrospect interested us the most as we moved on to make other works.

Works we made in the next few years had a more explicit relationship to durational performance practice, but I think what remained was an interest in the potential for creating social events and moments of social exchange through using extended time frames. It had to do with finding a way to enter everyday life, to have performances located in public space that were simply around long enough to fold into the normal 'life' of the place. I'm not sure it had to do with thinking about the difference between time in performance and time in the everyday world; it had more to do with us just simply wanting our work to take place in the here and now, in the everyday world and that world is of course a peopled space. Time for us was always used in an effort to meet people, or for other people to meet other people – it was an opportunity and it was space, it created somewhere to be, and something to gather around.

Marina Abramovic has spoken about creating a special kind of time through her durational pieces, arguing that artist and spectator must 'meet in a completely new territory, and build from that timeless time spent together'. Is there similar thinking in your work, and the particular kind of relationships you establish with audiences over time?

Yes, it's similar, although there's something a little too precious for me about the idea of 'timeless time spent together.' In very real pragmatic terms, it isn't timeless; in fact, most Lone Twin performances begin discussing the end in the first few minutes of the piece beginning. *Ghost Dance* lasts for 12 hours, which isn't a timeless claim; it's clearly going to end. That piece, in one sense, is about that period ending, as are most of our more explicitly durational works. Time in all of them is limited. That, for some, might create another sort of preciousness, but for us it offers us something that's really important: drama. It is dramatic to end something that has been going on for what is largely considered a long time – this is true, I think, in any area of life. But the idea of an ending does create something of heightened sense of being together, perhaps that's what Abramovic is getting at, the fact that this time together is unusual and won't last and must be, in some sense, built on or extended, if only as a private act. But we can't let that get too much – we make lots of jokes about the end coming, about the relief of it, the moment when we'll all get to go home and do something else! I like Abramovic's idea of a 'new territory'. For us, I suppose, that territory is the social event that begins to happen around the work. Although it might be better to think that the social event is the work and what we're doing in performance terms is merely the activity that facilitates that event.

Many of your projects have been developed over extended periods, in particular locations and for/with particular communities, in labour- and time-intensive processes. Is dealing with these larger timescales a fundamental part of your work, or just a consequence of available opportunities? Is there an underlying ethos here rooted in an understanding of time?

It's a fundamental part of the work and perhaps, in that, there is an underlying ethos, as you say. That ethos would have to do with wanting something positive to happen, wanting something good to come of the event. Giving time to something, literally just giving something a lot of time, allows for all sorts of things to happen, it creates an opening – a field of possibilities. Even if the thing that's happening is a set of repeated dance steps, the longer it goes on, the more the singular act becomes multiple, open, available.

How did you first decide on how much time Ghost Dance *needed in order to be realized fully both for yourselves and for the spectators/participants? Why choose a durational form for this material in the first place?*

Ghost Dance began as a gallery piece, and the first time we did it the gallery told us they could stay open for 12 hours, opening at noon and closing at midnight – so we worked to that, we inherited that time frame from them. The piece also began as something we framed as an attempt – we would *attempt* to dance for twelve hours; we didn't know that first time if we could do it or not. So, we had that time period to fill and we'd have a go at filling it, that was the plan. If we made two hours and then had to stop that would have been entirely fine, the piece would have been two hours long. As it was, we kept going and did the full 12 hours. And because people danced with us we decided we'd do it again, if anything just to find out if they'd dance again. They dance to support us in some way – or simply just to pass the time, which is also why we're dancing, I suppose. But the piece – which we thought initially was about the folly of heroic endeavour – became to be about people coming together, which is a much better thing to be involved in, as jobs go.

What processes did you find yourselves going through or otherwise experiencing as a result of the extended time of the piece that couldn't have been experienced in any other way?

Well, it's not that interesting to answer that on our behalf, because for us it's privately intense and, in a way, what we or I go through is the least interesting part of the piece. That intensity is a bit unseemly from my perspective; it's my own business and perhaps should stay that way. But what happens that couldn't be experienced in any other way is the gathering of other people around the dancing and, indeed, those people beginning to dance. The idea that this is a long thing, that these two dancing cowboys might need a bit of help to get through it, to offer assistance in the unseemliness – and more potently, to come together and dance with strangers – is what happens that wouldn't happen if the piece didn't occur over an extended time frame.

How has your understanding of the piece changed through its various incarnations and the whole lifetime of the work, particularly with regard to the unique experience of time passing?

In very pragmatic terms the piece has become easier to perform in some respects and much harder to perform in others. Doing it many times over many years gives you a familiarity with it and so there's something very comfortable, and brilliantly and reassuringly inevitable about it – time will pass. But then there's the knowledge that its passing enacts a kind of madness on you, plays tricks with you, and that makes it difficult – it's difficult knowing that difficulty will come. But the really interesting part of it is how that time passes for those that come into contact with it. Their days, their time with it, even those that disliked it and walked away – what did their 12 hours hold? I sometimes think of it as a time frame only, as a line drawn around a period in any given city or town at any given time. We were about to begin the piece in Hull once and somebody said 'at least you know what you're doing all day', so that person saw it as an answer. The question being the next 12 hours ...

How have your experiences with durational pieces affected your approach to creating short-form theatre pieces, either as summations or encapsulations of longer projects (such as Sledge Hammer Songs*), or the Lone Twin theatre pieces in which you haven't performed yourselves?*

The durational element in some of our pieces definitely taught us something about narrative construction. An explicitly durational work has a very clear beginning, a very long middle and often a dramatically short end. It's a narrative shape; they create the shape – or the possibility – of a story. It made us very aware, in quite simple terms, of the efficiencies of that shape: beginning, middle and end. Perhaps surprisingly, durational performances are what took us towards narrative models of performance-making – that and the meetings with people they incurred.

The time structures in your theatre pieces are many-layered, and they play many games with interconnecting time sequences, cycles and symmetries within the over-all narratives. Could you comment on how repetition appears to be a privileged compositional device in your overall approach to making The Catastrophe Trilogy[8] *in particular?*

Repetition as a compositional tool is something we've always used, I think, in every piece. I think when we're making something, especially when we find ourselves writing something, we look for logics and motifs that begin to offer some support to the writing internally – bits of material that can be repeated, moved around, changed a bit and then re-used. Those bits become a framework of sorts that we can hang other material on that doesn't repeat. In a way, it might be the bits that don't repeat that we're most interested in, but they'd be too free-floating, too unframed for us to use if we didn't have an internal shape and structure to place them on. So, the repeating material is what starts to hold the piece up, it's what gives it some shape. It feels organic when it happens; it feels like the piece has started to reveal its own logic and we should attend to that. But we also like repetition as a quality in itself – we find something inherently comic about it, even as a structure; there's something silly about things being so insistent, so wanting to impress that they won't go away, won't shut up. It's funny to us, especially if that thing is mundane in some way, ordinary or everyday. I know for some audiences it doesn't work, and they find it deadening. But for us the opposite happens, repetition begins to bring a bit of life to something, and helps us understand what it is, because, quite pragmatically, it keeps explaining itself, or wanting to explain itself.

Simon McBurney commented: 'Theatre has a special relationship with time that no other art form has, in that it exists in the present, *and human beings have a need to be present in this life.' Do you agree?*

I partly agree, but texts, photographs and paintings – if they do their jobs well – exist in the present, don't they? I suppose McBurney means that in theatre we see people in front of us, alive, in the present and that has a relationship with the very condition we find ourselves in. And that is special, I suppose. I'd say sport's relationship to the present is a lot more special in that regard, because its live quality is much more lively: the outcome is contingent, the end is undecided when the piece begins, and what we see is people in front of us working to find out what the work is, what it will mean. Theatre and performance almost do that, but it's a kind of trick, a benign and completely honest con. An early influence on Lone Twin was the Olympic Games, specifically the moment when an athlete wins gold. What an end to a very, very long story – and what a great audience. It's enviable really.

4.3   The lives and times of performance

Tony Gardner

In the previous sections, both Steve Dixon and Gregg Whelan draw attention to two important realities of performance as a live art form. First, that notions of liveness are invariably bound to the present tense, and therefore to the *presence* of artist and audience in a collaborative and inherently social experience. Second, that this relationship to real time is by no means a slavish one. For Dixon, the understanding of what constitutes the present, along with its posited relationship to the past, history, memory and ideas about (or projections into) the future, are products of their historical and cultural contexts. They change constantly under the influence of political and social forces, as well as technological developments, and are capable of being contested through the unique possibilities presented by new media theatre practice. For Whelan, the extension of the present moment into an extended *duration* for both artist and audience opens up a privileged space within which to build communities of experience, and potentially establishes organic connections between performance and the larger rhythmic cycles of the seasons, environment, weather, and so on. Both contributions therefore invite further thinking about the nature of performance when considered from the perspective of time, and suggest important questions about the uniqueness of this connection.

The unique connection between performance and time

Simon McBurney, director of Complicite, has argued that an understanding of time is at the very core of our understanding of theatre in comparison with the other arts:

> Theatre has a special relationship with time that no other art form has, in that it exists in the *present*, and human beings have a need to be present in this life ... Theatre is unique in that everything happens in the present, and I think that the only way theatre can develop is to increase its acknowledgement of the present moment instead of emulating television. (McBurney, cited in Giannachi and Luckhurst 1999: 72–3)

To assert the 'presentness' of live performance, according to McBurney, is therefore to underscore its distinctiveness as a strategy for survival: creating works in a way that exposes and reinforces theatre's 'particularity of time' (cited in Giannachi and Luckhurst 1999: 71) necessarily involves asserting its separateness from the other art forms. On the face of it, this argument is difficult to dispute, and it reminds us first of all that, unlike the other art forms, the time in which the work can be experienced by an audience is not in the control of that audience: *being there* fundamentally means being there at the *right time*, and for as long as the work lasts. As stated at the beginning of this chapter, the binding of live performance to a framework of real time means that the present moment is constantly emptying out into the past, so that the work itself ceases to exist in all but the memories of its audience at the very time of its making. The film viewer has the privilege of knowing that, even if the time of the viewing were to be interrupted, it could be resumed later without the nature of the film being affected; recorded media also hold out the promise of repeat viewings or listenings, pausings and rewindings, fast forwards and slow motion replays that can be controlled completely. The reader of texts, whether novels or play texts, enjoys even more degrees of freedom when it comes to the time of their reading. As Hans-Thies Lehmann has observed, the historical entanglement of text and performance in theatre has served only to reinforce the time constraints imposed by the circumstances of production:

> While the text gives the reader the choice to read faster or slower, to repeat or to pause, in theatre the specific time of the performance with its particular rhythms and its individual dramaturgy (tempo of action and speech, duration, pauses, and silences, etc.) belongs to the 'work'. It is a matter of the time no longer of one (reading) subject but of the shared time of many subjects (collectively spending time). (Lehman 2006: 153)

In this generic model of the relationship between text and performance, the audience appears to give up individual control of time as part of the basic contract of live theatre, and submits to the 'shared time' of the performance. Without such a mutual participation in and voluntary yielding to a structure of real time, the model seems to suggest, live performance loses its distinctiveness and perhaps ceases to be such at all. However, this idea that the ephemerality and transience of live performance constitutes its essential identity in contrast with the other art forms needs to be approached carefully. A recent example may serve to expose some of the problems that are soon encountered when these assumptions are tested in practice.

Antony Gormley and the Fourth Plinth

One & Other was a 'living sculpture' created by Antony Gormley in collaboration with Artichoke for the Fourth Plinth in Trafalgar Square, London, between July and October 2009. The Fourth Plinth remained empty for a number of years, before a number of contemporary artists (including Mark Wallinger, Bill Woodrow and Rachel Whiteread) were commissioned to provide temporary pieces on a rotating basis that engaged both with the context of the site and its historical statuary, and with popular conceptions of public art itself. Gormley made two key choices that pushed *One & Other* beyond the boundaries of sculpture and into the territory of performance, if we are to follow the argument above: first, by deciding not to place an object on the plinth but, instead, to fill it with real people; and, second, by adding a dimension of real time through a tightly structured time scheme.

The piece was designed to last exactly 100 days, and to run continuously for this duration. The larger time scheme therefore spanned two seasons, from summer into autumn, and so operated at the macro level of *calendar time*, where time passes at a pace at which changes are too slow to be observed directly, but can only be experienced cumulatively, or in stages. Within this larger scheme, the piece was divided into one-hour periods, both night and day. During each period, a different member of the public was placed on the plinth and given free rein to express themselves in whatever way they chose. These individual actions by the 'plinthers' – 2,400 in total – made the Fourth Plinth into a space of performance, or an interconnected sequence of performances, obeying the strict rules of *clock time* within larger diurnal cycles and seasonal durations. The piece may be thought difficult to characterize as sculpture at all, as it engaged the impermanent and fleeting present of performance rather than the enduring solidity and unchanging materials of the type of sculptural object to be found elsewhere in Trafalgar Square. These other monuments to individuality are designed, in sharp contrast with *One & Other*, to survive the passage of time rather than yield to it, to persist in the present memory as an active *memorialization* of the past.

This is, of course, where the problems begin. While Gormley's piece appears to confirm the distinctiveness of performance in contrast with sculpture through its complex game with and over time, it is by no means certain where – or *when* – the real performance of this work is actually to be located. This is due mainly to the fact that each hour of the piece has been comprehensively documented: video recordings from mounted webcams (which ran 'live' throughout the piece) are archived online[9] and available to be viewed in their entirety, along with commentary by their creators. Not only that, but a second-by-second experience of the piece is depicted visually through a graph that tracks public voting on the popularity of individual moments, segments or 'scenes' within the larger work (for example, the moment where the plinther dressed in a Godzilla costume destroys the cardboard city that he has been carefully assembling up to that point), and these peaks and troughs map the lowest level time schema operating in *One & Other*. The audiovisual documentation as a whole connects the micro and macro levels of time directly, and this appears to have been a deliberate intention of the work; or, rather, it is a piece that seems to have been designed to be recorded for remote viewing as well as posterity right from the start of the process.

Grasping time

The public media event that was *One & Other* as a whole therefore played out in a number of arenas, only one of which was the 'actual' live performance in Trafalgar Square. If we consider that the work could be experienced variously online, through media reports, commentary and documentation as well as 'live', this raises the question of which 'shared time' was actually the operative one. This is particularly so if we agree with observers such as Jonathan Jones that experiencing the performances in person and in real time was, in many ways, the least authentic option, because the physical configuration of the plinth – its size and surrounding safety net – prevented a meaningful connection between spectator and performer, in contrast with the intimacy provided by the all-seeing web camera. 'It does not function as a grand, eloquent podium', Jones noted of the plinth, 'but on the contrary, removes the performers from the social world. It is not a stage. It's a hermit's platform' (Jones 2009: 6).

So, we need to recognize the complexity of McBurney's celebration of the fact that live performance 'exists in the *present*, and human beings have a need to be present in this life'. Different notions of what 'being present' means are at play here. In practice, contemporary performance frequently exhibits a richly complex, intertwined set of time schemas beyond simple conceptions of the 'real time' that might validate its uniqueness and distinctiveness. This way of thinking about time requires more finely-grained analytical tools than we have been used to applying, for reasons that are best explained by Anne Ubersfeld:

> Time in the theatre is not easily grasped, either at the level of the text or at the level of performance. It is difficult at the level of the text because … the temporal signifiers are all indirect and vague. It is difficult at the

level of performance because important elements such as rhythm, pauses and articulations are infinitely harder to grasp than elements that can be spatialized ... It is easier to grasp the dimensions of space than it is to grasp the dimensions of time. (Ubersfeld 1999: 126–7)

The first stage in helping us to 'grasp' time in performance with the same concreteness as space is to recognize the complexity of the audience's experience, and to try to catalogue the different layers, levels or schemas of time that are either worked with directly by artists, or otherwise engaged by specific examples of contemporary work. We can extend the broad distinction that Lehmann makes between two types – 'represented', 'dramaturgical' or 'fictional' time on the one hand, and 'performance time' or 'real time' on the other – while avoiding reductive binarisms by emphasizing that both are constantly in operation in any example of performance. They are combined in unique ways that vary from work to work and give each their distinctive identity. Performance analysis that focuses on the perspective of time therefore invites nuanced and layered descriptions of what makes one performance work differently from another. This process has important practical implications that have been spelled out by the American director Anne Bogart:

The theatre can straddle many kinds of time in a single production. From fictional time to real time, subjective time, linear time, nonlinear time, time suspended, time stopped, time sped up, a lifetime in an instant, rehearsal time, performance time, and so on, each segment requires the appropriate *time signature*. In a similar way that the palm of every hand has a unique pattern of lines and creases, a work of art contains an independent logic of time and space. (Bogart 2007: 131–2)

Discovering this logic – the particular 'time signature' that represents the DNA of a performance piece – is therefore, according to Bogart, the main goal of the artist as well as the critic. For this reason and others, Bogart developed a system of performer training used also in the rehearsal process that she termed 'Viewpoints', based on key terms that represent different ways of talking about and working with performance materials, as well as a general philosophical approach to making theatre. Adapted from the work of dancer Mary Overlie, Bogart's system now consists of nine Viewpoints, five relating to space (shape, gesture, architecture, spatial relationship and topography) and four relating to time (tempo, duration, kinesthetic response and repetition). What the Viewpoints provide is a precise, technical language through which the performer can expose time structures, isolate them, and work on them independently before re-inte-grating them with the other Viewpoints. In this process, the performer is able to develop a heightened consciousness of the relationship between what Bogart terms 'objective time' and 'subjective time', the former repre-sented by the clock and calendar, the latter by the personal, internalized and imaginative experience of the flow of time, which may contrast radi-cally with any objective time schemes operating in a work. As she notes: 'The feeling of this continuous passage varies from person to person and depends on changing moods and interests ... The theatre can uniquely and eloquently express subjective time' (Bogart 2007: 128). The pattern of choices that connects the objective time of the performance – how long, in how many sequences, with what tempo and rhythm, and so on – with the subjective experience of the audience is what provides the work with its unique overall 'time signature'.

It is also no coincidence that the language, as well as the process, here borrows from dance and music composition, each with their own more developed vocabularies for articulating how to work with time; indeed, Bogart identifies *Composition* as the second main component of her system after the Viewpoints and, in many ways, this is another example of what David Roesner has termed the 're-discovery of the musicality of theatrical process and event', or more generally its 'musicalization'. By this, he means a new emphasis on working processes that 'shifts attention from working on character, situation and narrative towards aspects of timing, sound and the polyphony of the theatrical media' (Roesner 2008: 109). Tina Landau made the same point about the Viewpoints in more blunt terms: 'By using the Viewpoints fully, we eliminate the actor's ability to state "my character would never do that"' (cited in Dixon and Smith 1995: 24). Obviously critical to this has been the opening of theatre practice to productive borrowings and cross-fertilizations from the other art forms, keeping a permeable border between them rather than strict disciplinary boundaries. For Anne Bogart, the uniqueness of performance therefore lies in its hybridity and porosity rather than what separates it from the other art forms.

Conclusion

While the immediacy and transience of performance is rightly asserted by McBurney as some of its defining characteristics, when we open out from this to engage with the variety and complexity of choices available to performance-makers working with the perspective of time, we find ourselves at the boundary line between theatre and the other art forms, as well as between theory and practice. Here, we can assert that performance enacts a crucial transformation in the audience's experience of time that intrudes upon and folds back in to the frameworks of real time within which works are constructed. When the relationship between subjective and objective time is properly engaged, the time of performance is experienced in a qualitatively different manner, as *occasion* or *event*. As Adrian Heathfield (2004: 9) argued: 'the varied deployments of altered time in contemporary performance invariably bring the artwork towards the condition of eventhood'. This complements the process by which space assumes an identity in performance as a *place*. In combination, these represent the means that artists have at their disposal to mark out, frame or otherwise capture space and time in a way that is unique to the form, whether this be a 'time out of time' of the type described by Dixon, or the virtual spaces of digital performances, or the mediatized event of *One & Other*, or the temporary communities located in specific times and places created by Lone Twin.

The task facing forward is to identify how different examples of performance achieve this transformation, by drilling down to their individual time signatures, or by detailing the relationship between 'fictional' and 'real' time that they propose from moment to moment. At one end of the spectrum, for example, we could consider the extensive repertoire of dramaturgical choices proposed by Alan Ayckbourn in his manual of playwriting, where he makes a distinction between 'elapsed time', 'time plays', 'time frame' and 'time perception' (Ayckbourn 2002: 20–8) as these might be worked with variously by the playwright. At the other end, it is also important to reflect on the increasing number of artists and companies who now work with the element of time more consciously, or as a strategy for composing new material, and how these choices have emerged from an continuing engagement with live art practices.[10] The Sheffield-based company Forced Entertainment is an especially useful case study in this regard, as they have continued to add durational performances to their programme of work alongside their short-form theatre pieces, with notable early examples being the six-hour *Quizoola!* (1996) and the 24-hour *Who Can Sing a Song to Unfrighten Me?* (1999). Of the former, writer and director Tim Etchells noted: 'Making this work, we are composing in a very different mode, and as performers we are present in a very different way' (Etchells, cited in Helmer and Malzacher 2004: 88). Precisely what is different about this way of being 'present' in performance, and the implications of it for an audience, is worth exploring in more detail. These should be contrasted with the durational works of, for example, Serbian artist Marina Abramovic, who blurred the boundary between art and everyday life by living for 12 days in New York's Sean Kelly Gallery for her durational piece *The House with the Ocean View* (2002), in a deliberate attempt to create a time *within* time, arguing that both artist and spectator must:

> meet in a completely new territory, and build from that timeless time spent together ... And really, that's the only way I can see: to have time is to create time in performance. (Abramovic, cited in Thompson and Weslien 2005: 48).

Tools such as those provided by Anne Bogart may help us to frame the discussions around time, technology and performance outlined by Steve Dixon, as well as the new kinds of performer/audience relationship that durational pieces of the type developed by Lone Twin seem to engage. Most importantly, they are also practical means of bridging the divide between theatre performance and the other art forms, and as such they help us to understand the range of possibility available to theatre-makers today as they invent the theatre of tomorrow.

Activities

➤ *Solo activity*

- Visit http://www.oneandother.co.uk, and especially the 'Plinthers' section, to explore information about any one of the one-hour performances, organized by calendar (the first is Week 1, 9.00 am Monday 6 July, and the last is Week 15, 8.00 am Wednesday 14 October). Video material is also directly available via the sponsor's website.
- Ask yourself what you might do given an hour on the plinth. You should think about how your choices might be affected by specific times of day or night, which month and season, and so on, and the implications of these for thinking about time in performance generally.
- Sketch out a calendar for a hypothetical 100-day performance inspired by *One & Other*. Map what actions and events could take place at different times, and what tasks or rules might be applied at different stages. Build up a collective 'score' of the durational performance.

➤ *Discussion activity*

When analyzing performance from the perspective of time, it is important to develop a working vocabulary for describing the various aspects of time that might be exposed in different examples of performance. This task encourages you to begin this process:

- Write the following six words at the top of a sheet of paper, in two columns: event, occasion, moment, rhythm, duration, tempo.
- In small groups, extend and elaborate on the list by adding new, related words – alongside another, or underneath, or otherwise in some kind of visual relation on the page.
- Keep this going for as long as possible, periodically stopping to discuss broad categories and groupings of terms that emerge.
- Compare these lists with Anne Bogart's Viewpoints of time (tempo, duration, kinesthetic response and repetition). Select groups of words from your lists (minimum four words per group) and discuss how these might be applied to the analysis of 'time signatures' for known examples of performances, or personalized for use in your rehearsal and making processes.

Durational works have become an increasingly popular choice for contemporary performance-makers, whether from theatre, dance, music or fine art backgrounds. The next task will help you to explore the possibilities of this mode of working by considering recent examples of practice.

A practical understanding of the different kinds of skills required in order to create durational performance is not easy to develop, since this necessarily involves a significant time commitment. You can, however, begin this process by exploring the dynamics of durational performance in a more concentrated fashion.

➤ *Practical activity 1*

- Read the extract of the 'text' for *Quizoola!* (available in Heathfield 2004: 106–11). This is a very long list of questions designed to be read by one performer, with answers freely improvised by another over a six-hour period. A useful task here is simply to answer the questions. That is, set up two people to work through at least one whole column of questions – one quizzing, the other improvising answers – within a predetermined time.
- You can also simply make a list of questions of your own to be answered. It's important in this case to write many of them. The ebb and flow of ideas only really becomes apparent after spending considerable time on this task. Continue past the point where you think you have no more questions to write down – that's when the work will begin to get really interesting.
- Once you have explored this simple set of tasks in practice, you should begin to get a sense of how rules and structures interact with improvisation and play in this kind of time-based work.
- You can continue these experiments by developing new rules for different kinds of materials and scenarios: a marathon sharing of invented confessions; 200 consecutive two-minute phone calls; gathering every photograph of yourself as a child and making up stories about them; documenting everything you eat or every person you meet over a one-week period, and so on.

The next task focuses attention on the performer's relationship both to their chosen tasks and to onlookers' or participants' engagement with them. Extending your practice to consider the larger social event of performance created in this way is an important goal here.

➤ *Practical activity 2*

• Research the performance history of Lone Twin's *Ghost Dance*. A short video of the piece is available on the DVD accompanying *The Many Headed Monster* (Sofaer 2010), among other sources.
• In groups of two, try to recreate the repeated line dancing sequence from *Ghost Dance* as closely as possible. You can also create your own short sequence from scratch, of course, based on what you imagine a line dance would be like. The imagined version is perhaps more important here than any real one.
• Explore what happens when this sequence is performed in successively longer sequences. Start with 10 minutes, then work up to an hour. Try performing the sequence in different locations, including outdoor spaces if you're able to and have the necessary permissions.
• What kind of attention did the piece generate from onlookers? Did anyone interact with the performers in any way? Explore how this element of social encounter with an audience could be increased or deepened through changing the nature of the tasks performed or rules followed.

Notes

1   The full version of this article was first published in the *International Journal of Performance Arts & Digital Media* (see Dixon 2005). Edited extracts are reproduced here with permission.
2   Editor's note: Postmodernism developed across Europe and America in the decades following World War II as a response to, rejection of or commentary on the principles of modernism in the arts as well as in theory. Here, Dixon refers to how postmodern theorists have questioned the earlier idea of history as representing a kind of perpetual march of progress through mostly technological development. Postmodern theorists propose, among other things, a radical type of scepticism toward time viewed in these linear terms, and often point to the great tragedies of the first half of the twentieth century as exemplifying the failures of this type of historical thinking.
3   Editor's note: Plato's 'Allegory of the Cave' from *The Republic* first developed the idea that the world of experience is a mere reflection or shadow of a perfect realm of Ideas, and Jameson compares it with Jean Baudrillard's reading of contemporary culture as driven primarily by simulations and mediatized representations of reality where the 'copy' threatens to replace the 'original'.

4   Editor's note: 'Posthuman' in the sense mainly, here, of a rejection of a *human-ist* outlook that emphasizes the idea of a universal human nature as the main subject of art. Postmodern theory frequently exposes how this idea of univer-sality – that people are essentially the same in all places and all times – is histor-ically constructed, and so may be interrogated through, for example, exploring how our understanding of what it means to be human may be drastically changed through the interventions and disruptions of technology.

5   The Dada movement began during World War I in Zürich and expanded during the 1920s and 1930s to Paris, Berlin and New York. This disparate group of artists, poets, painters and theatre-makers (led initially by Tristan Tzara) were first united by their anti-war stance. Later, this developed into a full-scale rejec-tion of European culture in what they termed *anti-art*, which revelled in performance as political provocation, scandal-mongering and the celebration of radical freedom from the rules of the past, emphasizing instead values such as chance and spontaneity. Members of the Dada group in Paris subsequently broke away to form the Surrealist movement, led by André Breton.

6   *Futurism* was an artistic movement developed mainly in Italy before World War I by artists such Filippo Tommaso Marinetti. Its celebration of technology, machinery, speed and creative innovation as a radical separation from the past was somewhat discredited by their glorification of war and the close association of many of its members with Fascist politics in the interwar years.

7   See, for example, the 'lifeworks' of Taiwanese-American performance artist Tehching Hsieh, documented beautifully in Heathfield and Hsieh (2009).

8   The trilogy consists of *Alice Bell* (2006), *Daniel Hit By a Train* (2008) and *The Festival* (2010). The whole trilogy was recently performed at the Barbican as part of the *bite10* season of international performance. This included two week-ends where the three performances were shown back to back – a durational experience in itself.

9   As at the time of writing, via: http://www.oneandother.co.uk

10 See, for example, Heathfield's suggestion that 'this encounter with and within time has marked the history of performance art from its diverse beginnings in the visual arts, theatre and in social practice' (2004: 8).

Further reading

Bogart, Anne and Landau, Tina (2005) *The Viewpoints Book: A Practical Guide to Viewpoints and Composition*. New York: Theatre Communications Group.

Heathfield, Adrian (ed.) (2004) *Live: Art and Performance*. London: Tate Publishing.

Heathfield, Adrian and Hsieh, Tehching (2009) *Out of Now: The Lifeworks of Tehching Hsieh*. London: Live Art Development Agency.

Richards, Mary (2010) *Marina Abramovic*. London: Routledge.

Sofaer, Joshua (2010) *The Many Headed Monster: The Audience of Contemporary Performance*, with accompanying DVD. London: Live Art Development Agency.

5   Technology

Introduced and edited by Sita Popat

Introduction

Social and cultural behaviours have changed dramatically in recent years with the proliferation of new media and digital technologies in everyday life. Knowledge is more freely and easily available than ever before via the Internet. Mobile phones, SMS/MMS and Skype have changed the ways in which we communicate on a daily basis. Online communities such as Facebook and Twitter allow us to present ourselves in a multitude of different ways to ever-increasing circles of friends and acquaintances. Computer games consoles are increasingly common in homes, and active entertainment choices have replaced the diet of three or four television channels only a few decades ago. Western first-world inhabitants are gradually becoming 'digital natives', particularly if they are less than 30 years of age. Some are more fluent in the languages of digital media, but all are deeply embedded in the culture.

The diverse potential identities granted by multiple communications media offer space to play and practise ourselves, and to observe and rehearse human behaviours. In this space, performance and everyday life can merge. Two examples may suffice to illustrate this development. In 1996, computer student Jennifer Ringley set up a webcam in her room so her mother could see her via the Internet. The webcam became known as Jennicam, and it broadcasted images of Ringley for 24 hours per day, seven days per week over nearly eight years. Barry Smith describes it as being 'the most publicized' webcam of its time:

> Ringley unwittingly created one of the most influential and longest running pieces of improvised endurance theatre ever, without the benefit of theatre or media training or any enhanced performance skills. (Smith 2005: 92)

Ringley became a performer by default, representing herself in a public arena via multi-media communications technologies. On a larger scale, an article in the journal *Lancet Infectious Diseases* (Lofgren and Fefferman

2007) explained how medical researchers could study human behaviour in real world epidemics by watching how the virtual disease 'Corrupted Blood' spread in the massively multi-player online (MMO) game *World of Warcraft*. Some people ran from infected areas, some went to offer aid, and some spread the disease purposefully to new areas in order to cause mischief. The behaviour of human players in the game environment mimicked real-world situations such as the cholera outbreaks in mid-nineteenth-century Europe, but fears and inhibitions were mediated by the knowledge that it was 'play', not 'real'.

Performance has embraced new technologies in a wide variety of forms, often layering them with older established technologies of costume, stage and theatre. This chapter will focus specifically on digital and new media technologies that affect our perceptions of presence and communication, changing or extending them through encounters in/with virtual, augmented and mixed realities. In recognition of the potential that computer games hold for rehearsal and playfulness, section 5.1 is an essay by performance design researcher Jessica Wood on gaming and performance. Wood considers how concepts of dramatic narrative and identity bridge the distance between computer games and performance practice, particularly in relation to representation and action in virtual worlds. Section 5.2 explores the integration of gaming and performance techniques in the installation *SwanQuake: House*, created by artists Ruth Gibson and Bruno Martelli (who work together as igloo).[1] *SwanQuake: House* combines game-engine design with site-specific location, highlighting the complex nature of the mediated environment. It plays with perceptions of the 'virtual' and the 'real', bleeding them together to create an immersive yet simultaneously disorientating experience. In section 5.3, I take a broader perspective on performance and technology through the register of augmented and mixed realities, examining how new technologies can affect the ways in which we perceive physicality, presence and location as concepts of performance practice.

5.1   Gaming and performance: narrative and identity

Jessica Wood

The first computer game was created when the computer was identified as something that could represent action with which people could participate. The development was made nearly forty years ago by a group of hackers at the Massachusetts Institute of Technology (MIT). Since then, computer games have rapidly developed from flat, two-dimensional representations to fully navigable, immersive and interactive three-dimensional worlds where gameplay can be a solo activity or an experience shared online with anyone, anywhere in the world. Gaming is now a multi-billion-dollar industry, and the potential of the gaming paradigm is becoming increasingly recognized as an important influence in the future of interactive arts and performance.

Computer games as drama

Narratology is the branch of game studies where emphasis is given to the importance of narrative experience as part of the pleasure of gameplay:

> Video games involve virtual and fantasy worlds which may seem technologically advanced but are largely constructed within the well-known parameters of narrative and theatre, simulation, and make believe. (Dixon 2007: 601)

Early gaming relied heavily on text-based action. For example, in the game *Adventure* (Atari 1979) the goal was to find the enchanted chalice and return it to the golden castle, using a series of worded commands which enabled the player to move from place to place, pick up and use objects, and to negotiate obstacles and creatures. The game's structure guided the player to progress in a linear fashion through a series of story-based episodes. The text-based interface gave way to the graphic adventure genre in the early 1980s, representing events through fast-paced dynamic visuals that placed stronger emphasis on action. Although more technically advanced, the games retained the linear narrative form that gave meaning and significance to their action. Generally, the aim is to reach the end of the game by achieving various tasks and goals which will eventually culminate in the defeat of a final 'boss' character in battle. Once the game is completed, it can be replayed, but variation is limited within the set story structures.

Gaming developed rapidly with many new genres evolving structured narrative, strategy and role-playing to offer alternative experiences. Massively multi-player online role playing games (MMORPGs) are defined as 'social storytelling, or collaborative fiction' by Celia Pearce (2004) as these games are played online by many players, who often do not know each other. Each player is represented by his or her game 'character' (also known as an 'avatar') and can communicate with other players via text or voice chat systems within the game environment. As with many genres, the game usually involves tasks – quests or activities to be completed – but social interaction becomes a major part of the experience, and games often include communal gathering places (for example, cities, inns) and trading of game items between players. Some games have guilds, clans or groups that players can join in order to gain allies to help them, or simply to make friends. The result is 'an emergent narrative, a story that evolves over time as a result of interplay between rules and players' (Pearce 2004: 149). Individuals play a part in the development of dramatic action, improvising with their character in a structured environment.

Brenda Laurel's *Computers as Theatre* (1993) was the first major study to draw attention to the theatrical quality of human-computer interaction (HCI), suggesting that the qualities of drama, action and intensification are highly relevant in the design of HCI systems. Drama has become accepted as an important critical frame for understanding the representation of action in computer games. Stories do not require us to do anything except pay attention as they are told, whereas games will always involve some kind of activity and the mastery of skills. Games are thus a form of 'symbolic drama' with the player as the protagonist 'of symbolic action' (Murray 1998: 42). Steve Dixon elaborates on this theme in his taxonomic text on digital performance:

> [*games and drama*] are time based; both engage in the telling of a repeatable fictional narrative with identifiable characters; the characters develop relationships and, to varying degrees, personalities; both undertake elaborately defined tasks or missions ... the participants who witness or engage in the time-based activities will be drawn through various responses and emotional states. (Dixon 2007: 601–2)

The performative aspects of playing videogames are noted here in relation to the performer and the action, but Dovey and Kennedy (2006: 116) go further to identify the entire computer game with a theatrical event, considering every gameplay experience as a live performance with set, characters and props provided by the game environment. How, then, is game play experienced through the representation of self, virtual reality and agency?

Self-representation and the avatar

Avatars are the means by which we occupy the worlds of gaming, the visual representations of self that we temporarily inhabit as part of gameplay. In many solo games, we experience the avatar as a fixed form chosen by the game's designer, such as the Lara Croft character in the *Tomb Raider* series (created in 1996 by Core Design). However, it is becoming increasingly common to be able to create or customize your avatar's appearance, basic skills and even its personality from a large palette of options. This is often the case in MMORPGs such as *World of Warcraft* (Blizzard, 2004 Australia/North America, 2005 EU) or *Dungeons and Dragons Online* (Atari 2006).

> How does the game represent the player? Are we a cursor, a figurative snake, a small furry animal, a recognizably humanoid character, an alien? (Dovey and Kennedy 2006: 121)

The avatar is not only how a player enters the game world, but also how we experience and engage with it. It is through the attributes of the avatar that we explore, fight, battle and live in the game world:

> When visiting a virtual world, one treats the avatar in that world like a vehicle of the self, a car that your mind is driving. You 'get in', look out of the window through your virtual eyes, and then drive around by making your virtual body move. The avatar mediates our self in the virtual world: we inhabit it; we receive all of our sensory information about the world from its view point. (Castronova 2003: 5)

The avatar becomes an extension of the physical self. Having a stronger influence over physical appearance and attributes in these game worlds offers us a choice of alternative modes of being. Avatars have evolved from crudely drawn cartoons to well-developed characters with personalities, likes, dislikes, and emotions. The *Sims 3* (Electronic Arts 2008) player control over character creation has become sufficiently intricate for players to determine not just physical appearance, but also the behaviour of their Sim and even the Sims they encounter in gameplay. This is possible via a list of traits enabling players to map the personalities of their Sims' friends as well as their own Sim avatar.

Game worlds allow us to take on different representations of self, and this is all the more evident in online environments. This choice of representation has a greater value in online communities, such as MMORPGs, as this is how other people perceive the player. Pearce (2004: 149) explains that, in MMORPGs, players chose roles rather than characters. Although these roles are often somewhat generic (for example, orc warrior, elf healer), they allow players to configure unique characters composed of various traits, with which the player can then identify and invest in action that leads to a sense of agency.

Being there, doing that

More often than not, when a player describes the events or experiences of a computer game they will refer to their avatar in the first person. You find yourself telling someone, 'this is where I got killed', without even giving it a second thought. This relates to feelings of agency, where the player feels involved as an agent within the action. The pleasure of agency in electronic environments is frequently confused with the mere ability to move a joystick or click a mouse. But simple activity alone is not agency. The action must relate directly to the player's intention, so that its achievement provides a sense of empowerment. Laurel (2004: 19) states that 'significance' is key to agency – 'that is, the effect the player's action has on the plot needs to be substantial.' In this sense, agency is deeply related to the experience of game virtual reality, combining player, avatar and character:

> a key distinguishing feature is that the audience's identification with the character is closer within a videogame than in traditional theatre (even though game characters tend to lack theatre characters' psychological complexities and depths): the audience is the participant, the participant is the player, the player is the character. (Dixon 2007: 601)

We tend not to empathise with a computer game avatar as we would with a character in a play. Rather, the relationship is one of investment. The player gains ownership and identity through creating and customizing their own avatar, and by investing time and energy in developing game skills and social status through that avatar. It is the feedback received through the avatar that places the player herself as 'being there, doing things':

> the experience will be fed back in the same way to the player through a combination of these haptic, sonic and visual cues, leading to a growing sense of being in the game. (Dovey and Kennedy 2006: 113)

Typically, feedback occurs kinaesthetically, visually and aurally. In many role-playing action games, action is accompanied by the sound of the avatar's breath and footsteps, whilst physical impacts are relayed to your hands through the rumble pack feature on the joypad. With the development of the Nintendo Wii gaming platform, the physical experience of a game extended from thumbs on a joy pad and adrenaline fuelled twitches to full gestural control. In recent months (at the time of writing), the Microsoft X-Box Kinect has begun to offer control through full body movements, tracked by a camera and mapped onto the avatar. Avatar/player association is achieved through investment in developing skills over time, personal progression in the game, and through the simulation of action and consequence. It is how we are re-embodied in the game world and the means by which our experiences are fed back to us that develop the sense of agency.

The fourth wall

Theatre has always been a virtual reality where performers conspire with the audience to transform bare spaces into other places through the willing suspension of disbelief. Virtual reality in a computer game, however, is different from this in the framing and nature of the engagement. In a traditional theatre environment, we sit in our seats as we watch characters perform in a different world. Within a computer game, we engage directly with the virtual world via an avatar that inhabits the space. The avatar is the representation of self by which one explores and experiences the virtual world. Upon entering a videogame environment, the player becomes part of the larger narrative of that game, actively involved in the construction of the emergent narrative. In other words, the player does not so much perform *in* it as *perform it*. The way we enter or inhabit this space is through the *hypersurface*. Giannachi (2004) describes the hypersurface as allowing the player to be in two places in one instant:

> The hypersurface is where the real and the virtual meet each other ... the viewer can double their presence and be in both the real and the virtual environment simultaneously ... In performing through the hypersurface, the viewer enters the world of the simulation while maintaining a direct rapport with their own environment. The theatre of the hypersurface is not immersive but it simulates immersiveness. (Giannachi 2004: 95)

The hypersurface can be likened to the reassuring fourth wall of the theatre. The wall becomes a boundary in which we can safely allow ourselves 'to surrender to the enticements of the virtual environment' in much the same way as we give ourselves to the game within the 'magic circle' (Murray 1998: 103) that permits or authorizes action outside normal behaviours. Laurel (1993: 113) states, 'it is the state of mind that we must attain in order to enjoy a representation of an action. Pretending that the action is real affords us the thrill of fear; knowing that the action is pretend saves us from the pain of real fear.'

We can now access virtual worlds through various platforms, in any location, as personal computers, handheld devices and consoles become wireless, allowing greater accessibility. Mobile phones provide another key platform for gaming on the move. Where we play contributes to the gaming experience. All gaming platforms operate within their own social spaces and the environment contributes to the gameplay. For example, 'arcade games are played in commercial spaces amongst the frenzy of other machines, mobile games incorporate the everyday as they can be played anywhere' (Bolter and Grusin 2000: 102). With home consoles and personal computers, early computer gameplay was essentially a solo experience. However, networking expands the social space beyond the confines of the office or bedroom. Social expansion can be seen through players' stories on *World of Warcraft*, a MMORPG where gamers describe how their social encounters in the game world have enabled them to forge friendships, giving players a sense of being in this virtual place with someone else. In accessing online communities, the player has the sense of being amongst others rather than alone. The sense of being present in another place with others creates the feeling of 'being there' as well as 'here'.

Conclusion

Computer games and performance share many of the same principles, in that they both take place outside everyday life within specified boundaries. They have the common characteristics of narrative and intensification of time for the dramatic event and both employ performance terminology; for example, character, set and plot. However, the role of audience differs from theatrical convention, as the viewer becomes an active agent in the creation of events – the player is both spectator and performer. Every day, computer games host millions of small-scale performance events that evolve through the collaboration of protagonist/player and emergent narrative in shared virtual worlds. The computer game genre holds great potential for the future of performance, and this is being increasingly recognized and explored by practitioners and theorists alike.

Introduction to 5.2

In section 5.1, Wood introduced some of the key parallel concepts across computer games and performance practice. Section 5.2 will demonstrate how some of these concepts can be applied through the piece *SwanQuake: House*, by Ruth Gibson and Bruno Martelli. It begins with a 'thick description' (Geertz 1973: 3–30) of *SwanQuake: House*, which details an encounter with the work from a personal perspective. This process of description is designed to give access to the experiential nature of this work as an installation, whilst also providing an explanation of the work itself as context. This is followed by an interview with Gibson and Martelli, in which they discuss the ideas behind *SwanQuake: House*, and some of the processes involved in designing and creating the work.

Before we move on to section 5.2, it is useful to revise the key points raised by Wood in section 5.1, and to anticipate how some of these will reappear in section 5.2. Wood highlights the function of dramatic narrative in the way that the game unfolds. The use of episodic structure affords the player a level of investment in the action, creating a sense of ownership and, thus, identity within the game. Critical to that investment is the way in which the player is represented by her avatar, which Wood describes as the character that the player is performing within the emergent narrative. In the interview in section 5.2, Martelli will discuss the importance of risk (and death) as part of that investment.

Wood refers briefly to first-person perspective, where the player sees the world through her avatar's eyes, and third-person perspective, where the 'camera' is positioned just behind the avatar so that the player sees her avatar interacting within the environment. This has an impact on the way in which the player experiences the game, as Martelli will discuss in relation to *SwanQuake: House*.

Wood also describes the importance of the feedback that the player receives in response to the actions that she undertakes through her avatar within the game. This feedback supports the sensation of 'being there' on the other side of the 'hypersurface', allowing the player to experience embodied location simultaneously both in the virtual world and in the real world. As a performance installation, *SwanQuake: House* challenges the separation inherent in this mode of thinking. Instead, it bleeds together visual and kinaesthetic signals from the real and virtual environments, immersing the 'visitor' (Gibson and Martelli's term) in an intense multireality experience.

5.2   *SwanQuake: House*: 'messing the system up'

Sita Popat

SwanQuake: House – a personal experience

It is a sunny September afternoon in 2008, and I have come to a back-street in East London to experience igloo's *SwanQuake: House* at the V22 Gallery. I know little about the piece except that it involves computer game aesthetics in some way, and I am slightly apprehensive about what awaits me. I knock on the door of an old warehouse building, and igloo artist Bruno Martelli opens it. He leads me to the top of a flight of stone steps, and I walk cautiously down into the semi-dark basement. Crumbling brickwork is exposed where the paint is peeling. The air is damp and cold. Incongruously, in the middle of the room there are a chair and a bare wooden dressing table with a wide mirror. I sit down and look into the mirror. I see a London underground station platform, with a burning train on the line. Slightly startled, I realize that I am looking into a virtual world through the eyes of an avatar. The dressing table is bare apart from a trackball flanked by two buttons. Experimenting, I find that I can make my avatar turn, walk forward and jump using the simple controls. My perspective is first-person, so I cannot see my avatar, but I notice that it casts the shadow of a female body and I can only walk at a slow pace through the virtual environment. I move along the platform and up into the station. By the escalators, I see a woman dancing – slowly turning, stepping, occasionally jittering or flicking between positions. She ignores me completely.[2] I approach her, but she fades as my avatar gets close. When I turn around, she is there again. I go back past the train and walk along the tunnel, but my avatar gets close to some sparking electric cables, and the screen dissolves into brilliant white. I emerge from the whiteness into a large silvery grey room with no windows or doors. Did I die? Is this heaven? Around the room are more dancers, each moving independently, ignoring me (Illustration 5.1). I realize that all the dancers look like igloo artist Ruth Gibson. I notice that my avatar's shadow is identical to the dancers. I feel my breathing physically slow as I accept my isolated existence amongst my ethereal, meditative sisters, and I listen to the haunting soundscape that permeates the room. It feels cold, although there is no temperature in the virtual world. Maybe it is the chill of the basement where my physical body is sitting on the other side of the hypersurface.

Illustration 5.1 *SwanQuake: House* (2008) Computer Installation with Sound, V22 Gallery London. Dancers in the 'Heaven' Room
[Copyright: igloo]

The 'heaven' room is a descriptive title coined from audience members' comments on the work.

Across the room I find a teleportation device, and my avatar is transported to an old, empty house. The paint is peeling to expose the brickwork, and the small rooms look dark and damp. My skin crawls, as the visceral feedback from the real basement matches the virtual world. I flick my eyes up into the corner of the basement room and then back into the virtual room, and the two look almost identical. I shiver. My avatar drifts upstairs where I find another dancer, apparently trapped in a tiny room, but unconcernedly going through her glitchy moves and ignoring me. I try to get her attention but she is oblivious to my avatar's existence and fades away as it approaches her too closely. The house has many stairs and rooms, and it is raining outside. The sound of the rain adds to the sinister feeling. (It is only much later after I leave the installation that I realize this house is an exact copy of the place where Gibson and Martelli live in real life, but rendered 'uncanny' in its virtual representation.)[3]

Another teleporter takes me to a high ledge over a lava-filled valley, and I experience sudden vertigo as my avatar looks down. I follow the narrow path, keeping close to the cliff face. There is a bridge over the valley and my avatar crosses it to get lost in tunnels of stone inside the mountain. I return to the bridge, and look down into the flowing red burning river far below. I am filled with a sudden urge to jump into the lava river. My avatar jumps and falls – and, again, the whiteness floats me into the silvery room with the dancers. There is no way out apart from the teleporter, and although the room is on a grand scale, it feels somehow claustrophobic. Is this Hell? I make my way to the teleporter, a little frustrated by the slow speed at which my avatar is able to walk across this large space. I arrive back on the station platform and listen to the crackle of flames in the burning tube train in front of me. I check the other platform to see if there is another train, but I find my avatar unexpectedly plummeting downwards as the second platform turns out to be vertical instead of horizontal. I am back in the silvery room.

Slightly unnerved, I stand up from the dressing table and look around. There is a corridor off the back of the room, so I go to explore – this time with my physical body, although it feels oddly similar to my virtual body, moving slowly through dark, damp rooms. At the end of the corridor is an old-fashioned oval mirror on the wall. I move closer and realize that the mirror is actually an oval screen. I appear to be looking back into the game world through it; one of the dancers is just in view. I turn off the corridor into a smaller room. At once I feel strange, although there is nothing in the room but the bare, peeling walls. I move closer to a wall, and the feeling gets stronger. I realize that the walls are not the same as the rest of the base-ment. They are images of the walls – texture maps – printed at full size but at a low resolution, and placed over the original walls (Illustration 5.2). As

Illustration 5.2 *SwanQuake: House* **(2008) Computer Installation with Sound, V22 Gallery London. The Texture-Mapped Room**
[Copyright: igloo]

I look closer, they appear out of focus. By now, I am uncertain what is real and what is not. The feedback from all my senses is telling me that the real and virtual worlds are bleeding into each other, and I am disorientated. I leave the basement and step out into the sunlight with some relief. As I take the train home, I am unusually aware of small details in the world around me.

Interview with Ruth Gibson and Bruno Martelli

Bruno Martelli and Ruth Gibson are the creators of igloo. They work in the field of electronic media and performance, championing the use of motion capture in real time 3D worlds. igloo's work includes gallery installations, video works, online projects and performances. Gibson and Martelli believe in growing pieces and exploring ideas of being in other people's stories, allowing audiences to join the dots, providing libraries of motion for play and provoking imagination so that certain things can be left unsaid. They experiment with different formats and new methods of interaction to develop ways of blurring the boundaries between spectator and participant. [4] In this interview, they talk about the concepts and processes behind *SwanQuake: House*.[5]

What inspired you to work with a computer game aesthetic for the SwanQuake *series?*
BM: I was playing a World War II shooter online with Scott deLahunta, and our avatars met in a French village. We started doing a sort of standy, crouchy dance with each other, and he could see me and I could see him and it was great. And I found I could exploit some of the glitches that characters have – like, if two of you threw a grenade at the same time, it went weird and kind of 'broke' the motion capture. Sometimes I've seen other people doing similar things. Once this person got everybody to stop fighting – which is no mean feat! And he got them all to gather in one area. And we were all doing this glitchy thing while he's running round taking screen shots. It probably sounds really crass but we thought there's more in there about how people might interact in a game environment if you subvert some of the conventions. So we started working on *SwanQuake*. But it's slowly, slowly, because we're not a big games company.

Viewers receive very little information about SwanQuake: House *before they come to see it. Why did you choose to frame the work in that way?*
BM: A lot of the user experience tends to come from how the whole thing's framed. When people go into the theatre, they expect the lights to go

down, stuff's going to happen on the stage, it'll last for around an hour and a half, the lights come on and it's time to go home. So it's heavily mediated by the framing of it. When people are walking in the street and stuff happens, it's unexpected – it's magical. We had to stop venues from describing the work as being 'interactive', because it's always disappointing when people have this idea about what the interaction's going to be. And, whatever it is, it doesn't do that. Whereas, if stuff just happens, and they can make it happen, they love it because it's completely unexpected. Doing the piece as a site-specific installation, that adds to it. Because in the theatre or cinema, the experience has a start, a middle and an end, and you get taken on this journey. The stuff we're trying to make is where you have to take yourself on a journey.

How far do you see the player as a performer?
BM: When a person is playing a computer game, they're somehow performing. In the 1970s and 1980s, when Space Invaders was really popular in arcades, the kids who were really cool would put their 10p in and they could be on the machine for a really long time. A crowd of people would gather to watch them playing, and in a way that was a kind of performance. I used to feel quite uncomfortable if someone was looking over my shoulder when I was playing – there is that kind of feeling as well. We made the *SwanQuake* controls for a single player, but it's not a single-person installation. People can watch while someone else is at the controls. And we don't feel bad if a visitor doesn't ever touch the controls.

Did you aim to create a specific type of experience for visitors to SwanQuake: House?
BM: I think, at first, we were making stuff for live work and we thought we'd have these virtual characters because it would give us an extra thing that we could manipulate on stage, and an interesting sort of relationship could develop. So we started working with motion capture and we made performances on the web. When you've got those characters, they're just like action figures that you're manipulating. You're out here and they're in there; it's like looking at a performance in a fish tank. The next step was to think 'It would be great if you could go into the performance as well – get away from the proscenium arch of the screen and just be in there'. So the correct answer to that problem is to use some sort of game engine technology.

We decided to recreate our own house as the virtual environment, because then we can look at it and look at the 3D model, and we can see how good the mapping is. A lot of the time in computer game worlds the

127

sense of embodiment, scaling and relationship to size is actually quite good, but you don't really experience it because a lot of environments are fantasy, like *Prince of Persia*. Or you're in a spaceship. But, actually, you've never been in a real spaceship or gone to Arabia in a fancy castle, so you don't know how accurate the computer game is. So we thought 'We'll make our place' because then we'll be able to see if it feels the right sort of size. Then, later on, we can deviate from realism. So the house is supposed to be natural, but it's empty – only the sofa and a chair – and it's got a strange feeling. I don't really like it very much – freaky.

RG: The history of the work is the sense of spontaneity and immediacy. I'm interested in experiences of visceral things and sensing them in different ways. I'm talking about the way in which the installation is seen as a whole. The four rooms, the dressing table and the mirror – it's a complete piece of work. We've not always given what an audience wants. There's no goal to this 'game' – instead, there's a kind of idea of being 'in the moment', which is what I love about dancing. Yet you're maybe sitting at the dressing table or you're walking around the space, and there are moments of having control and yet not being in control. I enjoy that flipping of perspectives, like the wall prints where the printing is of low-res bit maps, so when you get closer they go out of focus rather than come into focus – it feels the wrong way round. So it's constantly making the visitor feel alive and aware of themselves in a place where the 'real' and the 'virtual' coexist and bleed into each other.

The design of the control interface in the dressing table is simple but intuitive (see Illustration 5.3).
BM: We've tried different control schemes in a few shows. We're trying to find one that makes sense to everyone, and we found that the trackball and the two buttons are the minimum that actually allows you to engage with the world. A mouse can be very twitchy and people can get disorientated, especially when it's quite a big projection. The trackball has inertia to start with and we've deadened the response so you have to move the trackball a lot to turn the character a lot. So people who are not used to game controls find it easier to use, and it works for gamers. You can still have fine control – if you move it a little bit the viewpoint totally changes with just your fingertip. But if you spin it, it doesn't go horrible.

We made the dressing table because we tried stuff with large projections but we wanted it to be an intimate experience. And big projections were limiting the places we could show because there were problems working with front or back projection, and you needed a big blackout. We don't

**Illustration 5.3   *SwanQuake: House* (2008) Computer
Installation with Sound, V22 Gallery London. The Dressing
Table with Trackball and Two Buttons**
[Copyright: igloo]

need so much blackout with the dressing table because it's a smaller screen, but it still gives quite a widescreen point of view with a lot of peripheral vision, so it's still quite immersive. It changed the relationship with the work too, because you automatically sit close to the mirror/screen.

You chose to use first-person perspective, rather than third-person, for the virtual environment. What were the reasons behind that choice?
BM: Because this was the introduction level to *SwanQuake*, we thought it may be important to make the user feel more embodied, and I feel that first-person perspective is more embodying. Also, if you're watching some of the non-player characters (the dancers) it would be weird if you could also see yourself watching them. When you go to the cinema, you see the film – you don't sit behind yourself looking at yourself watching the film. I've always found that third-person perspective doesn't make any sense to me, and I feel disembodied. I'm not in there, I'm watching some little person in there – it's like a little puppet, and maybe you get attached to it. But you don't really care. It's not as visceral as if it's you. I know some people get really upset because 'Super Mario died'. But that's just some-thing on a screen. It makes a big separation for me.

So, instead, the player herself can die?

BM: Initially the player couldn't die. But that destroyed a lot of the tension, and some of the narrative structure as well, because there was no risk. If there's no risk, there's no real reward. So death was actually a useful mechanism for making people be a little bit cautious. Also it enabled us to use it as a mechanism for teleporting people from location to location. In computer games, the convention is you're starting at Point A and you have to get to Point B. When the enemies kill you or something happens, you go back to Point A. So you have another go, and another go, and eventually you get through to the end. But for us, because we don't really have a start or an end, it's just ongoing. We're not putting people back a step, we're just putting them somewhere else.

RG: The construction of the world is carefully considered, and the sounds and music tracks are plotted. There are very different types of constraints for that. So that ongoing journey has a sense of navigation, there's something brooding. Each place has its own intensity, so in some ways you're relieved to arrive but then desperate to get out. It's a constant pushing forwards of the action in a way. It's a chance to be teleported somewhere of contrast, when you die you float down to die, or you float in to die, it's not a sudden thing, but with the vertical station platform it feels like it's somehow faster to death, a warping of time and space. Death and teleporting are different sensations. But it's all about going to the next zone.

You used motion capture for the characters. How did you create the choreography?

RG: Originally, we wanted to have an avatar trapped in one of the rooms in the house. It seemed logical that I be the person. But the player is me as well, so that's an odd idea of identity. You have my physical appearance in my shadow, and you have my walking. But there were four dancers involved in the motion capture process. Putting together all the motion capture sequences, there was a point when I thought that all the moves from one person would have to be on the same model. But I found out that, actually, you could sew together different moves from lots of different performers – dancers of different sizes, for example. That was a thrill, because it's something you really can't do in any other way. That kind of variety of movement styles on one model is quite an odd thing. In the future, I'd like to explore further the relationship between the movement and the modelling, and how those things can work and how they can inhabit space, and how that can change how the player uses or understands that space.

Sometimes we would put movements on a character just to test it. They were either hilarious or they would conjure up so many different things just by changing the model and how the movement is seen through it. I've been working with motion capture for 15 years so I know what works and I know how to mess the system up, and I love messing the system up because of what comes from it. But when you're in a commercial situation, a lot of the nuances of the material will vanish because of time constraints or getting the game out or whatever. So there's no room to explore the weirdnesses, or the thing that didn't quite work how it was expected to. And sometimes, in the commercial world, it would look like mistakes because the movement is jittery, but it's different and you can do interesting stuff with it. As artists, we can take the time to play with that and follow creative ideas.

The sound is a key part of the experience. How did you go about choosing and designing it?
RG: I worked side by side with the two composers.

BM: Some of the sounds are based on background noises – there's traffic, rain, and things like that. But we said to the composers that we didn't want it all to be ambient and environmental. There's got to be music as well, but it can't just be regular game type music, you know, swelling orchestral overtures or whatever.

RG: The large room – the 'heaven' room – has music. We wanted a contrast with the re-creation of the house. But the rain track is composed, too. The sound builds up, so it actually is music. The music is really important to the feel of the whole piece. It heightens a sense of curiosity, anticipation and all those things which build up on the way to somewhere. It's beautiful to have two different composers as you get very different kinds of material, so it's not all in one style. We've worked with them both on previous pieces, so there's a nice relationship going on there, a constant.

Where does the SwanQuake *series go next?*
RG: We started working on the series in 2004, but I think it could be a life project in a way. There's always something new coming tech-wise that doesn't necessarily solve the problems but actually makes us think 'Oh, we could use that ending for that, and we could add another level to do that'. It's exciting – and it means the work is actually evolving. Each time we show it in a different location, that's changing it, too. But I was astonished

at some of the horror genre responses from visitors to the last showing at V22. I guess that's what keeps us going, because we're pleasantly surprised by the different reactions of people coming to each version afresh.

5.3 Performance and technology: the myth of disembodiment

Sita Popat

Introduction

In the description of *SwanQuake: House* at the start of section 5.2, I shifted between the terms 'I' and 'my avatar' when writing about my interaction with the virtual world. I was not always consistent with my usage, because I was not always able to determine objectively whether it was my avatar or myself in the relationship with the environment. This is partly attributable to the particular bleeding of virtual and real aspects in this piece, which sometimes triggers physical responses aligned with virtual (visual) stimuli. Yet, is it also a result of the hypersurface described in section 5.1, where the player exists simultaneously in two places. I was experiencing Murray's (1998) proposition of the avatar as a 'mask' worn to gain agency in the game world. The sensory feedback that I received in the virtual world was mirrored in my physical responses. This ranged from the uncomfortable feeling of being ignored when the dancer refused to look at my avatar, to the tightening in my stomach when my avatar jumped into the lava river or fell down the vertical station platform. The latter reflects the importance of risk that Martelli discusses as a part of investment in the player/avatar relationship.

Gibson and Martelli refer to the 'freaky' nature of the house in *SwanQuake: House*, and to some of the 'horror genre responses' that were reported by visitors to the installation. I found the installation 'slightly unnerving' and I was 'relieved' to get out into the sunshine. These responses were to different stimuli, but they shared a common source. The fact that the *House* is closely based on a real location has allowed the programmers to make it look almost real, but somehow 'freaky'. I experienced the alignment of the virtual and the physical when I felt the cold, damp basement whilst my avatar was in a similar environment in the virtual world. My sensory feedback matched the visual stimulus too closely. The world is real, but not real – *almost* real. As such it falls into the realm of Masahiro Mori's 'uncanny valley' (1970):

Mori conceives of a moment in the development of increasingly familiar and humanlike robots when our sense of fascination and investment gives way to unease and displeasure. (Surman, in Brenton *et al.* 2007: 94)

Mori uses the examples of the corpse and the zombie, both made frightening by the similarity to the living human. Surman suggests that Mori's term is equally applicable to 'photorealistic computer generated characters' (Surman, in Brenton *et al.* 2007: 94); when the film *Polar Express* (2004) was released, some children were scared by the computer generated train conductor's eyes. Extending the concept of the uncanny valley to the environment, it seems that the house in *SwanQuake: House* has become uncanny as a result of the attempt to reproduce the real house faithfully. The confusion between real and virtual signals resulted in my sense of the uncanny, and the replacement of the physical wall surfaces with low-resolution prints had a similar effect. As Surman notes, 'verisimilitude gives way to a crisis of definition' (Surman, in Brenton *et al.* 2007: 94): we become discomforted because we are no longer able to define where the boundaries between the real and the virtual lie.

In section 5.1, Wood explored virtual reality in relation to human experience and communication through the analysis of gaming as performance. In section 5.2, Gibson and Martelli played with perceptions of virtual reality and real life, sometimes colliding them to create uncanny moments for the installation visitor. There is another way of configuring this relationship between modes of reality as augmented, technologically enhanced, or 'mixed reality' (Hansen 2006), where virtual and real are seen less as separate and oppositional, and more as a continuum. This final section of the chapter examines a range of examples where performance and technology combine to occupy places on this continuum. As a dance academic, I am particularly interested in the nature of the body and technology, and I propose that the common myth that technology promotes disembodiment is false. Instead, I suggest that technology in performance can heighten and stimulate bodily awareness.

Cyberspace

Cyberspace – the final frontier! In 1984, William Gibson introduced the world to the concept of cyberspace in his science fiction novel *Neuromancer*. Cyberspace is a computer-generated world where the corporeal body is transcended, allowing the mind to escape into a place of pure consciousness. In this world, all of our dreams can come true, but also all

133

of our nightmares in many fictional representations (for example, *The Lawnmower Man* 1992, the *Matrix* trilogy 1999–2003). Even in real life (RL), according to cybernetics expert Kevin Warwick (2002), one day we might be able to harness machine intelligence and plug our brains directly into the Internet. In this vision of the future, we would, indeed, be in danger of succumbing to Hubert Dreyfus's bleak prediction of virtual reality as:

> a disembodied and dubious world [where] Descartes might make a successful last stand. (Dreyfus 2001: 63)

According to Dreyfus, Descartes' mind/body dualism (often called the Cartesian split) would be realized in virtual reality in a way that the seventeenth-century philosopher himself could never have envisaged.

However, it eventually became clear that cyberspace was not going to be the final frontier. By the turn of this millennium, it was evident that virtual reality was unable to deliver the ultimate alternative existence that it seemed to promise in the early 1990s. The 'VR-hype' gradually receded and it was replaced by other ways of configuring the virtual and the real, taking a less polemical perspective and, instead, envisaging our environment as a technologically enhanced or 'mixed' reality. Mark Hansen proposes that 'all reality is mixed reality' (2006: 5), since we encounter digital elements regularly, in the home, the office, social environments, entertainment, travelling, and so on. To Hansen, our bodies form the primary mode of access to a world where the physical and the virtual (or digital) are woven simultaneously into the fabric of everyday existence. That access is channelled through the sensation and perception of touch.

According to Hansen's premise, the body is not lost to us in the Cartesian manner that Dreyfus suggests. Instead, it is central to our discourse. But the nature of embodied engagement across the real/virtual spectrum is complex, and there remains much room for exploration. The following range of performance and technology works demonstrate some of the ways that artists have approached the processes of negotiating and inhabiting mixed reality environments in the last two decades.

'Touching with my eyes'

Roy Ascott (1990) asks in the title of one of his most famous essays: 'Is there love in the telematic embrace?' In 1992, artist Paul Sermon produced the first version of *Telematic Dreaming* in Kajaani, Finland. This was the start of a series of works using telecommunications to link remote spaces.[6] The work involved two beds in different locations. The first bed was covered with a blue-screen sheet on which Sermon lay. This bed was filmed from directly overhead by a single camera, and there were three monitors arranged around its sides. The second bed was in a public gallery. Sermon's image was relayed from the camera above the first bed to a projector above the second bed, so that the gallery visitors could see his projected image lying on the bed. There were three cameras around the second bed, relaying images back to the monitors around the first bed, so Sermon could see when the visitors approached the bed and interacted with his projected image (see Illustration 5.4). There were no instructions or expectations. Some people passed through the gallery, whilst others stopped to sit, lie or interact with Sermon. Critically there was no audio connection, so communication relied on non-verbal modes that encouraged physical engagement.

Artist and academic Susan Kozel took Sermon's place in *Telematic Dreaming* in Amsterdam in 1994. In a detailed analysis of her experience (Kozel 2007: 92–103), she reports that early movement interactions were 'hesitant' and 'slow', as she and the visitors became accustomed to working via her virtual representation, or avatar. However, over time Kozel developed a strong connection with her projected image, describing the experience as 'one of extending my body, not losing or substituting it' (Kozel 2007: 99). Some visitors undertook lengthy interactions with Kozel, in which they became open, playful and even tender. She observed:

> When movement moved through us in this way, based on openness and trust, the distinction between which bodies were real and which were virtual became irrelevant. (Kozel 2007: 94)

This lack of distinction for Kozel chimes with Hansen's assertion that the body is the primary mode of access to both virtual and physical realms. Touch was inherent to the experience of *Telematic Dreaming*, but Sermon described it as 'touching with my eyes', since there was no direct physical contact. Instead, the sensation of touch was experienced via the visual impact of virtual image against real skin.

In a more recent telematic work, *Unheimlich*[7] (2005), Sermon collaborated with three other digital arts and performance practitioners, Steve Dixon, Mathias Fuchs and Andrea Zapp. Two female performers were located in Manchester, UK, whilst the audience was in Brown University, USA. There were blue-screen stage areas in both locations, and the audience members were invited to step onto the stage to interact with the performers. Cameras filmed the two stages and the visual feeds were mixed together, so that it appeared as if everyone was on the same stage.

135

Illustration 5.4 *Telematic Dreaming*
[Copyright: Paul Sermon]

Graphical images were layered into the background, so the action appeared to be taking place against the backdrop of a beach, a church, a burning forest, a computer game, and so on. The combined images were relayed back into both spaces, so that the performers and audience could see the whole picture.[8] The performance included an audio connection, so verbal interaction was possible. However, it was notable that touch remained an important factor:

> participants seek to shake hands, embrace, push, physically fight with, or caress ... The sense of virtual touch is something that delights *Unheimlich* participants, a sense of the body being extended in space ... by way of technology ... This leads to some moments of real contact and intimacy across the networks, for example through the most delicate stroking of hair in one performance. (Dixon 2006: 70)

As Dixon describes, many people will attempt to make intimate contact with a complete stranger via telematic communications. Is this because we feel protected by the remoteness of our locations, or is it because we crave physical validation in a virtual world? Or do we just want to see what it feels like? Dreyfus (2001: 62) assures us that 'telehugs' are not like real hugs. Virtual contact is not the same as physical contact, just as stroking someone else's hand with your pen is not the same as touching it with your finger. You gain a haptic sense of quality and texture through your pen, as a blind man senses the ground with his stick, but you do not feel the subtlety and warmth of the contact – and neither does the other person. Yet, Dixon describes 'moments of real contact and intimacy' in *Unheimlich*: a description echoed strongly in Kozel's account of her interactions with visitors in *Telematic Dreaming*.

In telematic performances/installations, two or more people are located physically in remote places. However, Sermon proposes that there is a 'third space', a virtual space, where they meet and interact, using the projected body image as avatar (Sermon, in Dinkla and Leeker 2002). In the 'third space', the physical body and avatar exist as one extended entity. Kozel reports that in *Telematic Dreaming* the real/virtual distinction is unimportant when both participants invest in the embodied communication. Artist and academic Anna Fenemore elaborates on the processes that she experienced as one of the performers in *Unheimlich*, defining 'the visual sense of touch which interpenetrates visual and physical space' (2007: 49). This echoes Sermon's explanation of 'touching with my eyes'. In both of these works, the performers report the irrelevance of the real/virtual binary in the moment of touch between participants. Perhaps there can be love in the telematic embrace.

Liveness

One of the fundamental concerns facing performance and technology over the past couple of decades has been the notion of 'liveness'. Philip Auslander has written extensively on this topic, including his seminal work *Liveness: Performance in a Mediatized Culture* (1999). He deals with the complex relationships between the concepts of 'live' and 'recorded' performance in the face of digital technologies. An example of this complexity is evident in the Wooster Group's theatrical production of *Hamlet* (New York, 2007). It incorporates live actors alongside many recorded representations of *Hamlet*, including a digitally re-mastered version of Richard Burton's film of his own 1964 Broadway performance. The Burton film-of-a-play frames the Wooster Group's production and becomes a 'cinematic "master" text' (Parker-Starbuck 2009: 23), which the actors reconstruct as it is projected around them. Relationships between recorded media and live theatre are central to the meta-narrative of the performance.

In an essay about 'chatterbots' (computers using artificial intelligence to generate meaningful responses in conversation with humans), Auslander proposes that liveness is not simply about the presence of a live performer. 'Liveness is first and foremost a temporal relationship, a relationship of simultaneity' (2002: 21). Thus, the ontology of the performer is of less importance than the relationship that exists between the viewer and the performer (even if the performer is a chatterbot). In a critical response to Auslander, Kevin Brown (2006: 4) notes that: 'this viewpoint challenges traditional theories of performance that privilege the living human body as the determining criterion of what constitutes live performance'. The real/virtual chasm gapes wide in those 'traditional theories', as Brown describes them. In contrast, Auslander's perspective relates closely to our concern with mixed reality, where the body is the primary mode of access to a lived environment that incorporates digital and physical elements. This phenomenologically oriented perspective highlights the quality of the performance experience as the key factor. For *Unheimlich* and *Telematic Dreaming* participants, the distinction between virtual and physical bodies became immaterial, as the quality of contact was the primary concern. In the Wooster Group's *Hamlet*, the playful interchange between present and absent bodies is the very crux of the work. In another critical response to Auslander's essay, Herbert Blau (2002: 23) notes the chastening fact that, sometimes, one cannot tell whether the performer is human or not, and it can be possible to err in either direction!

Is any body out there?

Taking Blau's comment a little further, what happens when human and technology become intertwined or indistinguishable? In the concept of the cyborg, human and technology become fused as a single entity. Performance artist Stelarc explores the augmentation and alteration of his own body through science and technology. In his project *An Ear on An Arm*,[9] an ear made of cartilage was inserted under the skin on his forearm. His aim was to use computer chips, microphones or other devices to give that ear additional abilities, scaling up one of the body's senses (Stelarc 2007). There is much room here for debate concerning philosophy and ethics, but the cyborg is not as remote as it seems. As I type this text into my computer, I read it back through my contact lenses. I am cyborg – perhaps as much of a mixed reality as the world that I inhabit. But my technological enhancement is designed simply to restore my vision to normal levels. Stelarc wants to go beyond the norm and prefigure natural processes, seeking ways that we can improve the human body. Why wait for evolution, he asks. 'Why get stuck in an evolutionary trajectory?' (Stelarc 2007).[10]

The cyborg fuses body and technology, but motion capture extracts movement from the body and fuses the movement alone with technology. At first glance, this might seem to fall back into the realms of the real/virtual divide, since the outcome is an animated character. However, closer inspection reveals that the animation retains a complex link to its physical originator, troubling the concept of mixed reality in interesting ways. Writing about dance and motion capture, Dils (2002: 94) notes that portraitists 'pare away human attributes and environments to arrive at a representation of something essential, something telling about the person'. She suggests that motion capture is like creating a digital portrait of someone, in which the essential element is that person's movement.

Motion capture is the process of capturing movement from the body as data. Markers are placed at key points on the body, and infrared cameras around the space record the markers as dots. A computer programme reconstructs the links between these dots to create a basic figure, devoid of the physical features of the human originator. Only the movement is retained, and manipulation of parameters can map it onto a different shaped body or creature. As Gibson noted in the interview in section 5.2, the movement from dancers of different sizes and shapes could be used to animate the same virtual character. Human movement can be used to animate animals or monsters in computer games or films, probably the most widely known example being actor Andy Serkis's movement animating the character Gollum in the *Lord of the Rings* film trilogy (2001, 2002, 2003).

In 1999, digital artists Paul Kaiser and Shelley Eshkar collaborated with dancer Bill T. Jones to create a movie titled *Ghostcatching* (first exhibited at the Cooper Union School of Art, New York). Jones performed naked and his movement was captured using 24 markers placed on his body, including one on his penis. This data was used to animate a series of line-drawing figures dancing in virtual environments.[11] The figures appear hand-sketched in an elegant fashion. They split and merge, not overly troubled by the laws of physics, leaving trails of colour from their sweeping hands and feet. None of them look like Jones, or any other identifiable person, but they are male in general physique. Yet, for those who have seen Jones dancing, these figures are infused with his characteristic style to the extent that they are clearly in his movement-image. This is starkly at odds with Jones' own reactions on seeing the *Ghostcatching* dancers. 'Is it me?', he asked (Dils 2001). He is unable to identify himself in the animations on the screen, despite knowing the process by which they have been created. Perhaps this is simply because one does not generally watch oneself moving, although performers probably do this more than most via recording technologies. Or perhaps the movement is somehow compromised by the removal of all physical body references. Dils (2002: 94) recognizes the movement as originating from Jones, but she calls the animations 'gutless' and she misses 'Jones' often fierce movement'. (She also becomes embroiled in the fact that Jones usually improvises, and this is by nature a recorded work, but that argument is probably more concerned with the 'liveness' debate than with the ownership of the movement.) Yet, what is human movement if it is extracted completely from the body on which it was originally formed? If the computer captures the movement with detailed accuracy, why is there something missing in the resultant animation? Kaiser describes *Ghostcatching* as 'a kind of meditation on the possibilities and limitations of motion capture' (Spain and Kaiser 2000: 20). Human and technology are joined in the capture of movement essence, but the mixing of these realities asks more questions about the nature of physicality than it answers.

Conclusion

In defining 'liveness', Auslander places emphasis upon the relationship between spectator and performer, rather than on whether the performer is live or recorded, human or digital. Participants in *Telematic Dreaming* and *Unheimlich* agreed that the focus is on human contact, rather than the virtual or the physical body. These examples point towards the mixed reality of lived experience, and the primacy of our physical and perceptual senses in engaging with it. Hansen (2006: 2) acknowledges the essential function of embodied agency in the construction of mixed reality. He proposes that body motor activity lies at the heart of connections between physical and virtual worlds, since agency is created when we move and see our avatars move as a corresponding result. There are essential ties that connect my physical senses directly to my digital representation in the virtual world. Indeed, my presence in that world is severed if my extended embodiment is not borne out by my sensory experience.

Returning to the concept of the hypersurface (see section 5.1), we can understand telematic space as a place where 'the viewer can *double* their presence and be in both the real and the virtual environments simultaneously' (Giannachi 2004: 95, original italics). This doubling is a key concept for understanding relationships between bodies and avatars:

> It helps us to understand that we are embodied subjects whilst engaged in our experiences of 'virtual reality'. But we are also re-embodied and

gain a sense of presence and agency in these virtual spaces through the interface and the avatar. (Dovey and Kennedy 2006: 106)

Being both embodied and re-embodied does not imply a split subject but, rather, a doubled subject. The physical body is conjoined with its (identical or non-identical) twin image in the virtual realm, linked by the loops of intention, action and feedback. Yet, *Ghostcatching* still refuses to fit neatly into either the real/virtual binary or the definition of mixed reality. The telematic pieces are concerned with real-time human communication, whereas *Ghostcatching* is, in effect, an aesthetic exercise in movement abstraction. The question remains as to whether *Ghostcatching* is a performance or a visual artwork, and how far technological enhancement of the body renders such distinctions irrelevant. When defining 'liveness', does Auslander's willingness to ignore the ontology of the performer inevitably lead us into a post-human age? And would that necessarily be problematic to performance as a field of practice and study?

In section 5.2, Gibson and Martelli noted some of the ways that performance differs from commercial work. They felt that this occurred particularly in relation to their own work through their interest in the unexpected, the non-perfect, the error that might lead to new ways of thinking and working. They referred to the constraints often experienced by artists working with expensive commercial technologies within tight time frames, which can mitigate against the creative experimentation of improvisation-based methods. Performance is naturally a 'magic space', a place where reality and representation meet, overlap and merge. It can be profitably employed in design processes for technological innovation, as demonstrated by Billy Klüver's seminal 'Experiments in Art and Technology' (EAT) in the 1960s (Popat and Palmer 2005). In a recent example, researchers at the University of Leeds used performance techniques to explore how robots can be programmed to perform expressive movement in interactions with humans (Wallis *et al.*, 2010). Current projects funded by the Technology Strategy Board include choreographers working alongside architects to design buildings with a low impact on the environment.

Performers are accustomed to playing with realities, and to inhabiting the 'not-me' and the 'not-not-me' of performance (Schechner 1985: 112), where the avatar (character) and the player (actor) are one and the same (Popat and Palmer 2008). One might call the performance space a place of mixed reality, where real and virtual have intertwined since long before the advent of technological virtual reality. Performance has much to offer as a way of understanding and modelling the philosophies and practices of human/technology relationships. There is also much that performance practitioners and theorists can learn about the nature of extended physicality, communication and presence from exploring those relationships at the technological interface of the real and virtual.

> ### Activities

In the Introduction to this chapter, I mentioned Jennifer Ringley, who presented her life 24/7 via a webcam called *Jennicam* (Smith 2005). Communications technologies are prevalent in today's society, and you will probably use some form(s) of digital communication in your daily life. These forms of communication affect the ways in which we communicate, sometimes subtly and sometimes quite profoundly. They have a basic impact on the shape of the dialogue, and they also tend to affect the kinds of information that we use them to transmit.

➤ *Solo activity*

Consider the following questions:

- Do you Facebook? Do you play MMORPGs? Do you Skype, or text? Do you have a web page?
- How do you (re)present yourself in these contexts?
- Who is receiving that (re)presentation?
- Do different types of technology affect the way in which you behave or communicate?
- Where are you located when you use these different types of technologies?
- Do you tend to use different types of technology to present yourself to different people? If yes, why?

➤ *Discussion activity*

Use the questions in the Solo activity as the starting point for a discussion via real-time text chat or Skype. How does the communications medium (for example, text chat, Skype) affect the way that you communicate?

There are many different kinds of technologies, and you have discussed in the previous activity how some of these affect your communication channels, patterns and content. Different types of technologies (or media) affect the ways in which we communicate, as well as what we communicate. It is easier or more appropriate to communicate certain types of message in particular media. Ruth Gibson, in section 5.2, mentions that she has been working with motion capture for 15 years, so she knows how to use it to get different types of effects. If you are using a new type of technology in your practical work, then you need to allow yourself plenty of time to learn how to use it effectively.

➤ *Practical activity 1*

This activity is based on the game of Chinese whispers. First, play Chinese whispers, and notice how the message can get garbled, even when you are all using one medium (speech) and the same language.

Now try the following exercise:

1 Get into groups of five, and number yourselves 1–5.
2 Number 1 thinks of a short sentence and whispers it to Number 2.
3 Number 2 mimes the message to Number 3. (Numbers 4 and 5 must not watch).
4 Number 3 draws the message for Number 4. (Number 5 must not look at the drawing).
5 Number 4 writes the message down for Number 5.
6 Number 5 reads the message back to the rest of the group.

Compare notes and discuss where the message broke down (or, possibly, how it didn't – although that is rare). Compare the properties of the different media and how the message was or wasn't suited to the medium where it broke down.

• Did you have the right skills for your communications medium?
• Did that affect the way that the message was communicated?

Performances using digital and new media require performance skill sets, but they also require other skills in the understanding and practice of the media concerned. Sometimes, collaboration between people with different skill sets can help. This is one of the reasons why so many performance and technology productions involve collaborations between artists.

Section 5.3 of this chapter described some examples of telematic performance, and explored ways that real and virtual bodies might relate to each other through this medium. Giannachi describes how the real and the virtual are 'doubled' at the hypersurface.

➤ *Practical activity 2*

Set up a basic telematic environment and explore the nature of touch between two participants.

You will need:

• a camcorder;
• a dataprojector;
• a cable to connect your camcorder to the projector (this may vary according to the make and model of the camcorder);

- a screen or white wall to project onto (if you can back-project, then you will avoid shadows).

Performer A stands in front of the projection surface. Performer B stands somewhere else in the space where he or she can see the projection surface. The camcorder is focused on Performer B. The dataprojector projects the image of Performer B onto the projection surface.

- Experiment with touch. Can the two performers touch fingertips? How does that feel? What does it feel like to touch different body parts?
- Experiment with size. What happens to the relationship between the two performers if one is larger than the other?
- Practise moving together. Keep it slow and simple, at first. How do you experience your body, depending on whether you are Performer A or B? Do you experience the doubling that Giannachi describes? If you keep practising over a long period, do you experience some of the reactions that Kozel describes from her experiences of *Telematic Dreaming*? (Remember that Kozel took part in the installation regularly over a four-week period, so she became used to it and developed skills in working with her extended body.)

Take turns in the different roles and discuss your experiences.

Notes

1 http://www.igloo.org.uk
2 Note that the description shifts between the perspective of the person (for example, 'I can make my avatar turn') and the perspective of the avatar (for example, 'Did I die?').
3 See section 5.3, for further discussion of the 'uncanny'.
4 See Jefferies (2009), for a broad overview of igloo's work.
5 See igloo (2007), for a range of discursive papers and interviews concerning *SwanQuake: House*, and the concepts behind it.
6 Paul Sermon has made numerous other works using telematic principles. See http://www.paulsermon.org, for a comprehensive archive.
7 Literally translated, this means 'unhomely', or uncanny.
8 http://creativetechnology.salford.ac.uk/unheimlich/ [Accessed 22 February 2010].
9 http://web.stelarc.org/projects/earonarm/index.html [Accessed January 2011].
10 Other performance artists working with body augmentation include Orlan and Guillermo Gómez-Peña.
11 Movie available online at http://www.lumeneclipse.com/gallery/18/oeg/index.html [Accessed 24 February 2010] or on excerpts on DVD resource in Mitoma (2002).

Further reading

Chatzichristodoulou, Maria, Jefferies, Janis and Zerihan, Rachel (2009) *Interfaces of Performance*. Surrey: Ashgate.

Broadhurst, Susan and Machon, Josephine (eds) (2006) *Performance and Technology: Practices of Virtual Embodiment and Interactivity*. Basingstoke: Palgrave Macmillan.

Dixon, Steve (2007) *Digital Performance: A History of New Media in Theatre, Dance, Performance Art and Installation*. Cambridge, MA: MIT Press.

Giannachi, Gabriella (2004) *Virtual Theatres: An Introduction*. London: Routledge.

Kozel, Susan (2007) *Closer: Performance, Technologies, Phenomenology*. Cambridge, MA: MIT Press.

Popat, Sita (2006) *Invisible Connections: Dance, Choreography and Internet Communities*. London and New York: Routledge.

6   Interactivity

Introduced and edited by Alice O'Grady

Introduction

To be 'interactive' has become a twenty-first-century preoccupation. Frequent usage of the term within our language points towards (and often promises) a sense of empowerment of the 'user' and equality of ownership. There is the implication of a reciprocal relationship between the individual and the larger institutions with which we come into contact (the broadcast media, arts organizations, our employers, the information highway, and so on). However, achieving meaningful interactions in order to facilitate truly equal exchanges of communication and influence between individuals or groups is not always of primary concern. Indeed, the term 'interactivity' is used so widely, and often so imprecisely, that it has become somewhat devoid of meaning. Often, how one can interact is given priority over the *quality* or *significance* of the interactions taking place.

Interactivity is frequently linked with technology and its new applications, which are now deeply embedded in our daily lives in ways that hitherto would have been impossible. However, leaving to one side any technological focus, the numerous social interactions that occur on a day-to-day basis are the fundamental building blocks of how we understand the world and our place within it. How we perform and experience interactions with others provides an additional layer to how we experience and shape our own existence and identity. This chapter focuses on the principles involved in making work that can genuinely be experienced as interactive performance in the twenty-first century.

Two perspectives on interaction

The chapter is organized into three main sections that explore how interactivity can function as both aesthetic principle and political ideology. Sections 6.1 and 6.2 look in detail at two apparently contrasting performance perspectives. Placing these two examples side by side will enable us to consider how concepts and practices of interactivity can be applied in different contexts.

In section 6.1, university lecturer and practitioner John Somers discusses a model of participation and interaction that emphasizes concepts and practices of social responsibility and choice. This form of interactive theatre grows out of the work of the Brazilian theatre practitioner Augusto Boal, who developed a style of theatre involving direct participation from the audience, with the aim of achieving social change. Somers explores how this type of theatre practice engages audience members as active players within the drama. It offers ways in which they may find a voice, responsibility and moral involvement through interaction with the performers and each other, in the presentation, discussion and re-configuring of a performed social situation or narrative. Somers considers how Boalian practice has been adopted by educators wishing to use interactivity as a means for affecting attitude change in audiences. Technology is not implicit in this form of interactive theatre. Rather, Somers is concerned with interactivity as a way of engaging audiences in shared meaning-making, with flexible outcomes that are negotiated and co-owned through reciprocal exchange and communication.

Section 6.2 presents an interview with Matt Adams, co-founder and core artist of Blast Theory (www.blasttheory.co.uk). Blast Theory are best known for their experimental use of new technologies (such as GPS and mobile phone technology) in the creation of interactive performance pieces that take place across cities and on the Internet. They engage audience members as participants through various types of technological interfaces, including text messages and avatars in virtual environments. Participants can affect or be affected by the performers and other participants, negotiating their location or identity (or both) by making choices and communicating with others. Whilst their work has a very different aesthetic to the type of work discussed by Somers, they still share the same fundamental interest in interactivity as a process of shared meaning-making. The interview focuses on the ideas and creative processes behind Blast Theory's performance practice.

In the final section of this chapter, I discuss common themes arising from these two approaches to interactive performance, drawing out some of the key terms and ideas that run parallel between them.

6.1   Boalian perspectives on interactivity in theatre

John Somers

Introduction

The primary aim of interactive theatre is to involve the audience in a number of different ways, so that they may engage with the performance and its themes physically as well as intellectually. It is often used as a form of intervention and as a means of bringing about a shift in perspective for those experiencing it. Interactive theatre practitioners strive for engagement that will have lasting and meaningful impact on the participants. They do this by encouraging participants to take some responsibility for the final outcome, or by giving them the ability to affect how the work develops. This dialogic approach – where performers and participants work together to create new meanings, or to explore particular issues or problems through the dramatic mode – is often utilized by those working within education or community arts.

Research into underage alcohol misuse shows interactive dramatic experience to be one of the most effective interventions in attitude change; more than critical incident discussion and the use of video (Fox 1997). Interestingly, this research discovered that teachers who use didactic approaches are the least effective agents for changing students' attitudes. My own research shows that dramatic experience significantly altered the attitudes to disability of 13- and 14-year-olds (Somers 1996).

So, how does drama achieve this? Fundamentally, the underpinning theory concerns narrative. Effective theatre, novels, films and TV drama work by involving us in stories that matter to us, containing characters by whose concerns and problems we become intrigued. This enhances the chances of audience members coming to share the moral responsibility for the actions of the characters – we care. They become our surrogates in the situations in which they operate. In novels, films and TV drama, the feedback loop between audience and performer is limited by time and distance. However, in theatre there is opportunity for interactivity – communication between audience and performer – to take place. It is this interactivity that provides the potential for new meaning-making.

The real and the fictional

The relationship between the real and the fictional is crucial. We live in a world in which story structures form a major – perhaps *the* major –

framework by which we make meaning of experience, and by which we are informed of things that we cannot experience first hand:

> By neither being tied to fact nor quite separate, fiction is a tool, necessary for thought and intelligence, and for considering and planning possibilities. Fiction is vitally important – indeed we may live more by fiction than by fact. It is living by fiction which makes the higher organisms special. (Gregory, in Rosen 1985: 16)

How can theatre achieve the greatest penetration in involving an audience in its stories, and so maximize its chances of achieving participant change? Interactivity attempts to narrow the gap that can exist in more conventional forms of theatre, where the tacit codes of behaviour for an audience require them to be still and silent whilst the performance takes place. By facilitating two-way exchange, practitioners committed to interactivity give audience members permission to take a more active and concerned part in understanding what is happening in the lives of the people in the story, and in finding possible routes for the characters to ameliorate the problems they face.

In most interactive drama contexts, the material prepared and offered to participants has the quality of 'incompleteness'. In a 'well-made' play, the performance generally involves the audience meeting the characters, the exposition of the problem, the characters wrestling with the problem before some form of climax, followed by the dénouement – the resolution of the problem, or its accommodation by the characters. Interactive theatre, by contrast, often stops at the climax and audience members are invited to understand the factors involved in creating the problem, and to assist the protagonist and others in finding positive ways forward.

What kinds of interactivity are there?

Interactivity can take many forms. The following examples are meant to show the degree of interactivity and do not represent exclusive models. I have chosen not to cover the use of digital and other media, but to focus on live theatre and, specifically, on work which relates to Augusto Boal's practice.

Boal had a major influence on a style of theatre which seeks to engage audiences more directly in the dilemmas experienced by people in theatrical stories. His principal contribution was to remove the 'fourth wall', which in most theatre forms through time had clearly separated audience and actor spaces. His early work focused on creating contexts in which audience members could become active participants in a variety of interventions that could ameliorate the problems depicted in performances. His theory and practice developed during the post-World War II period when many theatre people, motivated by the urge to make theatre more relevant to a wider audience, were looking for new forms of audience engagement.[1]

When we visit a conventional performance, other than applauding, or laughing, we are usually assigned to a part of the theatre – the auditorium – which signals clearly that it is different and separate from the space – stage – on which the artist will work. In this form of theatre, the performer – often because of the stage lighting context – cannot even see the audience. Clearly, there is some exchange and feedback taking place between audience and performers, but this is at a cerebral and emotional level rather than a vocal or physical level. Audiences watch the action unfold, take on its meaning and respond within the accepted convention. Actors may feel the intensity that the drama has established within the room, or they may hear appreciation for their work through audience applause. The physical gulf between stage and auditorium, however, is not breached and the fourth wall remains intact.

In the next level of interactivity, the demarcation between audience and artist spaces is less rigid. The artist may also make forays into the auditorium or invite audience members into their space. Typically, this happens when magicians or stand-up comedians perform. They can see and talk directly to the audience. Here, the demarcation by lighting is softened and the architecture of the performance space tends to signal that interaction may take place – a nightclub space, for example. The majority of the performance usually maintains the strict demarcation between artist and audience. Certain performers – solo clowns, for example – spend much of their time in the audience space. They can only perform if they use audience members as direct receptors of and reactors to their physical and verbal routine. Whilst these performers may improvise regularly, depending on the audience responses, their routine relies on a set stock of material. Similarly, other performances in this mode place a certain amount of responsibility onto audience members who may be invited up onto the stage to take part (in pantomime, for example) or who are required to give input within a pre-determined framework. Some one-to-one performances – or 'intimate' performance – situated mainly within the field of live art would also fall into this category.[2]

Interactive theatre – where it is applied for the purposes of attitudinal shift, education or social change – usually presents a human context through prepared enactment. The audience is invited to critique what they have seen, usually in ways that seek reasons for and causes of problems encountered by the protagonist. Forum Theatre is a theatre form developed originally by Augusto Boal. Boal contested the ideas of classical theatre which had at its centre the notion of catharsis, which he believed reconciled audience members to the *status quo*. Forum Theatre encouraged audience members to become actors (spect-actors) and not spectators, using theatre as a way to seek and practise solutions to their problems (Boal 1979: 139–42).

Typically, a short scenario is performed in which the protagonist is thwarted and oppressed. The scenario is re-enacted and the audience invited to say 'stop' when a crucial statement is made, attitude shown or decision taken by the protagonist. The process of interactivity is directed, governed and guided by a 'joker', who acts as a link between the audience and the scenario. Typically, when an audience member states that the protagonist ought to have behaved differently – been more assertive, helped a character in need, for example – that member is invited to take the role of the actor in the scene to show how they *should* have responded; that is, to interact with the performers in order to play out an alternative version of the action. The joker usually stimulates audience applause to congratulate the audience member who has performed.[3]

What does the audience contribute?

The aim is to engage an audience in ways which employ their empathetic responses. In these situations, audience members are encouraged to 'care' for those whose needs they witness within the drama. Knowing that the event is not 'real' but acknowledging its authenticity and relevance, given that the dramatic event and its accompanying pedagogic and dramatic techniques as outlined above have been effectively constructed, audience members are usually most willing to contribute in ways which enable the theatre programme to fulfil its potential.[4] Participation flows from a natural interest in the human conditions depicted, and is not disguised with trickery or gimmicks.[5] Although the event is set up to deal with genuine problems, situations or issues, the audience explores these through the dramatic mode, which affords them a degree of distance from the subject matter. They are able to engage with the material at a position of safety through what is known as 'one step removed' (Baim *et al.* 2002). This offers the participants a more objective perspective and one which avoids personal disclosure or exposure.

Attempts are often made to engage audience members *prior* to them seeing the performance element. They may, for example, receive an invitation to be a member of a jury, and be given basic information about the procedures and the case.[6] They may be directed to a website where introductory material is available. I often use a device I call a 'compound stimulus'. This is a collection of artefacts – documents, photographs, objects – in a container. The container – back-pack, shoebox, archaeologist's box – may contain a mobile phone with text messages which may ring with a message for the owner whilst audience members are examining it. There may also be an e-mail address and password which allows audience members to access the owner's in-box to discover the kinds of messages they are receiving – intimidatory, for example, in the case of a protagonist who is being bullied.

Examining this at least a week before they see the performance element, audience members explore the possible owner of the container and its artefacts, and the background to his or her life. The questions which focus this exploration are 'Who are the people in this story?' and 'What is happening to them?' They form hypotheses which can only be tested when they witness the performance element. Experience shows that this successfully orientates audience members to the story, and begins to set up interactive expectations and processes prior to the moment of performance. In one school-based project, I was able to create a complete room and its contents. This was explored by audience members before they saw, the next week, actors perform the events in the room about which they had conjectured in the previous week. Thus, actors now inhabited a space that they had already occupied, enhancing interactivity between them and the story.

At best, the audience experiences close engagement with real-life issues set in the context of a believable story. Within the safety of the performed fiction and the structure created by the facilitator, audience members are able to speak and ask questions about potentially sensitive topics. The consideration of the topic should be situated within a detailed scenario, allowing decisions to be made and advice given in the light of particular circumstances. In many ways, it is real life exposed in a social laboratory created within the dramatic medium. By deploying interactive strategies, the divisions between the three layers of real life, social exploration and dramatic medium are less distinct, allowing participants to move more freely between them. In this mode, each layer is in dialogue with the others, comments upon and informs the others. This form of interactive theatre does not pretend that illusion is real, or that fiction is somehow separate from how we live our day to day lives. Rather, there is an active conversation to be had that moves us from personal experience to a collective understanding that is constructed and verified in the presence of others.

Interactive theatre that has a 'real world' application (that is, seeks to promote social change) requires the audience to invest something of themselves in the event. As suggested, the audience become researchers in a social laboratory. It is the duty of the practitioner or facilitator to guide the participants through the work, and to take on a duty of care when the fiction begins to have an impact on how audience members start to address their reality. To this end, there are some key areas of concern worth identifying.

Sincerity

Where an audience is invited to become involved in the affairs of performed characters, they need to feel that they will not be taken advantage of. Those who invite their contribution therefore need to radiate a basic sincerity which is maintained throughout the experience. Only if this is achieved, will an audience 'trust' the performers and contribute. This is particularly true of predominantly vulnerable audiences.

Targeting

Unlike conventional theatre, where an audience may comprise a wide variety of ages and types, interactive theatre is often targeted at specific, generally homogenous groups – veterinarians, young offenders, 10-year-olds in a particular district, for example. This allows those developing the theatre programme to research and play to the common characteristics of an audience.

Authenticity

It is essential that, when a theatre programme is developed to represent the living context familiar to those experiencing it, that they regard it as authentic. If their response is 'nice try, but it isn't like that', then the drama-makers will have failed. This means that the programme developers have to conduct rigorous research on the topic they wish to deal with.

Relevance

The research should also reveal what the target group will find relevant to their personal or professional lives. It is essential that they recognize basic truths within the dramatic representations, and sense that the depictions deal with issues which occur, or may reasonably occur, in their worlds.

Validation

Audience members are more likely to become engaged with the story if it validates their experience. Many people who have defective well-being, for example, are embarrassed at their condition and do not wish to share the issues they are experiencing with those they feel may not understand. There can be something quite positive in witnessing the story created by a group of drama workers who have taken the trouble to capture aspects of a life circumstance of audience members. For this to be effective, the latter need to feel that the storyline and the characters within it reflect the verities of their own experience.

Audience size

Interactive theatre of this kind usually employs an intimate form where actors and audience inhabit a democratically arranged space and no audience member is distant from the action. For this reason, the audience numbers are restricted; it is more difficult to engage the moral concern of very large groups, as individuals feel less compunction to 'care' when many others are in a position to do so. There is also a negative correlation between distance from the action and engagement – so, audience members in the sixth row, for instance, are less likely to be engaged than those nearer the action.

What are the challenges for the actors?

The style of acting used in interactive theatre may be highly naturalistic. Because of the intimacy of the context, the actors might appear to be behaving as if in a normal room, rather than projecting their voice and physical messages to the back of an auditorium. Actors may narrate directly to audience members who, due to feeling that actors and audience inhabit a mutual space, feel they are being directly addressed. In any interactive phase, where the audience is invited to take part in a variety of ways, the actors make themselves accessible to audience members. Although much of the interactivity will take place within structures understood by both actors and audience, unpredictability of audience response ensures that actors must remain alert and respond in role to audience demands and suggestions.

The need for closure and for support post-event

Having drawn in audience members to the, often troubled, lives of the people in the story, theatre practitioners have a duty to bring about some release from the obligations felt. This might happen at the end of a theatre company's visit when actors are introduced to the audience as their real selves, or by a communication which thanks the participants for their concern and involvement, and signals that the programme has now ended. Many sensitive topics are dealt with through interactive theatre. In the recent past, for example, I have made programmes on self-harm, eating disorders, psychosis and teenage runaways. A significant number of audience members may have direct or indirect experience of the issue, and others may become deeply involved with the characters and the issues they experience. It is important, therefore, that participants are advised how they can seek help. This can be as wide as providing national and local helpline telephone numbers or, as in the case of the psychosis programme, the introduction at the end of the visit of the local Early Intervention mental health workers. In education contexts, institutions will have their own support systems but, for reasons of confidentiality, participants may prefer to approach outside organizations.

Conclusion

'Story' in its many manifestations – within artefacts as in the compound stimulus, in the hypotheses of the audience, or in the performed story – acts as a meeting ground on which audience members come to experience and become involved in aspects of the characters' lives. Interactive theatre of this kind has explicit aims. These aims can be achieved only if they are embedded in an effective dramatic event. The aim is to achieve the best possible levels of artistic merit and social efficacy. The theatrical quality of what is presented therefore must be high, and the attendant pedagogical devices deployed must be well-chosen and delivered. The target audience must feel that they are experiencing a story which they judge to be authentic in relation to their experience of the topic. The initial research phase is extremely important in ensuring that those making the programme understand the issues and the specific contexts in which they will be displayed. It is essential that the programme is made with the co-operation of experts by profession and experts by experience.

Successfully engaging the audience in the lives of the characters and their dilemmas is crucial to the success of any programme. Orientating them to the story through the use of the compound stimulus facilitates

Illustration 6.1   Engaging with the Audience
[Copyright: Jonathan Wall of Blue House Media]

Prior to the performance, the facilitator invites an audience member to take an object, in this case a trophy, from the compound stimulus

this process (see Illustration 6.1). It is important that the facilitator maintains sincerity and flexibility in providing the link between the audience and the story. Interactivity can be relatively superficial – such as that demanded by the clown, or profound – such as a situation where a girl is about to cut her wrists and audience intervention is required to avoid this and to take her to a safer psychological place.[7] Having brought the audience to the state of being involved, the theatre company has a duty to support any individual who has been affected by the event.

Introduction to 6.2

In attempting to explain the fundamental nature of interaction, the human communications theorist Berlo (1960: 131) suggests that 'interaction involves reciprocal role-taking, the mutual employment of empathetic skills ...We can define interaction as the ideal of communication, the goal of human communication.' For him, the process of communication is intrinsically circular in shape. Any interaction consists of a series of feedback loops where the communicator (or *performer*) demonstrates a response to the recipient (or *audience member*) and the recipient responds back. The process is self-sustaining and constantly in a state of negotiation or flux, until one or both parties decides to end the interaction by closing the feedback loop or disengaging their participation. Such interaction is evident in the processes described by Somers in section 6.1, where the feedback loop between performer and audience member is used to enact alternative versions of the story until a point of closure is reached. Berlo's 'mutual employment of empathic skills' is central to this mode of interaction, and the joker fulfils a critical role in facilitating communication between the parties involved. There is a clear sense in which the work is not complete without the audience, as their participation in constructing the story is key to the entire process.

The prefix 'inter' comes from the Latin meaning 'between', 'among', 'mutual' and 'reciprocal'. At its simplest, interaction can be understood as a deed or process which is undertaken together. The collaborative aspect, in performance terms, is particularly significant when we consider that this means activity *between* audience and performer. A commitment to something that might be termed as *the inbetweenness of things* brings to the fore notions of flux, co-authorship and shared meaning-making. These are pertinent issues for practitioners making work that seeks to implicate the public in the performed outcome; that is, involve them in making decisions or undertaking actions that directly affect the outcome. Prioritizing audience investment and participation in this way means certain sections of the work will remain unknown until the interaction is under way. To acknowledge and embrace flexibility, degrees of uncertainty and unpredictable outcomes is a prerequisite for this type of performance work. These are key concepts behind the interview in section 6.2, and we will return to them for further discussion in section 6.3.

The next section is an interview with Matt Adams, co-founder of Blast Theory. Blast Theory is an internationally renowned company based in Brighton, UK. With their roots in live art, Blast Theory's performance work is collaborative, interdisciplinary and experimental in nature. Innovation and risk lie at the heart of the company's work. They are, perhaps, best known for their application of new technologies, such as locative media and mixed reality to performance work which is often context- or site-specific. This interview examines the philosophy and some of the practices behind their practice. Whilst Blast Theory's work is very different from that discussed by Somers, the design of the interactive experience remains a critical factor in both contexts, with the *inbetweeness of things* playing a central role.

6.2 Interactivity and the work of Blast Theory

Matt Adams in conversation with Alice O'Grady

Was it the desire to be interactive that came first for Blast Theory – to engage an audience physically?
Yes. It's hard, in retrospect, to trace all of the different origins of where that decision was taken, but it was an absolutely fundamental building block of the company from the start.

One of the things that runs through our work is an interest in how you might problematize the line between the audience and the artist or the theatre-maker, and invite people to be conscious of that boundary between those two groups who are so regularly portrayed as entirely separate. So much discourse in art and theatre is around unique, talented, inspired individuals who have the decency to create wonderful things for us to partake in. Our view has always been to say 'I wonder how much that's true and how much that's a device into which everyone willingly buys?' We try to make work which, in some way, draws attention to some of those tensions.

Clearly, the history of theatre from the 1920s onwards – Brecht, Piscator, Mayakovsky, the Russian Constructivists – is interested in the relationship between the audience and the performer. There's a solid strand that runs through ideas about how you confound those relationships. They come from a number of different perspectives – Marxist, from the avant garde and from the strong communal ideas in the 1960s and 1970s. I was very aware of all those things doing my degree. I wrote my dissertation on David Hare, and looked at experimental British theatre of the 1960s and 1970s. That was clearly a leaping off point.

Theatres themselves are inherently conservative structures. The very architecture is all about familiarity and repetition, and the understood codes of bells and moving from foyers to auditoria and programmes, ice creams, etc. So, if you were going to create a new kind of theatre, where would you do it? For us, as we have done a number of times in our history, we looked to a popular cultural form. At that time it was clubs, then it became technology and the Internet, and then I think perhaps we did it again with games. Here are natural languages of interaction and natural spaces in which people are experiencing two-way structures. That's very much linked to developments in visual art in the last 15 years with artists who are interested in social structures and social interactions.

Ju Row Far, who is one of the three artists in our company, went to Goldsmiths College, University of London, at the same time as the YBA [Young British Art] generation, so her lineage is very much through a visual art trajectory. She brought an awareness of Sophie Calle, Christian Boltanski's work and thinking about how you might make work which is elusive in some way, or invites different forms of participation. We were strongly influenced by Boltanski's *Children In Search of Their Parents*, a work in which he handed out flyers with pictures of children at a railway station asking people to get in touch if you had seen them. He was very interested in how memory, particularly in relation to the Holocaust, would be perpetuated. Those sorts of pieces that were done in the 1980s and early 1990s had a real influence on our work, so that interaction side of it is always important to emphasize. We stepped across those different artistic and cultural trajectories.

So you have a particular ideological, political, social background – a particular ethic?
We've never had an explicitly political agenda that would link back to some of the more self-consciously socialist forms of theatre. We've always had a tremendous interest in interaction, dialogue, what it means to talk and to speak, how you might engage other people in a conversation. Is it possible, in a theatrical context, to engage an audience in conversation? Does that always involve a diminution of what can be said, or is it possible to do it in such a way that your audience can, however collectively, articulate things that have a precision or a specificity or a voice?

How you interact with people around you as you get on and off the bus is perhaps the most political thing you do all day. If you show people respect, care and attention in those minute transactions, in your awareness of your own body space, helping someone get their pushchair onto the bus is actually more political than wearing a badge about the war in Iraq. And yet, talking about that in political terms is to narrow it dramatically. How that manifests itself in the work we're making is in that set of interests.

An interest in strangers and how you deal with strangers can be seen way back in our work. It's very strong in *Kidnap* (1998), where we put two strangers into a room together for 48 hours, videoed them and streamed their interaction. Then it's incredibly strong in *Uncle Roy All Around You* (2003), *Day of the Figurines* (2006) and *Rider Spoke* (2007) – thinking about how we, as artists, interact with strangers who are simultaneously our audience, and how, when you bring an audience into a space, they are strangers to each other.

We've also made a number of less well-known works that are highly interactive, but that operate either without technology or with much less technology. *Route 12:36* was a commission for the South London Gallery. We were invited to make an interactive project for two bus routes, which ended up being a series of four posters that went up on buses with a question and an 0800 free-phone number. One of us manned the 0800 number for two weeks, picking up the phone and having a conversation with whoever called. The questions were things like, 'How do you watch people without them knowing?' 'Is there someone you saw once who you've never forgotten?' We'd have a conversation with the caller and record it. We still have all the recordings. At the time, we took the decision that we would make them private, and that's always been an interesting discussion for our work. We're having it right now with *Rider Spoke*, where we've already got several thousand recordings of people out in the city. But, this time, we've been very explicit in saying we would like the option to allow people to access these in the future.

There's a very strong ethical demand in what we do. If I ask you a question, then the context in which I ask it and your expectation of what I'm going to do with your answer determines everything. For that reason, even though the *Route 12:36* project had these beautiful recordings, we've never published them, because you can't renegotiate afterwards. At the moment that person rings, what holds true then has to hold true for perpetuity. That's one of the biggest challenges. Of course, people are being drawn into specious interactions all the time, and theatre has a long and noble tradition of bullshit-style interaction and shameless exploitation of people's trust and that sort of stuff.

Is your interest in the public and private realms the reason why you site a lot of your work in the city?
Yes, it is, but there are a whole bundle of strands of interest there. Clearly, there's a long tradition of work taking place in urban spaces. Although I never saw it, *You – The City* by Fiona Templeton was the most amazing idea for me and was always an inspiration in terms of how you might stage work within urban spaces. It's not clearly understood where the line begins and ends between representation and reality. That's another strong thread that you can see through our work – between the real and the virtual, between the fictional and the imaginary as different categories of knowledge or understanding of osmosis-ridden zones, and how you can leech backwards and forwards between the different places.

A big part of our interest in the city was about the use of mobile devices. Around 1999, we were touring *Desert Rain*, which took 10 tonnes of equipment on an articulated lorry to tour, and we thought there must be a better way to do this. At that same time, we realized that mobile phones were a completely different category of technology and that they were, in fact, cultural devices. I went to a couple of conferences in 2000 and was introduced to the idea that these phones would always be connected to the network, and that phones would be Internet devices. It occurred to me immediately that this was a new cultural space that was opening up. At the same time, the whole discussion at these conferences was around marketing and new commercial opportunities, and we saw an opportunity to make an insertion into this debate. There's a whole bunch of other things going on when you start having phones that work in this way. At the same time, we also found GPS, this military technology that tracks you wherever you are on the surface of the earth, hypothetically. These devices have tremendous potential.

When you, as a company, started to view those new technologies as a potential conceptual space in which to make work, was it their ability to connect people that interested you?

I think the original insight was that phones are social things. They're not technical platforms. They're not games devices. They're not productivity enhancement aids. They're actually about how you talk. Sadie Plant's writing[8] was always eye-opening in terms of her articulation of these things very early on, and her persuasive arguments that, for example, the mobile phone privatizes the phone book. To have someone in your phone book is a symbol of social transaction. If I give you my mobile number, I give you a direct line to me, more or less, 24 hours a day.

They impact on face-to-face conversation, too. If I do that (*places mobile phone on table*) as we sit down to talk, I've just sent quite a powerful message, and if I do this (*picks up mobile phone and looks at its screen*) I'm sending another powerful message. You know, that sense that we could be sitting here talking like this and then all of a sudden I could be in that corner with my back to you in about a two- or three-second gap. A lot of people would do that without even breathing a word to you. And I don't say that and mean 'How rude'. That's just a new shift.

Amongst a whole host of subtle changes, we began asking what's being gained and what's being lost? How are we changing the ways in which we talk to one another? How could theatre respond to these kinds of fundamental transformations? A performance space is the worst possible place to be trying to do that. It's antithetical in every way to the nature of the technologies that you're interested in.

Because people are now more used to interacting from afar, does that mean that they are more willing to accept interactive art, rather than sitting passively in a theatre?
I think we're in the middle of a major, seismic realignment of how people engage with culture. Television-viewing is about to fall off the edge of a cliff. Among people under the age of 20, it already has, and broadcasters can't understand it but they're scared by it. You've got to appreciate that participation and interaction are what those people want to do. They don't want to be sitting at home watching a TV programme. They want to be directly engaging with that TV programme. Why would you want to watch a clipped comedy programme when there are 25,000 comedy clips on YouTube and you can take your pick, or watch ones your friends have suggested and passed on to you? None of us really understand whether that's a fad, or how profound that is. You could see it as deterioration in cultural attention, a kind of snack food perspective. I would say it just reflects the way in which we live our life. People's lives are crammed with multiple interactions via multiple media, with varying forms of negotiation and interaction. Culture surely has to respond to that.

Do you think there's an interactivity backlash going on in some corners?
I think it's to do with the hugely generic term 'interactivity', because it is, essentially, meaningless. Everyone can be 'interactive'. It's all a question of degree, and it all gets lost in a big soup. Which brings me back to that question – in what way are you levelling the perspective between the speaker and the spoken to? Brian Eno[9] said a nice thing about interactive work – that, by definition, it has to be unfinished. And what's nice about that is that it speaks very precisely to the way in which you are actually giving up control. This is why the Labour Party struggles with people power because, actually, it's quite hard to do and artists are no different.

Do you give up control to the extent that people can start speaking within your work and say, 'This is pretentious, I fucking hate this'? How do you deal with that? Do you try and exculpate that from the work because that kind of comment is completely destructive? Or do you say, 'OK, if someone wants to say that, then let's have the discussion and that comment can sit alongside someone else's who's completely into it'? Where do you set those boundaries? And we wrestle with that all the time.

How do you, as a company, deal with that? I make interactive work for club spaces and you might get a very positive response, or you might get a punch in the face. That is the great risk in creating interactive work.
The city is similar. It's an inherently chaotic and entropic space where anything you set up and try to control will inevitably get screwed around

Illustration 6.2   *Rider Spoke* (2007) by Blast Theory in Collaboration with the Mixed Reality Lab, University of Nottingham
[Copyright: Blast Theory]

with. And, of course, with the technologies we work with, there is always the risk of dysfunction. Go through a tunnel, take your GPS inside – it doesn't work. You have to make work that can trade off that unpredictability and chaotic nature. The other thing that we've found is that people often will have incredibly powerful experiences within our work but it's not visible to anyone else. That sense of how you make that visible not just to us but to each other has been a critical part of the work we've made.

Rider Spoke has been an interesting journey in terms of those questions. How do you make the public private and the private public? How do you enable people to control that? What kind of threshold do you set to enable people to come in and listen? In *Rider Spoke*, you cannot come in and listen until you've spoken (see Illustration 6.2). We make that simple threshold that you're not allowed to just come and surf around in here, clicking and listening. You have to put yourself on the line and therefore you understand that everyone's done it, and that sets the tone for the discussion.

Illustration 6.3 *Can You See Me Now?* **(2001) by Blast Theory in Collaboration with the Mixed Reality Lab, University of Nottingham**
[Copyright: Blast Theory]

Would you say that play and interactivity are intimately linked?
That's why we started working with computer games. We realized that here is the fundamental language of interaction. A three-year-old kid understands how to play a game. We don't have to make up a new thing. You can employ a series of modes and icons that are totally familiar.

Desert Rain, originally, and *Can You See Me Now?* (see Illustration 6.3) are simple game structures. In *Desert Rain*, you go into space and look around until you find someone. In *Can You See Me Now?*, you run around and don't get caught. They are playground-type games which are then threaded through with other sorts of concerns. Games will come to be seen as a central part of cultural engagement because of interaction.

Where do you see the future of interactivity and technological interaction heading?
In terms of our work, it's hard to say. We consciously don't try to plan more than a few months ahead. We're at a stage now where we are kind of established. Our ability to continue to make work into the next year or two is secure. The danger is that people settle and it ossifies a little. While having a body of work where one piece relates to another is a real satisfaction, we

always want to be open to the possibility that a tangent can be the best possible way forwards.

Also, when working with interaction, you have to have a very tight iterative process between the technological possibility and the creative desire. We've learnt the hard way that you build something quick and dirty, test it, get feedback from what works, look at where the technology is giving you freedom to manoeuvre, and go that way. We've been collaborating with the University of Nottingham for nearly 11 years now, so they are a major part of our practice. Dialogue with them and other collaborators is a critical part of how we think about what we do. We collaborate regularly with a very wide group of people. For *You Get Me*, which is a piece for the Royal Opera House, we had our first workshop on Saturday working with the community in Mile End, who are connected to the park in some way. There, we've got 17-year-old local kids on an animation course through to postgraduates in their 20s. They will set the context in which that work unfolds. So, it's all of those collaborations that determine those iterations.

It's also true of interactive work that, until the day you first launch it, you don't know what you've got. The first few weeks of a new work are a massive effort of constantly reworking and reworking and reworking. That's a tremendously high risk. We premiered *Rider Spoke* last year at the Barbican. On the first night, eight or 10 traditional theatre reviewers from the broadsheet newspapers came and gave us an absolute kicking, partly because it wasn't polished in the way they wanted, and partly because they couldn't make head nor tail of it, and partly because they just didn't have enough experience of work that has that dynamic, and partly because we shouldn't have premiered it in such a high-profile way. We won't do that again!

You have to be quite a centred person, I would imagine, to do the kind of work you do. You can't be too precious.
It's why collaboration is so important to the three of us. It gives us the strength to take those risks and the strength to deal with it. That's why we've enjoyed collaborating so much, because all three of us, for different reasons, need it.

6.3 Interactivity: functions and risks

Alice O'Grady

The type of interactive theatre discussed by Somers in section 6.1 is very much rooted in pedagogy. The function of a piece of interactive theatre is, by necessity, carefully articulated, defined and linked to an explicit peda-gogical purpose. The intention of a piece which, for example, attempts to bring about a change in attitude in its audience members will be planned and worked though with learning objectives and educational aims from the start. The goal here is to engage the audience members in an interac-tive experience for which they feel partly responsible. This follows the Brechtian tradition of finding the antidote to 'culinary theatre', where audiences are seduced by illusion and ultimately dispossessed of their crit-ical faculties (Brecht 1964: 89) and, as such, associates itself with politics rooted in the Marxist tradition.

Whilst not steeped in an explicitly political agenda, Matt Adams expresses a similar commitment to meaning-making which has an ideolog-ical basis closely linked to Somers' notions of interactivity. For Blast Theory, meaning-making is a process not confined to the artist. They seek to involve wide audiences in the construction of meaning. Their subject matter asks what it means to talk, to speak, to converse, to engage in dialogue. Their search is to find appropriate forms for that type of ques-tioning to take place. If, like Blast Theory, you are interested in the signif-icance of dialogue, then you need to find dialogic forms in order to explore it. For practitioners working with interactivity, form and content are inter-connected. This interconnection is consciously constructed and applied to achieve both artistic and political results.

In this section, I consider some key philosophical issues in relation to interactive performance, identifying common factors in the two perspec-tives presented by Somers and Adams.

Interactivity and performance

In contemporary practice, much interactive performance is technologi-cally facilitated. However, interaction is primarily a psychological phenomenon, rather than a technical one. Robert Wechsler is a choreogra-pher who specializes in live performance and motion tracking, but he is at pains to point out the fundamental characteristics of interaction from which technological developments spring:

> One certainly does not need cameras and computers to be interactive. Interactivity is simply the instinctive back and forth energy which occurs when animals come together to speak, gesture, touch, or, in the case of humans, create art. (Wechsler 2006: 63)

It can, of course, be argued that an audience is never completely passive, regardless of whether the work that they are watching is described as 'interactive' or not. A performance only becomes a performance in the presence of an audience:

> in the theatre, due to the live presence of both spectators and perform-ers, the energy circulates from performer to spectator and back again, from spectator to performer and back again (McAuley 2000: 246)

In other words, even if an audience's side of the interaction is largely silent, there is still an integral reciprocity in the relationship between audience and live performer. Communication and exchange is implicit in their pres-ence there together, engaging in and sharing the experience. The extent to which that sense of interactivity is prioritized or made visible, however, is variable. Undoubtedly, interactive performance manifests itself in many ways and uses varying means to shape the exchanges that may take place. It might range from intensely physical performance such as De La Guarda's *Villa Villa* through to Paul Sermon's highly technical series of telematic works which he began in the early 1990s with *Telematic Dreaming* (1992) and continues to develop today.[10] As Popat points out:

> In interactive artworks the power given to the audience is far greater, and they are made aware of its existence. If the communication between artists(s) and viewers is to be two-way with mutual effect, then the focus of the artwork shifts. Instead of a completed product, the interactive artist designs a framework that contains the potential for the creative experience of the participant. (Popat 2006: 34)

Whatever shape it may take, for interactive work the artist is responsible for creating the structure, the framework, the environment within which the participant plays. However, the input of the participant, or the dialogue to which he or she contributes, is a central element of the work itself. The performance receives a greater proportion of its meaning from the audience, and audience participation becomes vital to the content of it. Interactivity is therefore a mechanism through which the distinctions between artist and audience may be blurred. Both parties are co-creators in the work, breaking down the boundaries between the roles (Barry 1996: 139).

In a performance setting, there exists the potential for a number of different channels of interaction. Interaction may occur between artists, between artists and audience, between audience members, and between the artist or audience member and a computer system. In addition, inter-action can be understood as existing on a continuum. Performance theo-rist and practitioner, Steve Dixon (2007: 563) offers four categories of interaction that indicate varying depths of engagement and, in relation to digital performance, 'user' intervention. At one end of the continuum is *navigation*, where users may respond to simple 'yes' or 'no' binaries, steer themselves through a narrative or, in the case of the Internet, 'surf' a computer system. The second category is *participation*, literally a 'joining in', where audiences might vote, input ideas or respond to the action without altering it significantly. The next level is *conversation*. This category provides the opportunity for genuine dialogue, reciprocity and two-way exchange within the artwork. The fourth and final category in the continuum is *collaboration*. Here, the framework of interactivity allows audience members or users to alter the artwork to the point that they become co-authors of the outcome and intended meaning. As Söke Dinkla (2002) puts it, at this end of the interactivity spectrum, highly flexible, open practice may be conceived as a 'floating work of art' – in other words, one which resists fixity.

Interactive performance is always incomplete

In a similar vein to Dixon's technological categorization of interactivity, academic and educationist Jonothan Neelands offers a continuum of theatrical engagement that he calls the 'Scale of Formal Participation' (2000). Here, he charts six degrees of participation which range from the total immersion of 'players' who are both physically and psychically engaged in the dramatic action through to the passivity and privacy of the individual 'observer' hidden within the darkened auditorium. Consider where you would place the examples of practice in sections 6.1 and 6.2 on Dixon's continuum. This is a key issue for makers of contemporary performance. How much of the performance can be predetermined, and how much can be left open, unfinished or incomplete?

In interactive theatre, performances are usually planned or structured in a very tight manner, but with creative gaps to allow for interaction to take place. These creative gaps are places in which the audience members are able to insert or implicate themselves in how the drama then unfolds. In this sense, interaction is intervention by the audience. The piece often stops at the climax and the audience are then asked to work out a resolution for the characters in the manner of Boal's Forum Theatre, for instance. The work cannot progress without audience involvement. However, it is usually a particular kind of interaction that is sought and the next step of the work will be known once the creative gap has been closed.

In work with a less defined or prescriptive outcome, large elements of the work will remain unknown until the audience have begun to engage.

A company might not know exactly what they have until performers and audience come together in conversation. Parts of the work may be impossible to rehearse, and certainly the outcome will be difficult to predict. With that comes notions of risk. Anything flexible or open runs the risk of collapse. Beryl Graham describes the nature of the artist's role:

> The skills needed by artists if they are to truly loosen control over the audience, but still share their pleasure, are perhaps less like the traditional art skills, and more like the social interaction skills of 'throwing a good party'. (Graham 1996: 171)

However, what happens when you have gatecrashers or plates start to get smashed? At what point do you lock the door and call the police? Within interactive performance, there is a constant negotiation between maintaining a structure and allowing for fluidity. When you invite people into your home, your space, your performance, you cannot always legislate for how they might behave or what they might do. If you invite people to play with you, there has to be some negotiation of rules. Undoubtedly, interactive work requires flexible structures, flexible performers and flexible spaces – it is this flexibility and risk-laden dimension which makes it dynamic for participants, performers, observers alike.

Interactivity in practice

From the outset, in section 6.1 of this chapter, John Somers establishes his belief that theatre has a duty to stimulate deeper thinking about the meaning of human existence. For him, the theatre is a debating chamber where we work out together our understanding of the world and how it might be imagined or shaped differently, and ultimately transformed. 'Interactive theatre' in this context offers an active way for performers and audience members to question and re-assemble that world in a process that Dixon would define as *collaborative*.

From a pedagogical angle, the clear function of interactive theatre is to bring about some kind of change or new awareness in the participants. This change is made more effective and lasting by the experiential quality of the interaction. Whilst framed by fiction, the exchanges that take place are authentic. Rather than merely bearing witness to unfolding events that are kept at a distance by theatrical architecture and convention, audience members are encouraged to talk to the characters, to question them, to engage physically with them. They are able to alter events as they happen. They are encouraged to change the direction of the fiction and to become co-authors of the outcome. For Somers, this is achieved through narrative, and he prioritizes story and story-making as the heart of this particular practice. The audience achieves an intimacy with the characters of the fiction through involvement, which may be physical, emotional and/or intellectual. Through their interaction with the performers, the audience begins to care for the characters and, ultimately, take responsibility for them and their course of action within the story. Audiences invest in the story and implicate themselves in it. Straightaway, we can begin to see a tension that creates the basic dynamic of interactive work of this kind. The exchanges are genuine but operate within the given circumstances of the fiction. Often, participants will bring their own experiences to bear on the situation. Thus, the relationship between real events and fictional ones is integral to how the issue is dealt with, and needs careful handling by facilitators.

Matt Adams of Blast Theory also expresses interest in the tensions between the real and virtual and the flow between these two states, albeit in very different terms. Whilst many participants of Blast Theory's work may well be teenagers, the company is not working within an educational context, and so are able to problematize and play with these concepts a little more freely. In *Uncle Roy All Around Me* (2003) and *Can You See Me Now?* (2001), Adams talks about the relationship between people playing live on the streets and those playing online. The very structure of the performance invites participants accessing it through their computers to ask how real are these people? How much can I mess around with them? What is real and what is fictional?

From this, the question of ethics arises. Somers states clearly the need for clarifying the distinction between the real and the fictional in his particular context, whereas for Adams this blurriness is to be embraced. In a pedagogical setting, there is the need for sensitivity and care when dealing with issues which may have personal implications. There may be the need for follow-up support, debriefing and so on. Adams talks about the political dimension of how we take 'care' of others in our everyday interactions on the street. Notions of respect, trust, responsibility and care are reiterated by both authors. For Adams, this is linked also to the documentation of work and how interactions might be framed. If you draw someone into an interaction, you need to be clear about how that conversation might be used later. How do you make private interactions visible? Should you? The ethical considerations when creating interactive work are multiple and change according to context.

A further challenge for interactive work concerns audience size. Somers talks about facilitating exchanges between, typically, smaller audience groups. Even then, he points out that someone sitting several rows back will have a significantly different experience from someone sitting in the first row who may feel more connected physically to the unfolding drama. Adams talks about the problem of sharing exchanges with much larger groups and concludes that new technologies, the Internet and other forms of mass communication are obvious spaces in which to attempt that. In both cases, the imperative to interact comes first: the methods of interaction are developed to fulfil that intention but the process is iterative, cyclical and self-propagating. To engage in debate means to allow for two-way exchanges. What form might that take in the theatre? What methodologies can be developed to facilitate that in a meaningful way? Certainly, there is a fine line that one must walk between artistry and efficacy (that is, positive social/political effect, or influence upon the audience member). This is a particular challenge for interactive work when the aesthetic is often open to disruption or intervention by an audience member, and the efficacy of a piece is not always easily seen, documented or proven.

Spaces of interactivity

Any work that involves interactivity is, by its very nature, going to blur and bring into question the relationship between audience and performer. Most artists engaged in interactive performance practice are fundamentally interested in challenging assumptions about the role of audience and the role of artist, and in breaking down barriers and divides between them. Interactive practice brings into question the hierarchies of performance structures and social structures too. This challenge to hierarchy is most clearly visible in spatial terms.

For Somers, the educational focus of interactive theatre means that more active involvement via experiential learning will lead to greater understanding. Here, the interactive space is democratic where actors and participants work collaboratively to reach a resolution. There is a certain flow between auditorium and stage where audience members are encouraged to breach verbally or physically any concept of a 'fourth wall'. Both Somers and Adams express interest in spaces which operate horizontally rather than vertically, where participants can move across spaces with more freedom than the physically restricted zone of the traditional theatre auditorium. As Baz Kershaw (1999: 52) says, 'within the theatre's walls, consumption of theatre is increasingly an abdication of authority and a relinquishing of power'. By arranging space differently, interactive practice blends the playing space of the theatrical experience with the everyday space of participants' existence. For Blast Theory, this translates often into situating work in urban spaces where daily life continues as the performance work unfolds.

For interactive theatre, participants are asked to bring their own experience and understanding to bear on the drama as it progresses and illusion is kept to a minimum.

Interactive work changes our understanding of playing space, both in terms of the theatre building as playhouse and performers as players. Cultural interest in play has developed exponentially over the past few decades, and performance practices reflect that growing field. The development of new technologies means we can play around with the parameters of our existence in new and interesting ways. We can go further than ever before in asking how rule-bound we want our playing spaces to be. Blast Theory consciously uses play structures and gaming models to inform their work. As Adams says, games are already invested with the fundamental language of interaction. Certainly, we learn through play – but we learn also through breaking rules and testing the limits of any given structure. There is a subversive, dark edge to much play which is one of the motivating facets of interaction. If interactive work can be seen as an invitation to play, perhaps the most fascinating questions to ask are: 'By whose rules are we playing?' and 'To what extent are those rules open to negotiation?'

Conclusion

The discussion in this chapter has centred around the notion of interactivity – how it pervades our language and shapes our expectations of how we might experience varying forms of media, mass communication and performance. By placing the pedagogical work of interactive theatre alongside the largely technological practice of Blast Theory, we can begin to draw parallels and distinctions between Boal's notion of the 'spect-actor' and the concept of what we might call the 'inter-actor'. To create interactive work, one has to be committed to the potential creativity of the state of being 'inbetween'. This liminal space is a slippery area of unpredictability, uncertainty and movement. It has clear implications for artists who want to make work that is flexible and dynamic, but that does not run the risk of total collapse.

By prioritizing audience involvement, one is making a statement about the very nature of meaning-making. To offer open frameworks that allow for audience intervention and collaboration, performance itself becomes a vehicle for co-authorship. It begins to function as a challenge to hierarchical structures and reflects the increased instances of horizontally organized systems as characterized by the Internet. In this sense, the performance structures or forms that we choose to employ for the purposes of interactivity become intimately connected to the attitudes that inform the content of the work.

Considering the model of circularity from Berlo and Dixon's continuum from navigation to collaboration, you should now be able to analyze how those systems operate in practice and in relation to particular performance pieces that you may have experienced or made. How can we use these theoretical frameworks to inform our own practice? The categories of inter-action and participation discussed in this chapter give us new methods for considering not only the form and content of performance, but also the function, efficacy and effect it may have on an audience. Whilst gaining control over and developing new methods by which interaction may be achieved is essential, understanding the social, cultural and theatrical implications of interactivity is the intellectual imperative that drives the work.

Activities

At the beginning of this chapter, we noted that 'interactivity' is becoming a ubiq-uitous term in our technologically-enhanced society. Its frequent – and often inaccurate – usage is in danger of devaluing the philosophies that underpin interactive processes.

➤ *Solo activity*

Begin to pay attention to the use of the word 'interactive'. Make a note over the course of one week each time you encounter this term. Become attuned to where, when and how this key word is applied. Start to unpick who is using the term, whether it is being applied appropriately, and to what end it is being used in various contexts.

One of the key concepts arising from interactive processes is the need for flexibility, degrees of uncertainty and unpredictable outcomes. Söke Dinkla (2002: 28) has described interactive work as 'a floating work of art'. Such work requires a level of risk-taking, and potentially puts the participants (performers and audi-ence members) in a vulnerable position. Somers and Adams both refer to social and ethical issues in relation to interactive work, and Adams also points out some of the aesthetic issues associated with shared ownership in the creative process.

➤ *Discussion activity*

- Consider the implications of interactive performance for:
  - ○ performance practitioners;
  - ○ audience members.
- What might be the purpose(s) for employing interactivity as a strategy?
- What might it enable you to achieve?
- What might be the drawbacks?

Having considered the nature of interactivity and its implications, benefits and challenges in the discussion activity, now try exploring how you would put this into practice.

➤ *Practical activity*

In preparation for this group activity, choose a scripted play with which you are all familiar. It is important to work with a text that would normally be staged with little explicit interaction between performer and audience. Plays by Arthur Miller, Caryl Churchill, Edward Bond or Mark Ravenhill would be suitable examples but there are, of course, many more.

Sketch out a plan for an interactive performance based on this text which attempts any or all of Steve Dixon's four categories of interaction (2007: 563), as discussed in the last part of this chapter:

1 navigation
2 participation
3 conversation
4 collaboration

Dixon applies these categories to technological interaction, but they are useful terms that can be applied to all interactive work. Thinking through these categories might help us to determine what an interactive work might look like, and how it might operate.

Remember that these categories may blur, overlap and intersect.

- Take one scene from your chosen text and rehearse it in a manner suitable for presentation in a proscenium theatre.
- Now rework it in the studio, opening and loosening its form to make it 'interactive'.
- Play the two versions side by side.
- How do the two versions differ? How does each version provide a different experience for audience and performer?
- What new discoveries did you make by working with the text in this way?

Having gone through and analyzed the practical activity, now consider the following three questions:

- What can be gained from using interactive strategies within performance work?
- What are the challenges and benefits in creating interactive work, which requires practitioners to loosen a fixed theatrical structure in order to make room for audience intervention?
- How does the notion of risk infiltrate interactive work, and what are the ultimate pay-offs in terms of engagement and collaborative meaning-making?

Notes

1   For more on Boal, see, for example, Babbage (2004).
2   For more information on one-to-one performance, see Rachel Zerihan's 'Study Room Guide', provided online by the Live Art Development Agency at www.thisisliveart.co.uk
3   For a definiton of Boal's Joker, see Babbage (2004: 142–3); for a detailed description, read Boal's 'Need for the Joker' and 'Structures of the Joker' (1979: 167–90).
4   It is called a 'programme', not a performance, play or 'show' because the performance element is only one phase of a multi-phase structure that comprises a range of pedagogic and dramatic approaches.
5   For further discussion of the pedagogic uses of interactive theatre, see Gallagher and Booth (2003). For a comprehensive guide to the varying techniques and conventions utilized in drama education, see Neelands (1991).
6   School students who were to experience a reconstruction of the events on the roof of a Croydon warehouse that led to the death of a policeman were invited by letter to attend the procedure, and were given certain witness statements and trial exhibits. This programme dealt with the infamous Craig and Bentley murder trial of 1952 that resulted in Derek Bentley's hanging. In 1998, the Court of Appeal set aside his conviction for murder.
7   This was the opening scene in the performance element of an interactive theatre programme I made recently in the Czech Republic. The facilitator persuaded the protagonist to stay her action and to tell/show us the events that had led her to this state.
8   Sadie Plant is a British author and philosopher, and founded the Cybernetic Culture Research Unit at the University of Warwick. She left the University of Warwick in 1997 to write full time.
9   Brian Eno is an English musician, composer, record producer, music theorist, singer and visual artist, best known as one of the principal innovators of ambient music (AllMusic, Explore Music, 'Ambient').
10 For more examples of interactive art works and a detailed discussion of how these pieces are constructed, see Dixon (2007): ch. 6.

Further reading

Boal, Augusto (1979) *Theatre of the Oppressed*, (trans. Charles A. and Maria-Odilia Leal McBride). London: Pluto Press.
Bolter, Jay David and Gromala, Diane (2003) *Windows and Mirrors: Interactive Art, Digital Design and the Myth of Transparency*. Cambridge, MA: MIT Press.
Creeber, Glen and Martin, Royston (2009) *Digital Cultures: Understanding New Media*. Maidenhead: Open University Press.
Dixon, Steve (2007) *Digital Performance: A History of New Media in Theatre, Dance, Performance Art and Installation*. Cambridge, MA: MIT Press.
Jackson, Anthony (2007) *Theatre, Education and the Making of Meanings*. Manchester: Manchester University Press.

7   Organization

Introduced and edited by Calvin Taylor

Introduction

One of the major intellectual contributions made by performance as a discipline within the arts is the explicit role it ascribes to the forms and processes of organization. This is explicit, for example, in the emphasis on collaboration in performance; perhaps more implicit in the roles of, for example, direction and text; and more implicit still in the ways in which we can say that performances organize their reception by audiences. This idea of organization *within* performance is an important topic of this chapter. It looks at the different senses in which performance is an organized creative activity, and explores the practical and intellectual implications of this.

As you have already seen in earlier chapters, performance is an unusual discipline in that it explicitly embraces an inter-disciplinary perspective, drawing on ideas, constructs and processes typically associated with other fields. Whilst, at its extreme, this can make performance look borderless, what it does is give performance a refined sense of its dual existence as both a discipline and practice on the one hand, and as a way of looking at the world outside its own immediate concerns on the other. Alongside the idea of organization within performance, this chapter is also interested in how performance itself exists within larger systems of organization, and the perspectives that performance might bring to our understanding of them.

So, in what ways is performance 'organized'? Perhaps the simplest way to think about this is to imagine a visit to the theatre. This demands organization. Who has the tickets? How are we getting there? Do we know where we are going? Do we know what time the performance begins? This experience is dominated by organizational considerations even before it has begun – and then, at 19.30 precisely, the curtain rises, the stage is set, a figure walks on, the performance begins and another set of organizational considerations come into play.

This apparently simple familiar scenario contains the major senses in which performance and organization are connected. The first is that, in a very practical sense, performance is an organized activity. Staging a production brings together performers, a script or choreography (in most cases), a location (typically a theatre, but not always) and an audience. All of these practical elements are organized. Their interactions with each other are planned and orchestrated. That organization can be more or less detailed (and may even include elements of spontaneous self-organization) but, however they come together, we can call that process a *process* of organization.

This attention to how characters present themselves invokes another important connection between performance and organization. Performers organize their bodies to work in certain ways. This process of embodiment is one of the most fundamental ways in which performance organization can be said to be a *structured* process. The ordering of the body (flesh, muscle) and its movement in patterned and structured ways represents a second sense in which we can say performance is organized. Actors and dancers typically train for many years to establish the level of control and organization required to perform. What can seem to us in the audience to be the most natural of movements may very well have taken years to perfect.

The presence of a text or choreography brings another sense of organization. Scripts contain both narrative and vision – providing an unfolding structure within which the action takes place. The script may specify time, place, duration, character, the plot – all of which not only organize the practical action, but also contain important information that helps to organize the audience's understanding of and participation in the performance. This sense of organization, which contains both process and structure, is the dramaturgical organization of performance.

Performance is also spatially organized. The performance space is organized in two ways. First, it is organized as a material space. The physical construction of the performance space has important organizational characteristics. What size is the performance space? Is it enclosed? Is it open? Where does the action take place? How does the audience view it? From where do they view it – above or on the same level, for example? As has been argued in earlier chapters, this material organization of the performance space has important implications for another kind of organization. How the actors and the audience relate to one another is an important social *interaction* that is inscribed within the material organization of the space. Are the actors and the audience kept separate? Do they inhabit the same space? Are there physical barriers between them? Can they physically interact? These kinds of relationships shift and change, both as we move between different kinds of performance activity, and historically as performance itself evolves and changes.

This sense of performance as a socially structured activity introduces us to the second sense in which performance and organization are connected. Performance as a cultural practice is organized into discrete sets of artistic forms. A few common ones are durational performance, site-specific performance and immersive performance, each of which possesses its own artistic values, models and typical ways of working. Genres and styles also change over time – some may disappear altogether, whilst other new ones appear and develop. At any one time, there may be dominant genres representing a norm or orthodoxy, whilst others depart from such norms – possibly in a self-conscious rejection of them, as in many of the performance genres that contributed to the modernist and postmodernist movements in Western cultural history.

These critical considerations are important for another aspect of performance as an organized activity. Performance depends on resources, even if, as is often the case, the only resource is the body of the performer. However, even that requires organization. More typically, performance requires a complex assemblage of resources and their management. Over time, these activities of organizing resources have developed into an important activity. The theatre company typically requires funding, marketing, promotion, contract negotiations (with venues, actors, directors) and the ability to pay its bills. Historically, this takes many forms, but each has important impacts upon the ways in which performance is organized. For example, what effects might funding have on the production of performance when its source is the state, compared with, say, private patronage or business sponsorship? On the contemporary performance scene, organizations are being encouraged to reduce their reliance on public funds and draw in funds from ticket sales and secondary merchandizing, such as the sale of souvenirs, refreshments and programmes. This raises a set of critical questions about the function and purpose of performance in society, which, in turn, prompts equally critical questions about the most appropriate way to support it?

We can see even from this brief review that we have a number of ways in which the word 'organization' is being deployed in relation to performance. We can see pre-performance organization – both by the producers of the performance and the audience. We can see the dramaturgical organization of the elements of the performance itself – the role of the script, for example. We also have the scenographic organization of the performance space itself, which has important implications for the organization of the relationship between the performance, the performers and the audience. And all of those things depend upon the existence of a performance organization, its funding, marketing and management. In summary: first, we can see organization as a process – bringing different elements together to make a whole. Second, we can see it as a structure that underpins complex phenomena, for example, the development and evolution of a cultural practice; and, third, we can see it as an entity; for example, the theatre company as an organization. Organization as process, structure and entity are not mutually exclusive. The American sociologist Howard Becker uses the term 'art world' to describe the culturally, socially and economically integrated ways in which artistic practice is developed and art produced. He describes this process in the following eloquent terms:

> All artistic work, like all human activity, involves the joint activity of a number, often a large number, of people. Through their co-operation, the art work we eventually see or hear comes to be and continues to be. The work always shows signs of that co-operation. The forms of co-operation may be ephemeral, but often become more or less routine, producing patterns of collective activity we can call an art world. (Becker 1982:1)

In this chapter, we examine the ways in which performance and organization relate to one another to produce performance 'art worlds'. In section 7.1, Ralph Brown expands this discussion of the ways in which performance is organized by reference to recent thinking about the cultural and creative industries, ideas which originate in the UK, but which are now global in significance. They are important because they foreground new thinking about the principles of organization, and have particular implications for the art worlds of performance. Section 7.2 draws on the work and experience of the performance practitioner and consultant Teo Greenstreet, to examine how performance and organization interact with important implications for how we think of organization more broadly. In particular, he explains how different ideas about organization draw upon critical performance concepts to have an application to worlds beyond the immediate field of performance. In section 7.3, I reflect on the arguments raised in the two preceding sections through an exploration of·the theoretical heritage that has drawn performance and organization together over a period of approximately one hundred years. I explain how an explicit focus on the relationship between performance and organization raises important questions about how key social and economic activities are performatively – and culturally – inscribed.

7.1   Performance, culture, industry

Ralph Brown

The idea that the arts are somehow not about serious business, that they are frivolous or insignificant, was a commonly held view among politicians in the UK during the 1980s. This view is much less widely held now. What has become known as the 'creative industries' (Hartley 2005) has been recognized over the past decade as a distinctive and increasingly important area of the economy across the world. In the UK, for example, in the 1990s, the arts were incorporated within the remit of the British government's Department for Culture, Media and Sport (DCMS), and considered as a major leisure industry on a par with hospitality and tourism. As defined and promoted by the DCMS, the creative industry sector is the fastest growing professional sector in the UK (Department for Culture, Media and Sport 2008). Like the tourist industry, the creative sector is regarded as needing national and local government support and direction. It is also required to be driven by market forces. Arts organizations are now expected to operate like competitive commercial businesses. At the same time, they have to respond to the conditions that are attached to grant aid or sponsorship that involves the state and/or business defining and shaping concepts of 'art' by selecting who or what to subsidize (Holden 2007).

The current political and policy frameworks which have championed the creative industries are contested and challenged by many commentators and artists (O'Connor 2008). Most criticism tends to focus on an apparent change in language that has occurred in the UK over the last 20 years which appears to exclude or restrict the defining role of the artist. As a result of the introduction of 'value for money' economics and political agendas, priorities in the arts can appear to have moved away from the more experimental, provocative or controversial work towards more culturally and commercially 'safe' work. Critics of the concept of a 'cultural industry' also tend to highlight a perceived shift away from the historical emphasis on original creation towards the marketing and selling of a product. The current state of London theatre is vigorously debated – is it booming (mainly from ticket sales for high-profile musicals), or has the quest for 'blockbuster success' squeezed out the more modest hit, restricting the chances of a 'straight' play running in the West End without a well-known American film actor appearing in it?

Theatre and dance practitioners generally don't tend to view their work as being organized on the model of a core creative industry. Performance activity doesn't usually involve large-scale industrial production or the commercialization and sale of intellectual property that are characteristic of, for example, the music, computer gaming and digital media industries. There is little reproduction involving industrial methods, where the main activity consists of live performances and one-off works. Performance projects and companies are not usually established with the prime motivation of financial success. Tastes and fashions can change rapidly. Audience expectations are unpredictable and company objectives are not, in the main, driven by the pursuit of profit but, rather, more by a desire to be working at the cutting edge and to be creatively dynamic. The French sociologist Bernard Miege (1979) famously draws a distinction between Type 1 cultural products – the one-off, unique work of art, and Type 2 cultural products that are subject to the possibilities of reproduction on a large scale.

Value, assets and returns

In economic terminology, performance is a way of organizing for *value creation*. *Aesthetic value* is central; what economists refer to as *use value* (a commodity that is useful and has the potential to be sold) or *exchange-value* (the commercial price for a product) are subsidiary considerations, if considered at all. Performance art explicitly aims only for a sense of absolute artistic value. The value of a play or performance is also essentially dependent on the audience/consumer finding value in their meanings – value is dependent on audience perception as much as creative content, which may or may not ultimately translate into a commercial return. So, value, as it emerges in an arts organization, can involve a variety of factors – the goals of art itself, the development of identity, or creativity in individual artists, and the reactions of audiences and the investors/stakeholders in the organization, all of which may be quite different from purely economic or monetary value.

While mainstream businesses would typically, first, identify a market, and then produce a product to meet an existing demand, most artists create a work first, then need to cultivate an audience for it. Arts companies – again, unlike other businesses – operate with few tangible assets. For most theatre companies, their main assets take the form of creativity, imagination and individual talent. Companies tend to be small, individualistic, and running them involves a high level of risk. Producing new musical theatre, for example, can be a particularly risky venture. A recent case study of the innovative and controversial British theatre production *Jerry*

Springer: The Opera has analyzed how the team working on this production were able to manage risk, and considers the approaches they were able to use to develop their initial creative ideas into eventual commercial success (Dempster 2006). The producers' approach was to manage the development of the production through a number of iterations before live audiences. After each production, they would examine what worked and what didn't work and then adapt the production, sometimes quite radically, in preparation for the next audience. In this sense, the production was the product of an ever-evolving relationship between the producers and the audience.

In fact, many companies in the cultural and creative industries, especially those within the performance field, actively prefer to keep their organizations small in order to retain their independence and be able to focus on their own creativity. For most people working in performance, the financial rewards from artistic and cultural production tend to be small and are typically unpredictable. Working arrangements can be risky and precarious. It is personal artistic motivation that makes the enterprise worthwhile. There is an element of risk, as in any business, but, in artistic terms, the risk element is on a much more personal level – artists are staking their own individual reputations on an idea or performance. This capacity to take personal risks is one of the characteristics that distinguish the productive artist from the potential artist.

Entrepreneurship then, especially in the arts, isn't necessarily about the financial risks involved in starting a new business, and the possible financial returns, typified by the television series *Dragons' Den*. It can also mean someone taking primary responsibility for the processes of performance organization; for mobilizing people and resources to initiate, give purpose to, develop and manage a new artistic project or organization (Bilton 2007). 'Artist-entrepreneurs' may not necessarily have even set out to start a business, as such. Their main focus may have been on developing their own practice, but they then face a need to come to terms with a financial environment in order to be able to make enough money to continue their artistic work. Alternatively, they may see the commercial market as a means of communicating with a larger audience – which then involves developing the necessary management and organizational skills to facilitate the performance and promotion of their work (for example, organizing touring productions/companies, writing business plans and understanding of copyright and contractual issues). Thus, whilst the performance artist may have had to begin with the processes of performance organization, in order to make their activity sustainable, they will have to address the organizational (financial, critical) structures of performance organization, and that may require the creation of a perform-ance entity. In other words, the ability to perform rests on the existence of a performance art-world and the means to engage with it.

Communities of practice

Freelancing and self-employment are the most frequent types of employ-ment in the arts sector. There are particularly large concentrations of small enterprises and sole traders in music and the performing arts, film, TV and radio. Enterprises tend to remain small-scale because of the creative nature of the activities involved; 'artist-entrepreneurs' need to have control over their creativity and the integration of innovation into their practice. The dance sector, in particular, has a large number of individual solo artists, and dance companies also tend to be small, often touring, companies. The aesthetics of dance and physical theatre performance since the 1980s, and the infrastructure that has supported it, have created more opportunities for small-scale companies and individual artists to flourish. These compa-nies tend to be highly networked, organized as clusters of small companies and freelancers working on a project basis, where teams, partnerships and alliances dissolve and re-form constantly. Artistic communities and what have come to be called 'creative clusters' can promote intense and fruitful rivalry between artists, as well as collaboration. The process of collabora-tion and competition at a local level sometimes also fosters tacit knowl-edge and expertise within a local cluster, stimulating new trends; for example, Acid House, 'Madchester', and the work of the Royal Court Theatre, London.

This relationship between creative practice and organization has been described as artists working in 'communities of practice'. This idea comes from the field of sociology (Wenger 1999). Communities of practice are groups of people who share information, insight, experience, and knowl-edge about an area of common interest. The idea is based on a definition of knowledge that includes tacit knowledge that is shared informally in groups through processes such as storytelling, conversation and coaching or mentoring. The idea of tacit knowledge is based on the philosopher Michael Polanyi's idea that we know more than we can tell, and that it is through sharing practice that we transmit tacit knowledge (Polanyi 1967).[1] In the 'communities of practice' model, individuals self-select into groups that share ideas. They self-select, at least in part, on the basis of whom they like to work with, and whom they can potentially learn from. The greatest value lies in intangible outcomes, such as the relationships they form among people, the sense of belonging they create, the spirit of inquiry they generate, and the professional confidence and identity they confer to their members.

The capacity to broker deals is also especially important. Turning an idea into a performance requires a range of different types of thinking, and could draw upon a variety of specialist expertise – including agents, producers, actors, designers and technicians. Cultural entrepreneurs often need the ability to broker both their own talents and the talents of other people, and rely on informal networks to organize their work. So, while traditional ideas of artistic hierarchies measure success mainly according to performance activity and status or prestige, in reality, artists often work in multiple concurrent roles – perhaps, for example, as creators, producers, designers, retailers and promoters all at the same time (Leadbeater and Oakley 1999).

The substance of the performance itself is intimately connected to the performance organizational processes of making meaning – the interaction between producer, performer and audience through which meaning becomes formed, making sense of our world and its problems, understanding new experiences. This is an interactive process of production/consumption because there is a crucial element of active participation on the part of audience/consumer of performed art. The performance is an activity of communication; for example, between the playwright, the author of an original text, the interpretation of the text by performers, the response of the audience, and the interaction between audience and performers expressed in laughter, applause and sometimes disapproval.

Arts organizations in the past have been characterized by being very producer-centric in the way that they approach their business, their audiences and their external environment. Recent technological changes, social changes, fashions and trends have all undermined that producer-centredness. The music industry, for example, has been transformed from an industry that largely controlled the markets it supplied to an industry that is now predominantly consumer-led. As technology has developed, a new economy has emerged that is rooted in information, connectivity and the virtual world. This has led to shifts in participation as technology has enabled people to become producers, as well as consumers, of art. There has, for example, been a wide range of performances made available on YouTube, as podcasts and even mobile phone programmes. The emergence of new technologies and social media means that digitally promoting yourself is now easier, cheaper and has a vast selection of options. Emerging artists have a closer relationship with their audiences than ever before. The 'digital revolution', making these technologies of reproduction far more accessible to the everyday person, also coincided with what turned out to be the lasting legacy of the 'punk ethos', which stressed above all the 'do it yourself' impulse. Its later manifestation in 'rave culture' during the 1990s had also used technologies in this way – making the technologies of reproduction work for you.

Conclusion

New markets and new business models of distribution in new media are opening up, enabling more artists to work as cultural entrepreneurs themselves, independently and retaining their own copyright. As a result of this process, the cultural industries now tend to be described as cutting-edge, a template for the other organizations to follow in the twenty-first century. Workers in the arts are no longer simply described as eccentric creatives crushed by the wheels of a corporate sector whose values they avowedly challenge and resist as best they can. It is precisely these people who are increasingly being regarded as being in possession of the means to operate most effectively within contemporary social and economic environments. By the 1990s, 'creativity' had emerged as a prominent contemporary value, as an important resource for contemporary economic growth and social development (Seltzer and Bentley 1999). This kind of thinking was reflected in the British government-funded Cox Review of Creativity in Business (Her Majesty's Treasury 2005) and the setting up of the Creative Economy programme under the leadership of the then Creative Industries Minister James Purnell. The focus on creativity has embraced everything from schools to urban regeneration in cities such as Liverpool (the European Capital of Culture in 2008). Creativity has also been seen more broadly as a key model for the development of what has been characterized as the post-industrial 'knowledge' economy. This new economy is seen to be about innovation, creativity, flexibility and responsiveness – many of the qualities on which the arts flourish.

It has been suggested that responding to the challenges of the new economy means not only abandoning traditional organizational structures; it actually requires a wholly new way of thinking about organizational culture. Indeed, commentators have suggested that, without a cultural change involving all the personnel in a particular organization, companies may no longer flexibly compete and respond effectively to wider economic and social changes. The cultural industries are cited as a classic case of the new thinking, where employees are expected to participate in the entire ethos of the company and its goals, giving rise to a management style that could be applied to other types of organization.

The past decade has witnessed a growing interest in the area of working in the arts, alongside increased political and media attention on the creative industries sector, at a time when rapid technological changes have opened up new methods and opportunities for engagement with the arts. At the same time, there has also been a developing field of academic studies of 'cultural work', spanning a range of disciplines outside of the arts themselves, including geography, economics, politics and sociology. Research in this area emphasizes the key ideas discussed in this section of the chapter: the passionate involvement of artists with their work, together with the elements of risk, precariousness and entrepreneurial ways of working (Banks 2007).

Introduction to 7.2

Section 7.1 discussed the ways in which the growing importance of culture and creativity as socially valuable resources has re-designed the relationship between artistic practice, organization and industry. This has, in turn, placed the spotlight on how artistic practice is organized. This asks important questions about how a given form of artistic practice – in our case, performance – may have impacts on the way we think about organization as entity, process and structure. In section 7.1, Ralph Brown showed how we could move from considering performance as a distinct art-world towards thinking about how the performance art-world may have important implications for how we think about organization in other contexts. For example, the proliferation of small-scale entrepreneurial activity in the performance industries can increasingly be seen in other industries. The organizational processes typical of the performance organization – self-organization, self-management, intense collaboration and networking – are rapidly becoming typical of many other kinds of industries and organizations. And, indeed, the structures of such organizations are increasingly reflecting new types of structure based on the network model. In section 7.2, the performance practitioner and consultant Teo Greenstreet explores how his training and experience as a professional performer was an important preparation both for his organizational work in the creative industries and, more recently, for his work as a consultant to a wide range of organizations working within the public, voluntary and private sectors. In section 7.2, he talks about how the particular areas of knowledge and skill that he developed as a performer have provided him with a way to think about how organization works in the contemporary social, economic and cultural environment, particularly an environment in which organizational responsiveness and agility have become key qualities for working in a highly networked world.

7.2 Organizational agility and improvisation

Teo Greenstreet

After leaving university I became a professional performer and teacher, working as a clown for six years and in the field of performance more generally for 10 years. After that period, I became the chief executive of the Circus Space in East London, an organization that specialized in the training of circus performers and the development of creative enterprise skills. After more years than I care to recall, I decided that I was ready for a change and a new set of challenges. I was fortunate enough to win a one-year fellowship that allowed me the space to reflect and develop a new career plan. Following this year, I became absorbed in thinking about leadership in general, leadership in organizations and, in particular, the business of looking at how creativity can inform and influence the kinds of approaches to leadership that organizations in the contemporary world might need. I became the chief executive of the Kirklees Media Centre in Huddersfield in the north of England, which was one of the first and most successful attempts to create a centre that would be dedicated to supporting the kinds of small creative enterprises discussed by Ralph Brown in section 7.1.

Throughout my career, my performance training and experience have been central to how I have viewed the organizations I have worked in, their relationships to their audiences and clients, how they might work and how they might be led. In this section, I want to talk about what I see as the overlap between performance knowledge and skill on the one side, and key organizational questions such as resilience, effectiveness, flexibility and adaptability on the other. As we progress through this, I will draw out what for me have been the key attributes of performance that have influenced my thinking. However, first we need some context.

All organizations in the contemporary world face a common set of challenges. First, no organization is immune from the processes of globalization and faces increasing levels of complexity and risk. All organizations need to be aware of the forces and trends that will shape the world they work in. Those forces and trends are social, economic, political, technological and environmental, and all organizations need to be able to understand them, find their way through them and work out their implications for what the organization does, how it does it and why. If key demographic structures are changing, for example, what are their implications for organizations? If the global distribution of industry continues to change as fast it has done in the last decade, what are the implications for organizations that are fixed to specific locations? If governments change key policies, how will the organization be affected? If, as predicted, key traditional sources of energy – oil, for example – become uneconomic, how will organizations deal with the consequences? If this sense of global significance wasn't daunting enough, organizations find themselves dealing with changes in their environment that happen with ever-increasing pace and unpredictability. This can be especially seen in the impacts that new technologies have had on organizations in the last 10 years. Just think, for example, of the ways in which technology has become part of education, and the effects that it has had on how students deal with information, or present their ideas.

One of the key consequences of this rapid change is that individuals and organizations, more than ever, need narratives to help them work through this. Narratives, in the form of stories and organizational folk wisdom, provide meaning at a time when change can make things look meaningless to the point of randomness. However, meaning is not simply a by-product of anonymous processes of social change; it is made by people. Performance, in an important respect, is one way in which people make meaning, as active agents in the worlds in which they live and work. This is one of the reasons why, as Brown pointed out in the previous section, cultural processes involving creativity, symbolism and meaning have become even more important than they might have been in the past. In fact, they have become so important that they have become industries in their own right. Industries now not only depend on 'branding' – that is, the process of building value (both financial and symbolic) in a wide range of things, products and services, but also organizations, specific activities (such as the arts) and even individuals. This is well-illustrated in the foreword to a report for the organization Arts and Business (a UK national organization that promotes relationships between the arts and business), where it states: 'the world of business is fast realizing that creativity is too valuable to be left to the creatives' (Hunter 2009). So, the role of performance in meaning-making is important.

However, meaning-making draws on a wide repertoire of skills, a key one being the ability to improvise. Just as the improvisational performance artist works with the materials and ideas to hand (rather than from a script or set of instructions), organizations have to be capable of improvisation, and a large part of that depends on the improvisational agility of the people who work in them. However, successful improvisation is dependent upon a particular set of attributes or outlook. The first of these is a particular kind of attentiveness that might be captured in the theatrical term *'complicité'* (Murray 2003). In essence, this is the process of 'being with' the people you are working with; for example, your collaborators, your audience or customers. It means being willing to be spontaneous, to take on roles as needed or as desirable; it means to work with openness and élan. It also means being able to work productively, flexing in response to constant feedback, just as the performance artist works productively with an audience, being present, reading the signals and changing activity accordingly.

There is a second sense in which improvisational capabilities become important. One of the key features of the sorts of rapid social, economic and political change that we see around us is that organizational activities appear increasingly as one-off projects. As Brown pointed out in the previous section, one of the chief characteristics of the creative industries is that work is packaged into projects requiring teams that can be put together quickly and disbanded as each project is completed. This way of working is becoming typical of a wide range of industries. The performance company is the archetype of the project organization. Whilst there may be a small number of core people in the organization, much of the work is undertaken by teams of flexible specialists who cover key project activities between them – directing, acting, finance, marketing and so forth. The ability to collaborate – to be present with the other members of the team – becomes critically important to the successful outcome of the project. Project working instils a new kind of organizational rhythm, and the performance company exemplifies this. As a performer, it was common for me to run with something I've have never run with before, with a group of people I've never worked with before, run it for three weeks, then stop and never see the people I've just worked with so intensively ever again. This way of working has a distinct rhythm and pattern. It organizes the work and your individual thinking, your thought processes and patterns.

The reality of focusing organization around projects has directly influenced the structuring of part of my current work as creative Director of Encounters (www.encounters-arts.org.uk) – a coming together as a creative collective able to flex and respond to our own programmes and those tendered for. An exceptional outcome of this structuring of improvisation is the effectiveness of this as a learning mechanism, as it also is dependent on a high degree of *complicité* between its members.

Definitions of success also need to be looked at in this context. However skilled organizations are in their improvisation, and however resilient they are, they will not always get it right – often they will get things wrong. With ever-increasing levels of uncertainty and risk, this is likely to happen with increasing frequency. Organizations, therefore, also need to learn how to fail well – that is, to accept failure, learn from it and move on to the next thing.

Whilst reflection is important, there simply isn't time for extended self-analysis; we need to develop new ways of responding to failure. Performance artists constantly deal with creative failure and learn from it. This sense of constantly moving on reflects the need to meet the next show-time.

Alongside this direct route, these performance competencies and skills can lead to deeper insights that then reinforce the potency and relevance of these abilities for future organizations. Two concepts from performance are very important here: *presence* and *authenticity*, both of which help us to understand how organizations might get a better understanding of the complexities of the world they work in and lead to better decision-making. In performance, you are called to be present, in a state of non-distraction from the noise of the over-communicating world, to be focused on what's in the here and now. Attention and observation are strengthened from being more present, more in the moment, as a result of non-distraction. Stephen Nachmanovitch (1990) in considering improvisation describes faithfulness to the moment and present circumstances as continuous surrender: 'we have to give up our expectations and ... control' (Nachmanovitch 1990: 21). Performance is dominated by the mind, *complicité* is with all senses – integrating mind, heart and body. For organizations, maximizing the options that decision-makers can perceive extends the realm of responses. For future organizations, this has significant implications for innovation and organizational agility.

Part of the process of meaning-making is envisaging the future. *Complicité, presence* and *authenticity* all help to develop a shared vision of how the future may unfold and help to build reserves of resilience and adaptability that the agile organization can call upon to help it adapt. In considering how society can adapt to climate change, Rob Hopkins (2009) commented: 'we have a paucity of stories that articulate what a low energy world might look like. What is hard, but important, is to be able to articulate a vision of a post carbon world so enticing that people leap out of bed every morning ... to make it happen' (Hopkins 2009: 14). The capacity for envisaging is also being able to recognize opportunities before they arrive and are too abrupt to exploit. Good envisaging means being in the best possible space to take advantage of opportunities as they appear. The key to good envisaging is rehearsal – the particular skills of a performer being able to rehearse ideas, to take risks with characterization, to have empathy in role play and bringing the future forward, jumping in and out of it and being able to respond productively and profitably to events. This approach to scenario-playing in organizations is being harnessed heavily through leadership and management development tools such as *Lego Serious Play*[2] and *Mythodrama*.[3]

The importance of *empathy* is particularly apparent in organizations that have customers. Once upon a time, organizations with customers simply offered them a product or a service. However, important cultural trends that increasingly stress personal autonomy and the technologies that can underpin it are transforming the ways customers interact with organizations. Where previously a customer was a passive recipient of what the organization offered, customers are now so much more active. They are not only willing to tell an organization what they want, but they are also prepared to play a part in its production. Technologies, especially social networking tools, allow organizations and their audiences and customers to relate to each other in much more engaged and immersive ways.

However, this has also prompted an increasingly questioning stance. The modern world stresses the need for performativity – meaning, in this particular context, the ability to achieve results. The strongest concept that unites much of these reflections on the relationship between performance and organization is *play* and, after over 20 years of running organizations, I believe it is of greater importance now than ever. The response of organizations to an increasingly unpredictable world is to be adaptable. Play will become ever more important in the process of meaning-making, imagining and testing between individuals and organizations looking to deal with complexity and increased risk. This willingness to enter into play requires courage – the courage of the performer.

7.3   Performance, organization, theory

Calvin Taylor

In section 7.2, we saw how the three senses of organization play out in the contemporary world. We also saw how key performance concepts – *complicité*, authenticity, presence, improvisation and play can all be marshalled to examine the ways in which these three senses – entity, structure and process – can be examined. Organizational entities are now required to be much more agile, adaptable and permeable than their more rigid, monolithic precursors. This is perhaps captured effectively in the image of the agile independent performance company that develops work by calling on highly-networked skills and knowledge, moving from project to project, and changing shape and structure as required. This suggests that the processes of organization are now also much more de-centralized, with organizational capacity dispersed among a range of agents – performers, directors, producers, designers – many of whom are required to take on more than one role. This, in turn, implies a need for a new way of thinking about the type of organizational structure that supports this way of working. In contemporary thinking, the metaphor of the network is commonly used to describe the dense connections that exist between these agents. In this section, I examine the ways in which thinking about the relationship between organization and performance has changed over time.

The relationships between organization and performance are complex and multi-faceted, and take you from theatre as an organized art form all the way through to contemporary economics, politics, media, technology, lifestyles, the labour market and work. These sorts of shifts are also reflected in the theoretical concepts that have been dominant throughout the Western twentieth century and the beginning of the twenty-first, the period during which our ideas about organization have been developed. In this section, I will review the key developments in this history, foregrounding the particular ways in which performance and organization have come together, both practically and theoretically.

In organizational theory, the deployment of metaphors is a very useful way to capture the abstract idea of organization in more concrete terms. Metaphors enable complex ideas to be described and explained simply. The history of organizational thinking illustrates the extensive use of metaphor. In his famous book *Images of Organisation*, Gareth Morgan (2006: 3–8), for example, identifies as many as eight typical metaphors that have shaped ideas about organization. These are:

- organization as machine;
- organization as organism;
- organization as brain;
- organization as culture;
- organization as political system;
- organization as psychic prison;
- organization as flux and transformation;
- organization as instrument of domination.

However, in thinking about organization and its relationship with performance, three metaphors are particularly useful. Two are clearly part of Morgan's list. These are the ideas of:

- organization as machine;
- organization as organism.

However, to this I add a third that has some relationship to Morgan's ideas about organization as flux and transformation; I will call this model 'organization as network', to help us draw on a range of contemporary ideas.

Thinking about organization goes back as far as the Ancient Greeks and probably earlier. However, in this review I am interested in the modern period – approximately 1880 to today – a period when thinking about organization began to have major cultural, social and economic consequences. In this period, the first two metaphors – machine and organism – dominated thinking about organization until approximately the 1960s (although, in some ways, the 'organism' metaphor still continues to have influence today). Since then, the broader global shift to what we now call post-industrial society has given the other two metaphors prominence. These changes in ideas, however, are not simply the product of random intellectual currents; they appear to progress in a similar direction to each other which, in turn, maps onto the way we have understood important large-scale changes in society, economy and culture. In what follows, you will see how the earliest ideas about organization emphasized order, structure, centralization, regularity, hierarchy and fixity. Over time, these give way to alternatives that stress complexity (sometimes chaos), de-centralization, fluidity, contingency and heterarchy (parallel interconnectedness).

For our purposes, our ideas about organization undergo a number of other significant changes that are part of the important intellectual and cultural changes that took place during the same period. The earliest writers treated organization as it if it were a physical thing, with an existence that is independent of the human mind, with the important consequence that they thought it could be studied scientifically just like any other physical phenomenon. It is no coincidence that the new large-scale factories developed in the latter half of the nineteenth century and the associated processes of mechanization fascinated many of the earliest writers on organization. Over time, however, there has been a shift towards thinking of organization as a social construct created out of the interactions between people – expressed, for example, in the idea of organizational culture. This trend has been intensified by the pervasiveness of networking technologies that allow people to interact beyond face-to-face situations.

The trend towards seeing organization as a cultural product also opens up the possibility of thinking of organization as a reflexive product of the mind, especially since formal structures appear to be declining in importance and new ways of interacting based on the person have become more significant. These developments point towards another shift. Earlier thinkers emphasized the relative permanence of organizational structures;

Table 7.1   Modernist and Postmodernist Organizations Compared

	← ————— Characteristic ————— →	
Rigid	Organizational resilience	Flexible
Mass	Forms of consumption	Niche
Deterministic	Effect of technology	Choice
Specialized, low-skill	Employment type	Multi-skill and adaptable
Hierarchical	Control and authority	Heterarchical
Monolithic and imposing	Structure	Micro-scale and facilitating
Planned and predictable	Strategy	Improvised and contingent

(left axis: Modernist organization; right axis: Postmodernist organization)

[Copyright © Calvin Taylor]

for example, think of nations, states and large companies. Contemporary thinkers, on the other hand, emphasize change, both of the evolutionary and revolutionary kinds. Thus now, for example, we find writers emphasizing temporariness, mobility, nomadism and improvisation in their descriptions of organizational process.

Some writers (for example, Clegg 2007) have described these distinctions as being between modernist and postmodernist accounts of organization. Table 7.1 adapts what Clegg suggests are some of the important contrasts.

The machine metaphor

Some of the earliest writers on organization regarded it as an objective entity capable of being studied, measured and predicted. A key contributor here was one of the earliest management theorists Frederick Winslow Taylor (1856–1915), author of *The Principles of Scientific Management* (2003 [1911]). Taylor was famous for examining productivity in factories, arguing that performance could be studied scientifically. The advent of the modern factory with machine-dictated time and regularized production schedules required workers to work faster, and with greater regularity and efficiency. Taylor studied how this might be made possible by breaking work tasks (movements) into their simplest elements, and then measuring and reassembling them to give the combination that produced the optimum work rate. In Taylor's perspective, organization is a matter of applying scientific procedures to work tasks with the purpose of imprinting the optimum solution on the discipline of the worker. It emphasized order, predictability, measurability and efficiency. It also described a world in which the worker was managed within a system that provided structure, order and continuity by separating the *planning* of activity from the *execution* of activity.

Such approaches to organization of work transferred themselves into the performance world very quickly. Taylor himself applied his ideas to sport, and the idea of bodily discipline became a concern for social reformers in America in the 1920s. Taylor's ideas were also explicitly included in Meyerhold's actor training through the concept of biomechanics (Pitches 2005: 56–65). Advocates of mass participatory dance recommended communal dancing as vehicle for encouraging sociability and good health among the citizenry. In a somewhat more sinister appropriation of these ideas, the monumental spectacles mounted by the Nazi Party in Germany in the 1930s and 1940s owed much to ideas of mass discipline and order.

The idea of discipline can also be seen in the work of the dance theorist and choreographer Rudolph von Laban (1879–1958). Now, he is famous for developing a system of notation for describing, analyzing and quantifying dance movements, but he was also an advocate for mass dance events in Germany in the 1930s. Just before World War II he settled in England and, among other activities, turned his knowledge about human movement and its coordination to the problems of productivity in industry (Laban and Lawrence 1974; Reeves *et al.* 2001).

Organization as organism

The machine metaphor led organizational theorists to pre-occupy themselves with questions of functionality and efficiency; for example, trying to find the technically optimum solution to a given problem. This changed when organizational theorists began to think about not so much the functionality of organization, but its health. This led a wide range of thinkers, such as Abraham Maslow (1908–70) and Frederick Herzberg (1923–2000), to begin to think in terms of organizations as systems of 'needs' – both in terms of the individual members of an organization, and the organization as a whole. This opened organizational theory up to the idea that organizations behave like organisms that interact with environments. These interactions are what determine the health of the organism and its capacity to deal with, for example, changes in the environment. From these initial insights, organizational theorists began to look at what motivates individuals to work in the ways that they do, and why. From here, they then expanded their interests to thinking about organizations as 'open' systems that interact with environments, receiving feedback messages from the environment signalling, for example important changes, telling the organization if it is doing the right things in the right way.

This organic or ecological theorization of organization intersects with performance in a number of ways. Performance theorists have often been attracted by the proposition that a close relationship exists between theatrical staging and ritual (Shepherd and Wallis 2004). The origins of ritual are complex, but they mainly stem from the need for humans to mark publicly their important relationships with their environment, and, in the process, mark their relationships with each other. Thus, anthropologists have extensively discussed the significance of rituals associated with food, fertility, planetary motion and the passing of the seasons. When the American performance theorist Richard Schechner was developing his ideas for his famous book *Environmental Theatre* (Schechner 1973) in the 1960s and 1970s, he was heavily influenced by the cultural trends for ritual-like artistic and cultural events – which, in the values of the period, were closer to human needs, and particularly the human need to relate both to the environment and to each other in ways which dissolved what was seen as an artificial distinction between art and life. This gave rise to new theorizations of theatre and drama that argued for their close relationship to ritual. In a more contemporary account, the English performance theorist Baz Kershaw has argued that performance is a key discipline for understanding the deep ecology of the relationships of humans to both their physical and biological environments, and to other forms of life (Kershaw 2007).

How might this connect with more contemporary accounts of the relationship between performance and organization? The relationship is two-way. In viewing organizations as ecological systems in which communication and feedback (both internal and external) are important, we begin to understand their performative characteristics. For example, what organizational rituals need to be performed in order to ensure that the organization is aware of its environment and internal well-being? How do organizations affirm their purpose and communicate it? How do they understand when things are going wrong, and how do they acknowledge when things are working well? In the other direction, thinking about organization as an organism works for performance in a number of ways. For example, rituals as performative events nearly always involve bodily expression. The processes of embodiment in performance have been discussed elsewhere in this volume, but they connect very closely with the ecology of human needs and the processes of being. These are, of course, deeply ecological phenomena. They are also modes of organization in which the organic metaphor plays an important role. Performance as a discipline also behaves like an open system. It is in continual dialogue with its environment – adapting, evolving and expanding.

Organization as network

This sense of constant adaptation, evolution and expansion also points to the possible limitations of the organic metaphor, if it is taken too literally. Two limitations are of particular concern here. The organic metaphor tends to posit both the organization and its environment as 'givens'; that is, concretely objective entities that co-exist independently of the human agents that work within them. The problem with this is that it potentially underestimates the extent to which organizations and their environments are social products; that is, products of the values, ideologies and belief systems of the individuals and social groups that work within them. The ritual dimension of the organic metaphor actually points in the direction of this 'cultural' aspect of organization. The second problem is that it relies on a sense of wholeness – both of the organization and its environment – that may be more a product of the theory than the actuality. This sense of wholeness, of integration, and of the parts of the system pulling together for the benefit of the whole breaks down when actual organizations are examined. Empirical studies of actual organizations often find fragmentation, 'silo-ization', disconnection and divided purpose.

However, there are two ways of looking at this process of fragmentation. It can be seen as a departure from an ideal, or – as studies of what is called the postmodern condition put it – it can be seen as the emergence of a new socio-economic structure which may appear fragmentary and discontinuous on the surface, but which is held together by a new structuring principle based on the network model. The network characteristics of the post-industrial economy have been carefully mapped by Manuel Castells (2010). The network metaphor of organization shares some characteristics with the organic metaphor, but differs in some very important respects. As in the organic metaphor, the network metaphor of organization emphasizes the system-like nature of relationships, open-ness with regard to the flow of information and feedback, and the interest in and attention paid to processes of change and adaptation. The differences are, however, important. The organic metaphor implies a singularity – an entity – which, in turn, implies some form of structural integrity. Networks are composed of independent actors who interact with each other on the basis of different kinds of social ties. Some social ties are strong – for example, ties of community affiliation; others, however, are weak – for example, business relationships.

Network structures as a metaphor for organization emphasize the role of these kinds of 'weak ties' – ties between work colleagues, between business partners, between students in a class, between people who interact with each via the Internet around a common interest. This web of weak ties is what makes the network 'work'. Where the organic metaphor shared an assumption about centralized control with the machine metaphor, the network metaphor recognizes that, in networks, control, authority and decision-making are dispersed and de-centralized. Kevin Kelly (1998), writing just before the 'dot-com' boom and bust, saw this de-centralization as key to understanding the power of networks. He used the term 'swarming' to understand why it is that, in networks, individual agents have the propensity to gravitate autonomously towards things of common interest. The writers Deleuze and Guattari (2004) further develop a theory of connectedness and multiplicity that combines the organic metaphor of the rhizome (a root that typically extends underground to connect different entities together) with an account of knowledge that stresses its horizontal multiplex inter-connectedness, rather than its linear hierarchy. The writers Potts and Cunningham (2008) have taken these ideas further and argued that the typical organizational form of modern society is the social network market in which social actors, through their interactions (both with each other and with the mass of interactions), construct principles of organization out of the seemingly chaotic nature of such interactions. This model trades very heavily on the idea that complexity harbours within it important principles of simplicity, a key principle being that the network is never, as in the machine metaphor, a completed thing. It is always in a state of emergence.

The idea of organization as network has become important for performance. Performance itself as a discipline is characteristically rhizomatic. It extends and connects very diverse bodies of knowledge and practice – not into a neat, finished whole but into a constantly emergent field of theorization and practice. However, the network metaphor of organization is also important in the construction of performances. Performance work, however ostensibly simple it may appear, relies heavily on the mobilization of networked resources – skills, knowledge and material resources. Networks of informal connections are critical for the making of performance work. However, it is not just for the provision of functional resources that networked organization is important. The principle of collaboration –

both within and between different fields – is greatly facilitated by the network principle. It is only in the informal connections established by networks that the trust necessary for effective collaboration can be achieved. This is why the performance world is characterized by networks.

In this section, we have mapped some of the main ways in which ideas about performance and organization interact with each other. By taking a historical view, we can see how ideas about organization have changed – moving away from ideas of permanence, stability, regularity and boundedness towards temporariness, unpredictability, novelty and permeability. As networked technologies become more readily accepted, and networked forms of work become more typical of how we manage our careers, the idea of the network as the most appropriate metaphor for our ideas about organization has now become well-accepted.

Activities

In the Solo activity for this chapter, we ask you to investigate the relationship between performance and organization through a conversation or interview with a contemporary performance practitioner. (You will be able to compare these experiences with your own gleaned from Discussion activity 1.)

➤ *Solo activity*

Prepare an interview for a contemporary performer focusing on their working practices and how they are organized. Topics for discussion might include:

• What were their motives for developing a career in performance?
• What kind of work do they make?
• What are their artistic and cultural values?
• How did they get into this area of work?
• How do they work and with whom do they work?
• What are the typical patterns of working?
• What kinds of organization do they work with/in?

In this next activity, consider how different ideas about organization are implicit in your own workshop and group sessions. Such ideas are often hidden or assumed, and only become apparent by reviewing a practical case study – in this case, your own performance work.

➤ *Discussion activity 1*

Concentrating on a practical experience or workshop project you have been involved in, consider the following questions:

- How did your group make its decisions?
- What networks did your group mobilize in developing your piece?
- In what ways might your piece or your working methods have been different had you worked, in turn, within the machine, organic and network metaphors?

In this chapter, we have structured our ideas about organization around three metaphors: organization as machine, organization as organism and organization as network. These ideas have important consequences for how we think about how performance is actually constructed. In Discussion activity 2, look for different ways that these ideas about organization might impact on the ways in which you think and work, and especially about what kinds of skills they might encourage and/or inhibit.

➤ *Discussion activity 2*

Working in groups of four or five, consider the following questions:

- Have you had experience of organizations that appear to work like machines, organisms and networks?
- What are the key skills that you can take from performance and apply in other areas of your life?
- How does your course of study enable you to develop the knowledge and skills seemingly required for working in the networked economy of temporary organizations?
- Where can you see evidence of networks at work and how do they become visible?
- What are the potential problems of the network model as a way of understanding how people build careers?

➤ *Practical activity*

You will need a practical stimulus for devising – or access to it in the time allotted.

Split yourselves into three groups and decide on one of the three metaphors of organization for each group. Agree ground rules for how you will operate for the next 30 minutes of creative work, based on the characteristics of the machine, the organism and the network. Ensure that you follow these ground rules through the whole process, even if they feel alien to you (remember these moments and bring them to the final discussion). All groups should follow the general approach to devising a two-minute piece of performance:

- researching source materials;
- rehearsing;
- performing to the rest of the group.

Share the performances with the rest of the group, and then discuss how evident the organizational choices were in the performances produced. How did the working processes differ?

Notes

1   The concept of 'tacit knowledge' has been particularly influential in the performance practice-as-research world (Nelson 2009).
2   For details of the genesis of this methodology, see the announcement 'Lego launches "serious play" bricks to help businesses' (*Marketing Week*, 2001).
3   The use of Shakespearean grand narratives, such as *Henry V*, to develop models of good leadership.

Further reading

Bilton, C. (2006) *Management and Creativity: From Creative Industries to Creative Management*. Oxford: Wiley Blackwell.

Hartley, J. (ed.) (2005) *Creative Industries*. Oxford: Blackwell Publishing: especially part V (Creative Enterprises) and part VI (Creative Economy).

Leadbeater, C. and Oakley, K. (1999) *The Independents: Britain's New Cultural Entrepreneurs*. London: Demos (Available at: http://www.demos.co.uk/publications/independents [Accessed 1 February 2011])

Morgan, G. (2006) *Images of Organisation*. London: Sage.

O'Connor, J. (2008) *The Cultural and Creative Industries: A Literature Review*. London: Creative Partnerships.

8   Epilogue: A Perspective on Perspectives

Jonathan Pitches

Perspective is a powerful tool, as Leonardo and the Renaissance painters clearly understood. But its power can be double-edged: it can reveal or conceal, it can support measured analysis or encourage imbalance, it can provide new insights or grind out old arguments. In short, it needs skill and practice to apply its laws effectively. A central ambition of this book has been to help develop that skill by introducing you to a carefully selected range of ideas, voices and activities relating to the phenomenon of performance.

Looking at performance from different angles (and, in doing so, evaluating the pluses and minuses of alternative views) has been a central, if simple, premise of this book and you should now be highly proficient in moving around your subject in such a way. The crucial thing to recognize now is that the process of perspectival analysis is by definition *partial*, but that partiality (transparently owned up to and rationalized) is an invaluable tool in the process of performance analysis. By bringing together in each chapter a triumvirate of voices to discuss one subject, *Performance Perspectives* has addressed this idea of partiality in a number of ways. Distanced reflective discourse has been balanced with the immediacy of the interview, personal registers with more formal academic writing. As a critical introduction to the field, we have attempted to evidence singular practices, but from diverse sources – from live art and site specific performance, to circus, dance and applied theatre, from everyday and quotidian performance to virtual reality and cyber-performance, from devised and collaborative work to single-authored playwriting. Our book has implicated you, the reader, in this celebration of partiality, too, with detailed tasks to be explored as an individual and as a group, in the practical studio and in discussion spaces.

The Introduction to this book suggested that our six performance perspectives were not to be thought of in a linear arrangement or on a continuum but, instead, might be arranged together as concentric circles, rippling out from an original 'disturbance' made to the water by the body (Figure 8.1).

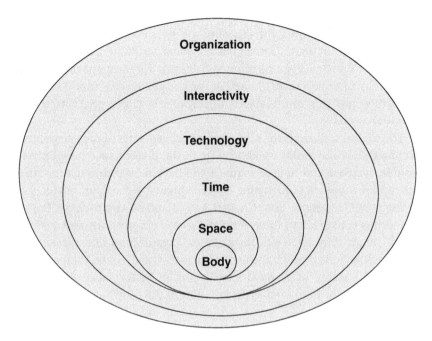

Figure 8.1 Concentric Circles Model of Performance Perspectives
[Copyright: Jonathan Pitches]

There are several advantages to such a view: it is holistic rather than linear, as each perspective is implicated (if not embedded) in the other; it suggests that the performer's own body is central, and that if you peel back the layers of a performance from its organizational outer membrane you ultimately arrive at a living corporeal core; and it gives us a visual sense of the logic of the book – from the materials of the performance itself (body, space, time and technology) to the conditions in which it sits (interactivity and organization). Perhaps most importantly this model restates the interconnectedness of our perspectives – a strong theme throughout this book.

But there are several ways to skin a performance, and it is worth considering the potential pitfalls of this view, now that you have been introduced to each perspective through the three-way conversations in the chapters.

The first complication is the question of *value* and its relationship to the surface-depth metaphor inherent in this model. I used the words 'outer membrane' carefully, as I was concerned not to present the organizational outer layer of this model as the superficial wrapping of performance – the first to go in any surgical unravelling of the work. Conversely, the core of this model is the body, as has been said, and this is entirely appropriate in signalling the centrality of 'liveness' to the performance phenomenon. But analysis must make explicit the value judgements it is making, and it should not be inferred from this arrangement that there is a hierarchy of importance 'hidden' in the perspectives, or that the deeper one drills into this multi-layered organism the closer one gets to the essential elements.

The second concern is the sense this model generates of the perspectives accruing: that one builds up knowledge of the performance progressively from body, space and time onwards. If you have moved through the book carefully, in sequence, then that indeed might be the case, but it is of course possible to move from Chapter 1 to Chapter 4 and back to Chapter 3, and this could lead to interesting and *partial* observations and analyses which might only focus on, for instance, organization and space. Such counter-directions through the book are equally valid, routes that resist the sequential layering or directed snowballing of performance knowledge, and which might been seen as deviating from the centrifugal direction of the concentric circles.

A third and related issue is one of *scale*: as it extends outwards, the size of each perspective clearly increases. What are the implications of this? There is, of course every reason why, in some cases, the singular body of the performer might profitably be contrasted with the organizational body at the level of scale, and this is evident in the model, as plain as Jupiter dwarves Mercury in the solar system. Consider an individual clown's relationship to the globalized corporate structures of a company like Cirque du Soleil, or the chorus member's place in an international opera company. But these kinds of hierarchies – and the political, economic and cultural issues associated with them – are not, in analytical terms, axiomatic or pre-prescribed in the perspectives model. There are many other permutations and alternative orderings of scale possible. Time, for instance, as a universal measure bracketing human behaviour might equally be positioned as the outer membrane or contextualizing perspective to performance. It is, after all, *the* factor in determining the liveness of the performance event. Interactivity might similarly be viewed as the largest frame, as the *interaction* of all the elements – audience, performers, designers, technical operators, environment – is crucial to an understanding of performance processes, as this book testifies. The point I am making here is not to debate the relative merits and demerits of these alternatives to decide on the 'best' arrangement, but to illustrate that the analytical *choice* lies with you and this kind of agency is a prerequisite of critical thinking in this field.

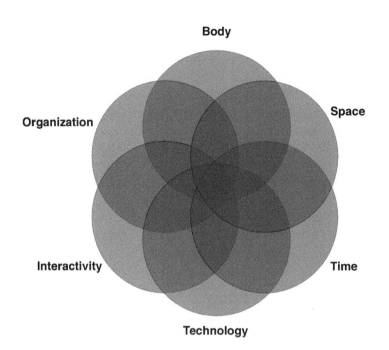

Figure 8.2   Flower Model of Performance Perspectives
[Copyright: Jonathan Pitches]

It might, then, be instructive to consider an alternative and complementary model (Figure 8.2), which addresses some of these potential misconceptions and offers an alternative perspective on perspectives.

In this arrangement, the place of *performance*, not any singular perspective, is at the nexus of the model, recalling the point made in the introduction that 'performance is central to the study of performance' (Huxley and Witts 2002: 3). Here, all six perspectives work in concert to *form* the very concept of performance itself and its complex interactions, as well as its collaborative nature, are effectively captured. That said, the perspectives retain an identity of their own as the outer edges of the model suggest ideal abstractions. Granted, there is no such thing as pure and unadulterated space without a relationship to the other elements, but there is virtue in beginning with these abstractions to develop a terminology or language to use when analyzing the rich and diverse work comprised in this book. This is another way of visualizing the idea of partiality introduced earlier.

Some brief examples here might serve to illustrate the usefulness of this flower model. When organisation interfaces with technology and interactivity, what kind of work might we be considering? A cyber-performance, perhaps, or an applied piece using new technology to facilitate its engagement with the audience. When time is solely allied to space, this brings to mind examples of durational performance and many types of immersive or environmental performance, as well as installation work. When body is related to technology along the flower's vertical axis, body art and specifically that which directly uses technological interventions and transformations, could be one of the performance forms under scrutiny. There are as many permutations as there are genres (and sub-genres) of performance but the discipline of foregrounding one or two elements can be helpful both for making new work in the studio and as an analytical tool when looking at existing material.

This suggests that the most fundamental of questions remains unasked: What instance of performance is it best to place in the *centre* of this model? That, of course, is the question that cannot be answered by this book. There are multiple examples of performance included in each chapter, and these are the starting points for a disciplined analysis. But these examples should not be viewed as definitive references: rather, as stepping-off points. Each manifestation of performance included here – from Alan Ayckbourn to *Zulu Time* – should prompt further questions and stimulate new research trajectories. Collectively, they stand not as a new canon of contemporary performance, but as a gallery of creative practice illustrating the utility of perspective. Ultimately, it is your choice what to place in the centre of this 'flower of perspectives' and your decision about what to do with the knowledge generated. What *may* be said is that, if the diverse creative practices documented in this book are any indication of that potential knowledge, then the vibrancy of contemporary performance practice in the future is assured.

Bibliography

Aarseth, E. (2004) 'Genre Trouble: Narrativism and the Art of Simulation.' in W. Wardrip-Fruin and P. Harrigan (eds), *First Person: New Media as Story, Performance, and Game*. Cambridge, MA: MIT Press: 45–55.

Agacinski, Sylviane (2003) *Time Passing: Modernity and Nostalgia* (trans. Jody Gladding). New York: Columbia University Press.

Aristotle (1932 [350 BC]) *The Poetics in Aristotle in 23 Volumes*, Volume 23, (trans. W.H. Fyfe). Cambridge, MA: Harvard University Press; London: William Heinemann.

Aronson, A. (2005) *Looking into the Abyss: Essays on Scenography*, Ann Arbor, MI: UMI Research Press.

Aronson, A. (1981) *The History and Theory of Environmental Scenography*. Ann Arbor, MI: UMI Research Press.

Ascott, Roy (1990) 'Is There Love in the Telematic Embrace?', *Art Journal*, 49(3): 241–7.

Aston, Elaine and Savona, George (1991) *Theatre as Sign System: A Semiotics of Text and Performance*. London and New York: Routledge.

Auslander, Philip (ed.) (2003) *Performance: Critical Concepts in Literary and Cultural Studies*. London and New York: Routledge.

Auslander, Philip (2002) 'Live from Cyberspace: Or, I Was Sitting at My Computer This Guy Appeared He Thought I Was a Bot', *PAJ: A Journal of Performance and Art*, 24(1): 16–21.

Auslander, Philip (1999) *Liveness: Performance in a Mediatized Culture*. London and New York: Routledge.

Auslander, Philip (1997) *From Acting to Performance: Essays in Modernism and Postmodernism*. London and New York: Routledge.

Ayckbourn, Alan (2004) *The Crafty Art of Playmaking*. London: Faber & Faber.

Babbage, Frances (2004) *Augusto Boal*. Abingdon: Routledge.

Bachelard, G. (1968) *The Psychoanalysis of Fire*, trans. Alan C.M. Ross, Boston, MA: Beacon Press.

Baim, C., Brookes, S. and Mountford, A. (2002) *The Geese Theatre Handbook: Drama with Offenders and People at Risk*. Winchester: Waterside Press.

Banes, S. and Lepecki, A. (2007) *The Senses in Performance*. Abingdon and New York: Routledge.

Banks, M. (2007) *The Politics of Cultural Work*. Basingstoke: Palgrave.

Barba, E. (1995) *The Paper Canoe: A Guide to Theatre Anthropology*, (trans. Richard Fowler). London and New York: Routledge.

Barba, E. and Savarese, N. (2006) *A Dictionary of Theatre Anthropology: The Secret Art of the Performer*, 2nd edn. Abingdon and New York: Routledge.

Barry, A. (1996) 'Who Gets to Play? Art, Access and the Margin', in Jon Dovey (ed.), *Fractal Dreams: New Media in Social Context*. London: Lawrence & Wishart: 136–53.

Bataille, Georges (1997) 'Architecture', in Neil Leach (ed.), *Rethinking Architecture*. London: Routledge: 20–3.

Baudrillard, Jean (1997) 'The End of the Millennium, or the Countdown', Lecture delivered at the Institute of Contemporary Arts, London, 8 May.

Baugh, Christopher (2005) *Theatre, Performance and Technology: the Development of Scenography in the 20th Century*. Basingstoke: Palgrave Macmillan.

Becker, H.S. (1982) *Art Worlds*. Berkeley: University of California Press.

Beer, J. (2004) *Sophocles and the Tragedy of Athenian Democracy*, Contributions in Drama and Theatre Studies 105. Westport, CT: Praeger: 26–7.

Benjamin, Walter (1996) 'This Space for Rent', in *One-Way Street, Selected Writings, Volume 1, 1913–1926*. Cambridge, MA: Harvard University Press: 240–58.

Berlo, David K. (1960) *The Process of Communication: An Introduction to Theory and Practice*. New York; London: Holt, Rinehart & Winston.

Bilton, C. (2007) *Management and Creativity: From Creative Industries to Creative Management*. Oxford: Wiley Blackwell.

Blaikie, A. (ed.) (2004) *The Body: Critical Concepts in Sociology, Volume 4: Living and Dying Bodies*. London and New York: Routledge.

Blau, Herbert (2002) 'The Human Nature of the Bot: A Response to Philip Auslander', *PAJ: A Journal of Performance and Art*, 24(1): 22–4.

Blau, Herbert (1964) *Impossible Theater: A Manifesto*. New York: Macmillan.

Boal, Augusto (1979) *Theatre of the Oppressed* (trans. Charles A. and Maria-Odilia Leal McBride). London: Pluto Press.

Bogart, Anne (2007) *And Then, You Act: Making Art in an Unpredictable World*. London: Routledge.

Bogart, Anne and Landau, Tina (2005) *The Viewpoints Book: A Practical Guide to Viewpoints and Composition*. New York: Theatre Communications Group.

Bolter, Jay David and Gromala, Diane (2003) *Windows and Mirrors: Interactive Art, Digital Design and the Myth of Transparency*. Cambridge, MA: MIT Press.

Bolter, Jay David and Grusin, Richard (2000) *Remediation: Understanding New Media*. Cambridge, MA; London: MIT.

Bourdieu, P. (1990) 'Structures, Habitus, Practices', in *The Logic of Practice*. Stanford, CA: Stanford University Press: 52–79.

Brand, J. and Teunissen, J. (eds) (2004) *The Ideal Woman*. Amsterdam: SUN.

Brecht, Bertolt (1964) *Brecht on Theatre: The Development of an Aesthetic* (ed. and trans. John Willett). London: Eyre Methuen.

Brenton, H., Gillies, M., Surman, D. and Sloan H. (2007) 'Uncanny Valley: Realism in Visualisation and Character Design', *SwanQuake: The User Manual*. Devon: Liquid Press: 93–100.

Breton, Gaëlle (1989) *Theaters*. New York: Princeton Architectural Press.

Broadhurst, Sue (2006) 'Digital Practices: An Aesthetic and Neuroaesthetic Approach to Virtuality and Embodiment', *Performance Research*, 11(4): 137–47.

Broadhurst, Sue and Machon, Josephine (eds) (2009) *Performance and Technology: Practices of Virtual Embodiment and Interactivity*. Basingstoke: Palgrave Macmillan.

Brook, Peter (1988) *The Shifting Point: Forty Years of Theatrical Exploration 1946–87*. London: Methuen.

Brook, Peter (1968) *The Empty Space*. London: Pelican/Penguin Books.

Brown, Kevin (2006) 'Auslander's Robot', *International Journal of Performance Arts & Digital Media*, 2(1): 3–21.

Butler, Judith (1999) *Gender Trouble: Feminism and the Subversion of Identity*. London and New York: Routledge.

Carlson, Marvin (2004) *Performance: A Critical Introduction*. New York: Routledge.

Cardullo, Bert and Knopf, Robert (2001) *Theater of the Avant-Garde: 1890–1950: A Critical Anthology*. Connecticut: Yale University Press.

Castells, M. (2010)) *The Rise of the Network Society: The Information Age, Economy, Society and Culture*, 2nd edn. Chichester: Wiley-Blackwell.

Castronova, E. (2003) *Theory of the Avatar*. CESIFO Working Paper 863. Available at http://ideas.repec.org/p/ces/ceswps/_863.html [Accessed 10 October 2007].

Certeau, M. de (1984 [1980]) *The Practice of Everyday Life* (trans. Steven Rendall). Berkeley: University of California Press.

Chatzichristodoulou, Maria, Jefferies, Janis and Zerihan, Rachel (2009) *Interfaces of Performance*. Surrey: Ashgate.

Chekhov, M. (2002) *To the Actor*, (ed. Mala Powers). London and New York: Routledge.

Clegg, S. (2007) 'Modernist and Postmodernist Organisation', in Derek S. Pugh (ed.), *Organisation Theory: Selected Classic Readings*, 5th edn. London: Penguin: 577–615.

Collins, J. and Nisbet, A. (eds) (2010) *Theatre and Performance Design: A Reader in Scenography*. London: Routledge.

Counsell, Colin and Mock, Roberta (eds) (2009) *Performance, Embodiment and Cultural Memory*. Newcastle-upon-Tyne: Cambridge Scholars Publishing.

Creeber, Glen and Martin, Royston (2009) *Digital Cultures: Understanding New Media*. Open University Press: Maidenhead.

Csordas, T.J. (ed.) (1994) *Embodiment and Experience: The Existential Ground of Culture and Self*. Cambridge: Cambridge University Press.

Damasio, Antonio (1999) *The Feeling of What Happens: Body, Emotion and the Making of Consciousness*. Orlando, FL: Harcourt.

Davis, K. (ed.) (1997) *Embodied Practices: Feminist Perspectives on the Body*. London, California and New Delhi: Sage.

Deleuze, G. and Guattari, F. (2004) *A Thousand Plateaus: Capitalism and Schizophrenia*. New York: Continuum Books.

Department for Culture, Media and Sport (2008) *Creative Britain – New Talents for the New Economy*. London: Department for Culture, Media and Sport.

Dempster, A. (2006) 'Managing Uncertainty in Creative Industries: Lessons from *Jerry Springer: The Opera*', *Creativity and Innovation Management*, 15(3): 224–33.

Derrida, J. (1990) *Writing and Difference* (trans. and intro. and notes by Alan Bass). London and New York: Routledge.

Diamond, Elin (1996) *Performance and Cultural Politics*. London and New York: Routledge.

Dils, Ann (2002) 'The Ghost in the Machine: Merce Cunningham and Bill T. Jones', *PAJ: A Journal of Performance and Art*, 24(1): 94–104.

Dils, Ann (2001) 'Absent/Presence', in A. Dils and A. Cooper-Albright (eds), *Moving History/Dancing Cultures: A Dance History Reader*. USA: Wesleyan University Press: 462–74.

Dinkla, Söke (2002) 'The Art of Narrative: Towards the "Floating Work of Art"', *New Screen Media Cinema/Art/Narrative*, Martin Rieser and Andrea Zapp (eds). British Film Institute: 28–39.

Dinkla, Söke and Leeker, Martina (eds) (2002) *Dance and Technology: Moving Towards Media Productions*. Berlin: Alexander Verlag.

Dixon, Michael and Smith, Joel (eds) (1995) *Anne Bogart: Viewpoints*. Lyme, NH: Smith & Kraus.

Dixon, Steve (2007) *Digital Performance: A History of New Media in Theater, Dance, Performance Art, and Installation*. Cambridge, MA: MIT Press.

Dixon, Steve (2006) 'Uncanny Interactions', *Performance Research*, 11(4): 67–75.

Dixon, Steve (2005) 'Theatre, Technology, and Time', *International Journal of Performance Arts & Digital Media*, 1(1): 11–29.

Dolnik, Adam and Pilch, Richard (2003) 'The Moscow Theater Hostage Crisis: The Perpetrators, Their Tactics and the Russian Response', *International Negotiation*, 8(3): 577–611.

Dovey, J and Kennedy H.W. (2006) *Game Cultures: Computer Games as New Media*. Maidenhead: Open University Press.

Drefus, Hubert (2001) 'Telepistemology: Descartes's Last Stand', in Ken Goldberg (ed.), *The Robot in the Garden: Telerobotics and Telepistemology in the Age of the Internet*. MA: MIT Press: 48–63.

Dutton, K.R. (1995) *The Perfectible Body: The Western Ideal of Male Physical Development*. New York: Continuum.

Dyson, F. (2009) *Sounding New Media: Immersion and Embodiment in the Arts and Culture*. Berkeley, Los Angeles and London: University of California Press.

Evans, M. (2009) *Movement Training for the Modern Actor*. London and New York: Routledge.

Evans, M. and Lee, E. (eds) (2002) *Real Bodies: A Sociological Introduction*. Basingstoke: Palgrave.

Feher, M., Naddaff, R. and Tazi, N. (1989) *Zone: Fragments for a History of the Human Body, Part II*. New York: Urzone.

Fenemore, Anna (2007) 'Dialogical Interaction and Social Participation in Physical and Virtual Performance Space', *International Journal of Performing Arts & Digital Media*, 3(1): 37–58.

Fischer-Lichte, E. (1989) 'Theatre and the Civilizing Process: An Approach to the History of Acting,' in T. Postlewait and B. McConachie (eds), *Interpreting the Theatrical Past: Essays in The Historiography of Performance*. Iowa: University of Iowa Press: 19–36.

Foner, Lenny (1993) *What's an Agent, Anyway? A Sociological Case Study*, http://foner.www.media.mit.edu/people/foner/Julia/Julia.html [Accessed 22 February 2010].

Foucault, M. (1991) *Discipline and Punish: The Birth of the Prison* (trans. Alan Sheridan). Hardsmondworth: Penguin Books.

Foucault, M. (1989) *The Order of Things: An Archaeology of the Human Sciences*. London: Routledge.

Foucault, Michel (1980) *Power/Knowledge: Selected Interviews and Other Writings: 1972–1977* (ed. Colin Gordon). New York: Pantheon Books.

Fox, K. (1997) *Taskforce on Underage Alcohol Misuse*. London: Portman Group.

Fraleigh, Sandra Horton (2004) *Dancing Identity: Metaphysics in Motion*. Pittsburgh: University of Pittsburgh Press.

Franko, Mark (2002) *The Work of Dance. Labor, Movement, and Identity in the 1930s*. Middletown, CT: Wesleyan University Press.

Freud, S. (1977) *On Sexuality: Three Essays on the Theory of Sexuality, and Other Works*, (trans. James Strachey, ed. Angela Richards). Harmondsworth: Penguin.

Fukuyama, Francis (1992) *The End of History and the Last Man*. Harmondsworth: Penguin.

Gallagher, S. (2005) *How the Body Shapes the Mind*. Oxford and New York: Oxford University Press.

Gallagher, K. and Booth, D. (2003) *How Theatre Educates: Convergences and Counterpoints*. Toronto: University of Toronto Press.

Garner, Stanton B. (1994) *Bodied Spaces: Phenomenology and Performance in Contemporary Drama*. Ithaca, NY: Cornell University Press.

Geertz, Clifford (1973) 'Thick Description: Toward an Interpretive Theory of Culture', in *The Interpretation of Cultures: Selected Essays*. New York: Basic Books: 3–30.

Giannachi, Gabriella (2004) *Virtual Theatres: An Introduction*. London: Routledge.

Giannachi, Gabriella and Luckhurst, Mary (1999) *On Directing: Interviews with Directors*. London: Faber & Faber.

Gibson, William (1984) *Neuromancer*. New York: Ace.

Graham, Beryl (1997) *A Study of Audience Relationships with Interactive Computer-Based Visual Artworks in Gallery Settings, through Observation, Art Practice and Curation*, University of Sunderland (unpublished PhD thesis, available online at http://www.sunderland.ac.uk/~as0bgr/thesis.pdf).

Graham, Beryl (1996) 'Playing with Yourself: Pleasure and Interactive Art', in J. Dovey (ed.), *Fractal Dreams: New Media in Social Context*, London: Lawrence & Wishart.

Grosz, Elizabeth (2001) *Architecture from the Outside: Essays on Virtual and Real Spaces*. Cambridge, MA: MIT Press.

Grosz, Elizabeth (1994) *Volatile Bodies: Toward A Corporeal Feminism*. Bloomington, IN: Indiana University Press.

Hall, Edward, T. (1966) *The Hidden Dimension*. Garden City, NY: Doubleday.

Hall, Edward T. (1959) *The Silent Language*. Garden City, NY: Doubleday.

Hansen, Mark (2006) *Bodies in Code: Interfaces with Digital Media*. London and New York: Routledge.

Hartley, J. (ed.) (2005) *Creative Industries*. Oxford: Blackwell Publishing.

Heathfield, A. (ed.) (2004) *Live: Art and Performance*. London: Tate Publishing.

Heathfield, Adrian and Hsieh, Tehching (2009) *Out of Now: The Lifeworks of Tehching Hsieh*. London: Live Art Development Agency.

Heidegger, Martin (1962 [1927]) *Being and Time* (trans. John Macquarrie and Edward Robinson). Oxford: Blackwell.

Heise, Ursula (1997) *Chronoschisms: Time, Narrative and Postmodernism*. Cambridge: Cambridge University Press.

Helmer, Judith and Malzacher, Florian (eds) (2004) *Not Even A Game Anymore: The Theatre of Forced Entertainment*. Berlin: Alexander Verlag.

Her Majesty's Treasury (2005) *The Cox Review of Creativity in Business*. London: Her Majesty's Treasury.

Hill, Leslie and Paris, Helen (eds) (2006) *Performance and Place*. Basingstoke: Palgrave Macmillan.

Holden, J. (2007) *Publicly-Funded Culture and the Creative Industries*. London: Arts Council England.

Hopkins, Rob (2009) 'Resilience Thinking', *Resurgence*, 257, November/December: 12–14.

Howard, Pamela (2002) *What is Scenography?* London: Routledge.

Hunter, M. (2009) 'Foreword', in *Beyond Experience, Culture, Consumer and Brand*. London: Arts and Business.

Huxley, Michael and Witts, Noel (2002) *The Twentieth Century Performance Reader* (2nd edn). London: Routledge.

Huyssen, Andreas (1995) *Twilight Memories: Marking Time in a Culture of Amnesia*. London: Routledge.

igloo (2007) *SwanQuake: The User Manual*. Devon: Liquid Press.

Irigaray, Luce (1985) *This Sex which is Not One*. New York: Cornell University Press.

Jackson, Anthony (2007) *Theatre, Education and the Making of Meanings*. Manchester: Manchester University Press.

Jackson, Shannon (2004) *Professing Performance: Theatre in the Academy from Philology to Performativity*. Cambridge: Cambridge University Press.

Jameson, Fredric (1991 [1984]) *Postmodernism: Or, the Cultural Logic of Late Capitalism*. London: Verso.

Jefferies, Janis (2009) 'Blurring the Boundaries: Performance, Technology and the Artificial Sublime – An Interview with Ruth Gibson and Bruno Martelli, igloo', in Maria Chatzichristodoulou, Janis Jefferies and Rachel Zerihan (eds), *Interfaces of Performance*. Surrey: Ashgate: 43–56.

Jones, Jonathan (2009) 'The Fourth Plinth: it was just Big Brother all over again', *The Guardian*, 9 October.

Kantor, Tadeusz (1993) *A Journey Through Other Spaces: Essays and Manifestos, 1944–1990*, (ed. and trans. Michael Kobialka). Berkeley, Los Angeles and London: University of California Press.

Kelly, Kevin (1998) *New Rules for the New Economy: Ten Radical Strategies for a Connected World*, London: Viking.

Kershaw, B. (2007) *Theatre Ecology: Environments and Performance Events*. Cambridge: Cambridge University Press.

Kershaw, Baz (1999) *The Radical in Performance: Between Brecht and Baudrillard*. London and New York: Routledge.

Khan, Omar and Hannah, Dorita (2008) 'Performance/Architecture: Interview with Bernard Tschumi', *Journal of Architectural Education*, 61(4): 52–8.

Kozel, Susan (2007) *Closer: Performance, Technologies, Phenomenology*. Cambridge, MA: MIT Press.

Kong, L. and O'Connor, J. (eds) (2009) *Creative Economies, Creative Cities: Asian-European Perspectives*. Berlin: Springer.

Kristeva, Julia (1995) *New Maladies of the Soul*. New York: Columbia University Press.

Laban, Rudolf von and Lawrence, F.C. (1974) *Effort: Economy in Body Movement*. Boston: Plays.

Lacan, J. (1980) *Ecrits: A Selection* (trans. Alan Sheridan). London: Tavistock Publications.

Lakoff, George and Johnson, Mark (1999) *Philosophy in the Flesh: The Embodied Mind and its Challenge to Western Thought*. New York: Basic Books.

Laurel, Brenda (2004) *Design Research: Methods and Perspectives*, Ann Arbor, MI: MIT Press.

Laurel, Brenda (1993) *Computers as Theatre*. Reading, MA: Addison-Wesley.

Leach, Neil (ed.) (1997) *Rethinking Architecture: A Reader in Cultural Theory*. London and New York: Routledge.

Leach, Robert (2008) *Theatre Studies: The Basics*. London and New York: Routledge.

Leadbeater, C. and Oakley, K. (1999) *The Independents: Britain's New Cultural Entrepreneurs*. London: Demos. Available at http://www.demos.co.uk/publications/independents [Accessed 1 February 2011].

Leder, D. (1990) *The Absent Body*. Chicago: University of Chicago Press.

Lefebvre, Henri (1991 [1974]) *The Production of Space* (trans, N. Donaldson-Smith). Oxford: Basil Blackwell.

Lehmann, Hans-Thies (2006) *Postdramatic Theatre* (trans. Karen Jürs-Munby). London: Routledge.

Levinas, Emmanuel (1991) *Le Temps et L'Autre*. Paris: Quadrige/PUF.

Libeskind, Daniel (2000) *The Space of Encounter*. New York: Universe Publishing.

Lofgren, Eric T. and Fefferman, Nina H. (2007) 'The Untapped Potential of Virtual Game Worlds to Shed Light on Real World Epidemics', *Lancet Infectious Diseases*, 7(9): 625–9.

Lyotard, Jean-François (1984) *The Postmodern Condition: A Report on Knowledge* (trans. Geoff Bennington and Brian Massumi). Manchester: Manchester University Press.

MacAloon, John J. (1984) 'Olympic Games and the Theory of Spectacle in Modern Societies', in John J. MacAloon (ed.), *Rite, Drama, Festival. Rehearsals towards a Theory of Cultural Performance*. Philadelphia: Institute for the Study of Human Issues: 241–80.

Machon, Josephine (2009) *(Syn)aesthetics: Redefining Visceral Performance*. Basingstoke: Palgrave Macmillan.

Mackintosh, I. (1993) *Architecture, Actor and Audience*. London and New York: Routledge.

Manifold (2007) Hays in an interview with Izabel Gass, *Manifold* (Rice University Publication), spring, 1: 82.

Manovich, Lev (2002) 'Spatial Computerisation and Film Language', in *New Screen Media: Cinema/Art/Narrative* (eds Martin Rieser and Andrea Zapp). London: British Film Institute: 64–76.

Marketing Week (2001) 'Lego launches "serious play" bricks to help businesses', 4 October: 6.

Massumi, Brian (2002) *Parables for the Virtual: Movement, Affect, Sensation*. Durham, NC: Duke University Press.

Mauss, M. (2004) 'Techniques of the Body', in A. Blaikie (ed.), *The Body: Critical Concepts in Sociology, Volume 4: Living and Dying Bodies*. London and New York: Routledge: 50–69.

McAuley, Gay (1999) *Space in Performance: Making Meaning in the Theatre*. Ann Arbor: University of Michigan Press.

McKenzie, Jon (2001) *Perform or Else*. London and New York: Routledge.

McKenzie, Jon, Roms, Heike and Wee, C.J.W.L. (2010) *Contesting Performance. Global Sites of Research*. Basingstoke: Palgrave Macmillan.

McKinney, Joslin and Butterworth, Philip (2009) *The Cambridge Introduction to Scenography*. Cambridge, UK: Cambridge University Press.

Melrose, S. (2006) ' "The Body" in Question: Expert Performance-making in the University and the Problem of Spectatorship', Seminar paper presented at

Middlesex University School of Computing. Available at http://www.sfmelrose.
u-net.com/.

Merleau-Ponty, M. (2002) *Phenomenology of Perception: An Introduction* (trans. Colin
Smith). London and New York: Routledge.

Merleau-Ponty, M. (1968) *The Visible and the Invisible*. Evanston: Northwest
University Press.

Merleau-Ponty, M. (1964) *The Primacy of Perception*. Evanston: Northwest University
Press.

Miege, B. (1979) The Cultural Commodity (trans. Nicholas Garnham), *Media,
Culture and Society*, 1(3): 297–311.

Mitoma, Judy (2002) *Envisioning Dance on Film and Video*. New York and London:
Routledge.

Mori, Masahiro (1970) Bukimi no tani [The Uncanny Valley], (trans. K.F.
MacDorman and T. Minato, Original in Japanese), *Energy* 7(4): 33–5.

Morgan, David (2002) 'The Body in Pain', in M. Evans and L. Ellie (eds), *Real Bodies:
A Sociological Introduction*. Basingstoke: Palgrave: 79–95.

Morgan, G. (2006) *Images of Organisation*. London: Sage.

Murray, J.H. (1998) *Hamlet on the Holodeck: The Future of Narrative in Cyberspace*.
Cambridge, MA: MIT Press.

Murray, S. (2003) *Jacques Lecoq*. London: Routledge.

Nachmanovitch, Stephen (1990) *Free Play: Improvisation in Life and Art*, New York:
Putnam.

Nachmanovitch, Stephen (2007) 'Improvisation and the Pattern which Connects',
Keynote address at *Improvisation Continuums Conference*, University of
Glamorgan, 11–14 April 2007.

Neelands, Jonothan (2000) 'In the Hands of Living People', Keynote address at the
National Drama Conference, York, UK, April 2000.

Neelands, Jonothan (1991) *Structuring Drama Work*. Cambridge: Cambridge
University Press.

Nelson, R. (2009) 'Modes of Practice as Research Knowledge and their Place in the
Academy', in Ludivine Allegue, Simon Jones, Baz Kershaw and Angela Piccini,
Practice as Research in Performance and Screen. Basingstoke: Palgrave Macmillan:
112–30.

Nietzsche, Friedrich (1974) *The Gay Science* (trans. Walter Kaufmann). New York:
Vintage

Noë, A. (2004) *Action in Perception*. Cambridge, MA: MIT.

O'Connor, Justin (2008) *The Cultural and Creative Industries: A Literature Review*.
London: Creative Partnerships.

Osborne, Peter (1999) 'The Politics of Time', in Roger Luckhurst and Peter Marks
(eds), *Literature and the Contemporary: Fictions and Theories of the Present*. Harlow,
Essex: Pearson/Longman: 36–49.

O'States, Bert (1987) *Great Reckonings in Little Rooms: On the Phenomenology of
Theater*. Berkeley and Los Angeles, CA: University of California Press.

Panofsky (1991) *Perspective as Symbolic Form*, (trans. C.S. Wood). New York: Zone
Books.

Parry, J. (1989) 'The End of the Body', in M. Feher, R. Naddaff and N. Tazi, *Zone:
Fragments for a History of the Human Body*, Part II. New York: Urzone: 490–517.

Parker-Starbuck, Jennifer (2009) 'The Play-within-the-film-within-the-play's the Thing: Re-transmitting Analogue Bodies in the Wooster Group's Hamlet', *International Journal of Performance Arts & Digital Media*, 5(1): 23–34.

Pavis, Patrice (2003) 'Afterword: Contemporary Dramatic Writings and the New Technologies', in Cariad Svich (ed.), *Trans-Global Readings: Crossing Theatrical Boundaries*. Manchester: Manchester University Press: 187–202.

Pearce, C. (2004) 'Toward a Game Theory of Game', in W. Wardrip-Fruin and P. Harrigan (eds), *First Person: New Media as Story, Performance, and Game*. Cambridge, MA: MIT Press: 143–53.

Pearson, Mike and Shanks, Michael (2001) *Theatre/Archaeology*. London and New York: Routledge.

Phelan, Peggy (2004) 'Marina Abramovic: Witnessing Shadows', *Performing Arts Journal*, 56(4): 569–77.

Phelan, Peggy (1997) *Mourning Sex: Performing Public Memories* London and New York: Routledge.

Phelan, Peggy (1993) *Unmarked: The Politics of Performance*. London and New York: Routledge.

Pitches, Jonathan, (2009) 'Spinal Snaps: Tracing a Backstory of European Actor Training', *Performance Research*, 14(2): 85–95.

Pitches, Jonathan (2005) *Science and the Stanislavsky Tradition of Acting*. London: Routledge.

Plato (1987) *The Republic* (trans. Desmond Lee). London: Penguin.

Polanyi, M. (1967) *The Tacit Dimension*. London: Routledge & Kegan Paul.

Popat, Sita (2006) *Invisible Connections: Dance, Choreography and Internet Communities*. London: Routledge.

Popat, Sita and Palmer, Scott (2008) 'Embodied Interfaces: Dancing with Digital Sprites', *Digital Creativity*, 19(2): 125–37.

Popat, Sita and Palmer, Scott (2005) 'Creating Common Ground: Dialogues between Performance and Digital Technologies', *International Journal of Performance Arts & Digital Media*, 1(1): 47–65.

Postlewait, T. and McConachie, B. (eds) (1989) *Interpreting the Theatrical Past: Essays in The Historiography of Performance*. Iowa: University of Iowa Press.

Potts, J. and Cunningham, S. (2008) 'Four Models of the Creative Industries', *International Journal of Cultural Policy*, 14(3): 233–47.

Read, A. (1993) *Theatre and Everyday Life: An Ethics of Performance*. London and New York: Routledge.

Reeves, T.C., Duncan, W.J. and Ginter, P.M. (2001) 'Motion Study in Management and the Arts: A Historical Example', *Journal of Management Inquiry*, 10: 137–49.

Richards, Mary (2010) *Marina Abramovic*. London: Routledge.

Richter, Irma (ed.) (2008) *Leonardo da Vinci: Notebooks*. Oxford and New York: Oxford University Press.

Roach, J.R. (1989) 'Theatre History and the Ideology of the Aesthetic,' *Theater Journal*, 41(2): 155–68.

Roesner, D. (2008) 'The Politics of the Polyphony of Performance: Musicalization in Contemporary German Theatre', *Contemporary Theatre Review*, 18(1).

Rosen, H. (1985) *Stories and Meanings*, NATE Papers in Education. London: National Association of the Teachers of English.

Rush, Michael (1999) *New Media in Late 20th-Century Art*. London: Thames & Hudson.

Sacks, Oliver (1985) *The Man Who Mistook his Wife for a Hat*. London: Picador.

Saussure, Ferdinand de (2006) *Writings in General Linguistics*, Oxford: Oxford University Press.

Scarry, E. (1985) *The Body in Pain*. Oxford: Oxford University Press.

Schechner, Richard (2006) *Performance Studies: An Introduction*. London: Routledge.

Schechner, Richard (1994) *Environmental Theater,* 2nd edn. New York and London, Applause.

Schechner, Richard (1988) *Performance Theory*. London: Routledge.

Schechner, Richard (1985) *Between Theater and Anthropology*. Pennsylvania, USA: University of Pennsylvania.

Schechner, Richard (1973) *Environmental Theater* New York: Hawthorn Books.

Seltzer, K. and Bentley, T. (1999) *The Creative Age: Knowledge and Skills for the New Economy*. London: Demos.

Sheets-Johnstone, M. (ed.) (1992) *Giving the Body Its Due*. Albany: SUNY Press.

Shepherd, Simon (2006) *Theatre, Body, Pleasure*. London and New York: Routledge.

Shepherd, Simon and Wallis, Mick (2004) *Drama/Theatre/Performance*. London: Routledge.

Simpson, L. (1995) *Technology, Time, and the Conversations of Modernity*, London: Routledge.

Smith, Barry (2005) 'Jennicam or the Telematic Theatre of a Real Life', *International Journal of Performance Arts & Digital Media* 1(2): 91–100.

Sobchack, V. (1992) *The Address of the Eye: A Phenomenology of Film Experience*. Princeton and Oxford: Princeton University Press.

Sofaer, Joshua (2010) *The Many Headed Monster: The Audience of Contemporary Performance*, with accompanying DVD. London: Live Art Development Agency.

Solà-Morales, Ignasi de (1997) *Differences: Topographies of Contemporary Architecture*, (trans. Graham Thompson, ed. Sarah Whiting). Cambridge, MA: MIT Press.

Somers, John (1996) *Drama and Theatre in Education: Contemporary Research*, York: Captus Press.

Spain, Kent de and Kaiser, Paul (2000) 'Digital Dance: The Computer Artistry of Paul Kaiser', *Dance Research Journal*, 32(1): 18–23.

Stanislavski, K. (2008) *An Actor's Work*, (trans. Jean Benedetti). London and New York: Routledge.

Stanislavski, K. (2010) *An Actor's Work on a Role*, (trans. Jean Benedetti). London and New York: Routledge.

Steinman, L. (1986) *The Knowing Body: Elements of Contemporary Performance*. Boston: Shambhala Publications.

Stelarc (2007) *Inaugural Lecture*, Brunel University, Monday 15 October 2007.

Strasberg, L. (1988) *A Dream of Passion: The Development of the Method*. London: Bloomsbury.

Swartz, David (1997) *Culture and Power: The Sociology of Pierre Bourdieu*. Chicago: University of Chicago Press.

Taylor, Frederick Winslow (2003 [1911]) *The Principles of Scientific Management*. USA: Dover Publications Inc.

Teunissen, J. *et al.* (eds) (2004) *The Ideal Woman*. Amsterdam: Uitgenerij Boom.

Thompson, C. and Weslien, K. (2005) 'Marina Abramovic Interviewed', *Performing Arts Journal*, 28(1): 29–50.

Tschumi, Bernard (1996) *Architecture and Disjunction*. Cambridge, MA: MIT Press.

Tuan, Y. (1977) *Space and Place – The Perspective of Experience*. Minneapolis: University of Minnesota Press.

Ubersfeld, Anne (1999) *Reading Theatre*, (trans. Frank Collins). Toronto: Toronto University Press.

Virilio, Paul (1991) *The Lost Dimension* (trans. Daniel Moshenberg). New York: Semiotext(e).

Virilio, Paul (1979) *Vitesse et politique*, Paris: Editions Galilée.

Wallis, Mick, Popat, Sita, McKinney, J, Bryden, John and Hogg, David (2010) 'Embodied Conversations: Performance and the Design of a Robotic Dancing Partner', *Design Studies: International Journal for Design Research in Engineering, Architecture, Products and Systems*, 31(2): 99–117.

Warwick, Kevin (2002) *I, Cyborg*. London: Century.

Wechsler, Robert (2006) 'Artistic Considerations in the Use of Motion Tracking with Live Performers: A Practical Guide', in Susan Broadhurst and Josephine Machon, *Performance and Technology*. Basingstoke: Palgrave Macmillan: 60–77.

Weiss (1995) *Mirrors of Infinity: The French Formal Garden and 17th-Century Metaphysics*. New York: Princeton Architectural Press.

Welton, D. (ed.) (1999) *The Body, Classic and Contemporary Readings*. Oxford: Blackwell.

Wenger, E. (1999) *Communities of Practice: Learning, Meaning and Identity*. Cambridge: Cambridge University Press.

Westcott, James (2003) 'Marina Abramovic's *The House with the Ocean View*: The View of the House from Some Drops in the Ocean', *The Drama Review*, 47(3): 129–36.

Williams, Raymond (1981) *Culture*. London: Fontana.

Yarrow, Ralph (2007) 'Improvising Scholarship', Keynote address at *Improvisation Continuums Conference*, University of Glamorgan, 11–14 April 2007.

Young, I. (1989) *Throwing like a Girl and other essays in Feminist Philosophy*. Bloomington and Indianapolis: Indiana University Press.

Zarrilli, P.B. (2009) *Psychophysical Acting: An Intercultural Approach after Stanislavski*. Abingdon and New York: Routledge.

Performances, artists and companies

(All websites accessed on 1 February 2011.)

Marina Abramovic – www.artnet.com/awc/marina-abramovic.html
Akram Khan – www.akramkhancompany.net
Rebecca Allen – www.rebeccaallen.com
Ron Athey – www.ronathey.com
Franko B – www.franko-b.com
DV8 Physical Theatre – www.dv8.co.uk
Fuerzabruta – www.fuerzabruta.net
Tim Etchells – www.timetchells.com
Forced Entertainment – www.forcedentertainment.com
Guillermo Gómez-Peña – www.pochanostra.com

Dominic Johnson – www.dominicjohnson.co.uk
La Fura dels Baus – www.lafura.com
Ludus Dance Company – www.ludusdance.org
Orlan – www.orlan.net
Punchdrunk – www.punchdrunk.org.uk
Kathleen Rogers – www.kathleenrogers.co.uk
Paul Sermon – http://creativetechnology.salford.ac.uk/paulsermon
Slung Low – http://web.me.com/slung.low/Slung_Low/slung_low_home.html
www.thisisliveart.co.uk
wilson+wilson website – http://www.wilsonandwilson.org.uk/
Louise Ann Wilson website – http://www.louiseannwilson.co.uk/

Index

Printed and bound in Great Britain by
CPI Group (UK) Ltd, Croydon, CR0 4YY